EATING
KOREA

ALSO BY GRAHAM HOLLIDAY

Eating Việt Nam

EATING KOREA

REPORTS ON A CULINARY RENAISSANCE

GRAHAM HOLLIDAY

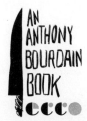

AN
ANTHONY
BOURDAIN
BOOK

ecco

An Imprint of HarperCollinsPublishers

Epigraph on page v from Kim Sung-Ok, "Seoul: 1964, Winter," Marshall R. Pihl Jr., trans., in *Land of Exile: Contemporary Korean Fiction,* Marshall R. Pihl, Bruce Fulton, and Ju-Chan Fulton, eds. (Armonk, NY: M.E. Sharpe, 1993).

HarperCollins books may be purchased for educational, business, or sales promotional use. For information please e-mail the Special Markets Department at SPsales@harpercollins.com.

FIRST EDITION

Designed by Suet Yee Chong
Photographs by Graham Holliday

Library of Congress Cataloging-in-Publication Data has been applied for.

ISBN 978-0-06-240076-5

17 18 19 20 21 LSC 10 9 8 7 6 5 4 3 2 1

Anyone who spent the winter of 1964 in Seoul would probably remember those wine shops that appeared on the streets at nightfall—the shops that sold hotchpotch, roasted sparrows and three kinds of wine, where the curtain you lifted to step in was flapping in a bitter wind that swept the frozen streets, where the flame of a carbide lamp inside fluttered in the gusts, and where a middle-aged man in a dyed army jacket poured wine and roasted snacks for you.

—KIM SUNG-OK

CONTENTS

THE CHANCE TO BEGIN AGAIN

A new life awaits you in the off-world colonies. The chance to begin again in a golden land of opportunity and adventure.

—Blade Runner

MARCH 26, 2015

I was sitting in a basement bar below a nondescript alley, off a nondescript side street, connected to a nondescript eight-lane highway in the downtown Jongno district of Seoul. There were six tables placed at angles, full of customers and illuminated by candlelight. I was with a friend. Some food arrived and he leaned forward. Wax dripped upon the table, his face glowed ghoulish in the gloom. He had a look almost of pride.

"This," he said, admiring the food that separated us, "is the future."

I looked at the grilled, disc-shaped object on the plate between us.

"It's a pizza," I said.

"No," he said, "it's the future of Korean food."

Twenty years had passed since I'd last seen Andy Salmon in this city; age now creased us and gray tickled our forelocks. Like me, he was British. We had both lived in Seoul back then, but I'd left and he'd stayed. He used to be a restaurant critic; these days he was a writer, journalist, and TV presenter.

"Try it," he said. It sounded like a dare.

I'd never seen anything good come out of South Korea in the shape of a pizza. And what gazed up at me from the plate at Bar Sanchez that night didn't look like it was going to change that. I took a bite. The crust was thin, and there was something odd there, something foreign to any pizza I'd ever known. Andy caught my flinch.

"What does it remind you of?" he asked.

It wasn't unpleasant, but it was savory and also somewhat sweet. It was like no pizza I had ever had a relationship with. It wasn't pizza, it was some kind of hermaphroditic food form.

"It's sweet," I said, putting the half-eaten slice back down on the plate. "That's no pizza." I shook my head. I couldn't place what it reminded me of. "No idea," I said. "It's an odd one."

"Fruit cake," said Andy. "A dessert pizza with a whiff of fruit cake."

He leaned back in his chair and waved a hand toward the bar.

"This Sanchez," he said, "He's an absolute genius."

Bar Sanchez was a modish crevice in downtown Seoul. Sanchez worked behind the small bar, and despite his name, Sanchez was Korean. He had one portable burner upon which he cooked and one person to help him prepare and serve. What this young Korean man was creating, Andy told me, was "nouveau Korean food."

"I'm telling you," Andy said, plucking a slice from the plate, repeating himself, "this is it. This is the future of Korean food."

My first night back in Korea with my oldest friend in Korea—a former restaurant reviewer, food guidebook writer, a man married to a recognized Korean food expert and chef—and he'd presented me with something he called "the future," but which to me looked like a mistake, and certainly not identifiable as Korean.

It was in 1994, midway along the noodle aisle of Pat's Chung Ying Chinese Supermarket on Edinburgh's Leith Walk, that I first became acquainted with Korean food.

At best, the one-dollar plastic vessel staring back at me from the dustier end of the "sell-by date expired" shelf was on life support. At worst, it was en route to being read its last rites at the local landfill.

Fate, if you believe in such things, comes in many forms. In my case, it arrived in the guise of a four-foot-tall Chinese grandmother with a tight, dyed-black perm and an insistent right elbow.

In hot pursuit of a half-price "maxi" soy sauce vat, this diminutive old lady knocked me sideways, sending herself clattering into the cheap shelf and much of Edinburgh's cast-off Asian edibles crashing to the floor.

Oyster sauce, pickles, fish sauce, and rice vinegar all made a leap for freedom, only to meet their sticky, broken end on the supermarket floor. I watched the glass, pickles, and sauces smash around me as a single bottle floated from its perch and dropped into my shopping basket. It lay there, cap covered in dust, nestled like an orphaned child in a blanket of instant noodles and shrimp crackers.

Clearly, it was meant to be. I bought it.

Back home, I sat in the kitchen and eyed this mysterious new arrival. Three words on the label gawped back at me: "Korean Bulgogi Marinade." "Bulgogi" sounded like a device you'd put in a baby's mouth to shut it up—it didn't sound like food. I knew nothing of Korean food, and I was ignorant of how it should sound. However, I *had* come across marinades.

Simple enough in theory: slop contents over dead animal, leave to fester, apply fire, serve when ready. Easy.

So that's what I did. With slices of cow.

I ate it quickly. The flavors of the beef—sweet, sesame oil, soy sauce, and garlic—unnerved my taste buds. Upon finishing, I swayed, slightly stunned, and surveyed the aftermath.

The empty plate glistened. Dark pathways of soy wiped their way across the secondhand porcelain. My head wrangled with the mass of mental rubble this meal had just bulldozed to one side of my brain. Within the space of a few short minutes, an unexpectedly desirable part of the culinary world had opened up a promising development in the part of my mind that prospected for tasty new real estate.

Two years later, having trained as a teacher, I relocated to the country from whence the dark, saucy genie had come. Ostensibly, I moved for work. In reality, I went to see what other Korean things I could eat. I ended up living and eating my way around the Hermit Kingdom for the better part of two years.

It was in the midnineties, while teaching at a state school in the southwest of the country, that I fell in love with South Korea and with Korean food. With the bubbling cauldrons and the pepper-and-garlic-steam-filled orange tents, called *pojangmacha*, that appeared on the streets and in parking lots from early evening to early morning. The Korean food I devoured daily detonated in my mouth like a pop art exhibition. It had never heard of cheese and would have grown nauseous at the thought of fruit cake.

When I first arrived in Korea in 1996, I had eaten only that self-made bulgogi and a chicken and potatoes dish called *dak dori tang* (닭도리탕) cooked by a Korean student of mine. There were no Korean restaurants where I lived in England. I arrived ignorant, and during a two-week induction in the central city of Cheongju, I went in search of the two dishes I "knew." I popped my head inside several small eateries and in pathetic Korean said, timidly, *"Dak dori tang?"*

That was how I ended up inside an old lady's living room, surrounded by dark brown wooden furniture, family portraits, a large, loudly ticking clock, and a TV. The woman slid a thin silk cushion my way and gestured for me to sit down. Looking back, I don't think she was running a restaurant business—she had just taken pity on me. She headed into the pantry and left me alone, facing the TV, tuned to the news in Korean. What she came out with ten minutes later was *dak dori tang*. It was huge, hot, and delicious, and it was to be the beginning of my journey into Korean food in South Korea. At the end of my induction period, I was asked where I would like to work. When I was informed that Jeolla province cooked the best food in Korea, I signed up immediately.

I soon learned that the Korean dining table was a rough-hewn, ramshackle, chaotic place where ruddy faces cracked tumblers of soju, the Korean firewater distilled from grain or potato. Where gallons of Hite and Cass, the watery local beers, vanished between bites of grilled pork and kimchi, slurps of bean paste soups, and scoops of rice. In those days, I traveled the country to taste as much as I could, though in reality, I barely sipped at the bounty. Even so, it rapidly became apparent to me, even in my inexperienced haze, that Korean food was regional. Few people outside of Korea are aware of that fact, as are many Koreans *in* Korea.

I decided to come back in 2015 to rediscover some of these differentiations for myself. My plan was to circumnavigate the country in a clockwise direction: I would start in the northwest, in the capital, Seoul, before heading to the northeast coast and down the southeastern seaboard to the city of Busan. By moving west along the southern coast, I would make my way to the city of Mokpo and sail over to Korea's largest island, Jeju. Back on the mainland, I would head north to Jeonju in Jeollabuk-do province, the food capital of Korea, before continuing north, back to Seoul.

I didn't want to see what had changed—I wanted to rewind the tape, to watch the same movie over again. But Andy had messed with my plan, and over the next six weeks, I intended to rectify that. I would learn more about the food, plot a route that others might follow, and eat a lot, but not too much. I would be picky, and fruit cake pizza was not on my list.

S eoul's skyline suffocates you. Angry apartment blocks stomp across the horizon like giant white tombstones. Almost all human life is crammed within these sprawling mass accommodation complexes. The capital is the same size as San Francisco, but it has ten times the population. Every street corner has a coffee shop or a small supermarket, or both. On the evening I arrived in Seoul, I took a stroll on my way to meet Andy.

A man with a van played a prerecorded message through a loudspeaker system attached to the roof. The tinny military staccato echo advertised the price of melons, apples, pears, and persimmons for sale from neatly stacked boxes in the back of his vehicle. School girls took selfies, or *selcas* (셀카), as Koreans call them, at a bus stop on an eight-lane highway. The wide thoroughfare was plugged with a concertina of cars.

An elderly activist in a sun visor and spectacles boasted a torso-length placard around her neck and shoulders. She walked in a tight circle and barked grievances about . . . something. Behind her, a chestnut seller, a fortune teller, a calligraphy writer, and a shoeshine man touted for trade. At the subway exit, there were orange, silver, black, and pink taxis. Hyundai and Kia sedans. The more affluent among the commuter throng drove Audis, Mercedes, and BMWs. The imported vehicles looked like fluffed-up peacocks among the Korean-made cars and buses that thundered through the concrete matrix.

The air was steeped in sour vinegar, tickled with kimchi, the deep-fat fryers of a thousand fried-chicken joints were sputtering into action, and the clink-clink, drink-drink of a hundred thousand shot glasses were beginning to smash across the capital.

After Bar Sanchez, we strolled around Seoul's epicenter. Andy had been a Seoul resident since 1989.

"It's heartbreaking," said Andy. He pointed at a hole in the ground next to a craft beer microbrewery near Gwanghwamun Gate. "So sad," he said. "The old *hanoks* just get ripped up and thrown away."

The hole was filled with dirt. All that remained of the *hanok*, the old bungalows with attractive, pointy, tiled roofs, were broken walls and shattered tiles. They used to fill the cities and the countryside. But now, apart from one or two preserved or renovated *hanok* areas, the Seoul of 2015 was almost free of original *hanoks*.

"No one gives a shit," he said. "It's a myth that Seoul was flattened during the Korean War. There was heavy fighting, but this was no Stalingrad. It was man to man, tank to tank. The city was badly damaged, but it wasn't leveled."

Andy knew his Korean history better than most: he had written two highly regarded books of Korean War history.

"The old Koreans say, 'But we hated growing up in those things,'" Andy said, referring to the *hanoks*. "'It was awful, they were filled with rats and snakes, there was no heat and no water.' But when they're gone, they're gone."

Like the workhouses of the British Industrial Revolution, or the grubby housing of the East End of London, these places were filled with good and bad memories. But in the west, they had found new life.

"Not here," said Andy. "It's rip it up and start again. Build new, build shiny, build high. The *hanoks* that are left are the second homes of the rich. They'll have a cello concerto party once a year, and for the rest of the year it remains barren, killing the district where life once thrived."

It wasn't just the *hanoks* that were under threat—I was worried about the food. What place did the Korean food I once knew and loved have in a country blitzkrieging its way into the future? Had the food survived? After my fruit cake pizza, I wasn't sure I was going to find an answer I would like.

For the past decade, the Korean government had been aggressively promoting Korean food and culture overseas. Andy wasn't impressed.

"The Koreans go on and on about kimchi and selling and promoting kimchi abroad," he said, as we nibbled inside the craft beer pub. "But they're missing a trick with *doenjang*. This is the stuff."

Doenjang (된장) is a bean paste. It is used as an accompaniment with grilled meat dishes like the marinated pork dish called *kalbi* (갈비), the grilled fatty pork *samgyeopsal* (삼겹살), and the sweet, sesame- and soy-rich beef bulgogi (불고기). It is also the base of a misolike soup called *doenjang-guk* (된장국) and it is the key ingredient in the cheap, popular, and delicious stew called *doenjang-jjigae* (된장 찌개).

"You see," said Andy. "*Doenjang* and cheese. It just works."

I looked at him. Had my old friend gone mad? Gotten cabin fever? Or was this what Korea had truly become? It was an unrecognizable place for me.

Koreans had long married the bizarre in the kitchen: shredded cabbage with a sweet cocktail dressing to accompany fried chicken, strawberry-flavored crisps, and kimchi chocolate. They all exist. McDonald's in Korea serves a Bulgogi Burger and even a Double Bulgogi Burger (which, actually, are not bad). For a two-month period in 2002, they also sold a Kimchi Burger. Korean pizza was, and still is if you look for it, the stuff of Italian nightmares. Bulgogi, wasabi, sweet tomato sauce, *gochujang* (고추장, Korea's potent red pepper paste), cream cheese, raisins, nuts, cheap canned pineapple, strawberries, kimchi, and potatoes . . . All these are legitimate Korean pizza toppings. And almost every standard-issue, nonartisanal pizza in Korea, whatever you order, comes with corn. If there truly were a loving and compassionate god, Korea's traditional pizza trade would have been erased from existence decades ago.

We went back to Bar Sanchez, where we were joined by Joe McPherson, an American food writer, TV and radio presenter, and founder of the blog Zen Kimchi. He wore a black leather jacket and sported a pale complexion. The Alabama native had moved to Seoul in the early part of the new millennium. He nodded agreement with Andy's bean paste and cheese theory.

"The Korean government likes to take credit for the upsurge of interest in Korean food," Joe said, referring to the increasing popularity of Korean food in the West. "They say their promotion of food is the major influence, but it's not true. The guys in LA doing the food trucks and fusion food, that's where it comes from. It's this outside bastardization of food, mostly by Korean Americans, that's pushing it. And that's what we're beginning to see happening back here."

Joe was referring to Roy Choi and David Chang. The Seoul-born, LA-raised Choi first rose to fame with his Korean taco truck, Kogi. He experimented with fusing cuisines, most notably Mexican, with Korean elements, whereas Chang was the mind behind Momofuku, the restaurant empire that singlehandedly put ramyun, noodles, center stage in the West. It was these punks who had catapulted Korean food to the attention of the non-Korean world and made it the voguish phenomenon it is today.

As Joe, Andy, and I talked, I had something of a revelation. I thought I might just be "getting" Bar Sanchez.

I'd often found that Koreans were embarrassed by their food. They would constantly apologize for it; it was too smelly, too spicy, too this, too that. Koreans did not believe that non-Koreans, especially non-Asians, could ever like it. They were fundamentally wrong—their food was amazing—but in 1996 I'd mostly found it a battle to convince them that I really meant it. Now, talking to Andy and Joe, I wondered whether Korea might just be learning to loosen up, give the world the finger and be proud and vocal about its food. Korea may not be in its punk period yet, I thought, but perhaps it was approaching it. This massive surge of interest in Korean food, music, and culture from overseas must have resulted in an increase in confidence in who Koreans are, what they eat, how they live, and how they feel they are seen from the outside.

In essence, I wondered out loud to Andy and Joe, "Are the Koreans becoming more French?"

It sounded odd to hear those words enter the ether. I was trying desperately to anchor this new Korea into a frame I could begin to understand.

"We're not there yet," said Andy. "But we're heading there. I've got a lot of hope in the younger generation in Korea. You'll see—they're completely different. You left this place. I've watched it change in real time."

Twenty years ago, Korea was a developing country. Most expats who arrived on its shores spent their time talking about when they were going to leave. In 2015, Korea was no longer a developing country; it was developed, and now the expats wanted to stay.

I didn't know Korea's younger generation. The Korean people I had kept in touch with all these years were either my own age or had just hit retirement, but I wanted to hear what young Koreans thought about their food, their culture, and their future. My expat friends' views were a helpful, if rather distressing, primer.

"He's a one-man show," said Andy, gesturing toward Sanchez.

His real name was Mr. Park Chang-hee. He came from Chung-cheong-namdo, south of Seoul, in the west of Korea, and had opened his bar in 2012. He seemed to have his head down permanently, preparing food behind the minuscule bar.

"Where did you learn to cook?" I asked.

"I had some earlier jobs," Sanchez said. "Mostly part-time work doing different things. They weren't particularly food-related jobs but they gave me some life experience to figure out what people like to cook."

He did have Korean items on his menu, but he said that the younger clientele gravitated toward fusion dishes.

"It's mostly fusion food I make here to appeal to younger customers," he said. "They crave Western-style dishes and flavor. I am a home cook with no food-related training. Korean food to me is my mother's cooking. Some of the Korean dishes I cook here are a reflection of what my mother used to cook, but as I said, it's mostly fusion that I do."

Another plate of pizza shipped to a table. And Sanchez got to work on his version of a Spanish omelet, or "American *pajeon*." It was his take on a traditional Korean *pajeon* (파전), or pancake, made with bacon, cheese, onions, and ketchup rather than the traditional spring onions, pork, kimchi, and squid.

"He has these young kids who help him out," said Andy. "They work here just because they love the concept of what he's doing. It's just one guy, one burner, and good, innovative, interesting food. This was unheard of before."

While I loved the concept and admired Sanchez for what he was doing, I pined for tabletop grills, for floors strewn with empty bottles, loud, rude customers, smoke, rough service, peeling walls, and stifling odors.

Andy looked at me. I think he could see that I was confused by this new Korea, but he had a suggestion for me.

"To understand what's happening here," he said, "you need to take a look at the 'new old.' Go see what Vivian Han's doing. She's going back to these old, forgotten Korean recipes and bringing them back to life in a really fresh, original way."

"Korean food gone chic-traditional?" I said.

"In a way," he said. "But in a good way. She calls what she does 'neo-Korean,' but it's really just very old Korean done better than it probably ever was."

Joe swooned at the mention of her place.

"Fantastic food," he said. "Amazing place, incredible woman."

Maybe I looked exasperated. I worried that my message wasn't getting through. Had I completely miscalculated where Korea was, culinarily? Had what I had come to see gone the way of the *hanok*s?

"Andy, it's not that kind of a book," I said. "This is a book about regular Korean food, not special food. And it's not about the best this or the best that, it's about food Koreans eat every day. I don't want the fancy, new, young, funky—I want the ordinary. In all parts of Korea, not just Seoul. In the canteens at bus stations, street stalls after dark, grilled meat shacks, and soju tents. Maybe you're right and it is disappearing, and maybe no one cares, but that's Korea to me, and that's where this country's heart is. Maybe one day the bulldozers will come along and remove it all. And maybe the Koreans won't even care, but that's the Korea I'm here to document. And I refuse to believe that fruit cake pizza and American *pajeon* and anything with the word *neo* in it is the future of Korean food."

I was surprised at my own emotion. My friends looked concerned.

"Look," I said, trying to calm down, "I hear everything you're saying, but does anyone here miss anything old? Is this the only country on the planet that doesn't do nostalgia?"

Andy looked at me, sagelike. I was seriously worried.

"For a country with such a seeming respect for customs, culture, family, and the like," he said, "they seem to be pretty adept at destroying everything from the past."

THIS IS SPECIAL

The owner has opened a number of places," Jin-Young told me as we walked up a slight incline to the front door of Hanok Jib Kimchi Jjim (한옥집-김치찜). "But this is the original."

Jin-Young was a thirtysomething Korean woman. I rented an apartment from her in Seoul; she insisted on taking me out to eat, and I was happy to accept.

We took off our shoes and left them in the collective pile at the step up to the wood-effect floor. A waitress wearing a yellow apron shepherded us to the only spare table, in the farthest corner of the restaurant. The place was lined with framed certificates, awards, newspaper and magazine clippings, reviews of the restaurant, and menus and pictures pinned haphazardly to the wall. If the name of the restaurant didn't already give away what they served, the aroma wafting through the interior most certainly did—kimchi (김치).

Ordinary air appeared to have vanished from inside this restaurant. It had simply run away. In its place was a thick, sour, garlic-laced miasma. The room shuddered with it. It seemed to shriek at me. *You're back, you wanted it, I'm here,* it said.

This was a first. To me, kimchi had always been a side dish or the basis of a stew called *kimchi-jjigae* (김치찌개). I'd never met the lone-gunman variety of kimchi restaurant before, and this one looked like it meant business.

I pinched my way past three tables of cross-legged eaters and sat down on the floor opposite Jin-Young.

"This place only serves aged kimchi," Jin-Young told me as the food began to arrive on a large, battered metal tray. "Old, stinky, and aged." It sounded like a geriatric bed wetter's lonely hearts ad.

The waitress placed each dish on the table as if she were laying out a display of shiny precious things in a jewelery shop. After the side dishes, she put the main event in the center. A long, bloody rag of kimchi spread out like a dead octopus on an oval plate. The glorious stench hazed me; my eyes leaked and my nose cried. The kimchi spirits bounced around the room like deranged pinballs. It was wonderful. Finally, I was back, and the panic of the previous evening at Bar Sanchez began to lift.

Our lunch oozed red. It was a very dead, very pickled vegetable, but it looked alive. And in a way it was. Fermented food like kimchi relies on microbes to turn it into the sour rocket assault that it is. There was life on this plate. Kimchi that has fermented for six months or more is known as *mugeunji* (묵은지). This *mugeunji* was a three-year-old.

Since when, I wondered, had the Koreans begun using the term *aged*? I'd heard it used to describe steaks and sherry, port, and whisky. But I'd never heard it used for kimchi. It sounded so un-Korean.

Most common kinds of kimchi are, by their very nature, "aged." Maybe by one winter, sometimes by more. Sure, fresh, unaged kimchi existed, made and served the same day—it's a sensible, sumptuous baby step into the often onerous arena that is kimchi love. But I'd never been served kimchi with a date stamp on it before. Was "aged" kimchi part of the "new old" Andy had hinted at?

"In Korea today," said Jin-Young, "very few of us can make this. We don't have the space and we don't have the time, but not so long ago, this kind of kimchi was normal, like for my parents' generation. But this is special for us now. That's why I like coming here."

The side dishes, called *banchan* (반찬), included a *pajeon* stuffed with spring onions and squid, a small bean sprout soup, dried seaweed, a plate of boiled pork, and some rice.

Jin-Young's father's job had taken the family overseas to Iran when she was nine years old. They then moved to Uzbekistan, where Jin-Young stayed until the end of high school. She went back to Korea for her first year of college, to the United States for the next two years, and back to Korea to finish her degree. She has lived in Korea ever since.

"At college in Korea," she said, "after Uzbekistan, I was called an outsider. There's a particular word in Korean used to describe outsiders, but it means outsiders who are from another country. Not just another country, but a poorer country. It's meant to put you down, to offend you."

Jin-Young picked up a pair of scissors the length of her forearm from the table. As she cut the kimchi into manageable sections, the scissors rasped as if they were going through coarse cardboard.

"I didn't care," she said. "I was an outsider by choice and I didn't want to be a part of those ignorant, old-fashioned Korean ways."

The severed portions of kimchi looked more like a sacrifice than a meal. I took a slice and placed it in my mouth. It was unlike any kimchi I'd ever tasted. It died on my tongue, like a melting spirit. It disappeared in a merry-go-round of garlic, vinegar, and chile. It whirled around and around; it tasted of the past, and I didn't want the ride to end.

"I was lucky that I escaped the Korean education system," she said. "Exam hell, private schools at night after normal school, ridiculous pressure from parents and teachers. I didn't have to go through any of that."

Students in Korea spend more time with personal tutors and in after-school classes than in any other Organisation for Economic Co-operation and Development country. Fourteen- to fifteen-hour days are the norm for Korean kids, days so long that students often bring their hair curlers, cell phone chargers, neck pillows, and blankets in their school bags.

The pressure to succeed is enormous, and students start to feel it from a young age. According to one study, South Korean children are the least happy among kids in developed countries. In 2013, suicide was the leading cause of death among South Korean teenagers and young people.

"However," Jin-Young said, "when I came back to Korea after living abroad, I still felt a need to fit in, so I got married. I thought I should. You know, 'I'm Korean, it's time,' that was my thinking."

The *pajeon* was greasy. I wrapped a piece of kimchi around it. Oil dribbled; I lapped it up.

"I was too young," she said. "It was a mistake, and we divorced. His mother expected us to come over every Saturday and Sunday. I would have to cook with her, like the sous chef, you know? To learn how to cook like her for her son."

Traditionally, most Korean women who marry are expected to go through this apprenticeship. It was often a cause of tension in a marriage.

"No, no, no . . . no way," Jin-Young said. "That life was not for me. If I wanted to learn to cook, I'd go to cooking school."

It was a sad fact that no matter how hard the Korean woman tried, she would never ever be able to make her *kimchi-jjigae* the way her mother-in-law made it. It was a lifelong competition in which the Korean daughter-in-law would always be second best.

"I just thought that if I got married, that would be it, you know?" she said. "I'd finally be 'in,' I'd be accepted and I could relax."

Jin-Young reflected upon her decision as she used a pair of metal chopsticks to wrap a sliver of kimchi around a cluster of rice and pop it into her mouth.

"It was a myth, of course," she said. "I could see it all lined up in front of me. I'd be expected to have kids, kids that had to do well at school and, of course, better than the neighbor's kids. Then we'd need to get a better house, a better car, then the kids would have to go to a good university and get good jobs. It never ends. Living abroad opened my mind to many things. Koreans are very closed-minded."

I never once met a Korean like Jin-Young when I was in the country in 1996. And here I was on my second day back, sitting down with someone I could have an enlightened, engaged conversation with. People like Jin-Young were the rarest commodity twenty years ago. Back then, I'd had trouble holding my tongue when a bigot labeled AIDS as "God's curse upon homosexuals" and homosexuality as a "disease." A disease that did not exist in Korea. The Korea of twenty years ago was a fascist, racist, ignorant place. One guy had even tried to seriously tell me that the latest model of the Hyundai Grandeur, Hyundai's top-of-the-range four-door sedan, was "just as good as an Aston Martin." I mean, really.

"Do you think they're closed-minded about food, too?" I said.

I was hopeful that she would tell me they were. They can open up to homosexuality and design better cars, but I didn't want Koreans to change their food habits.

"Less and less," she said. "They're experimenting, because they're traveling overseas more these days. And, tough luck for them, but they can't find kimchi everywhere they want to travel."

I noticed how she described her fellow Koreans as "they." It was something I had seen in Korean Americans, but not in Korean-born Koreans living in Korea. She really was an outsider.

"They come back," she said, "and they want what they ate in Spain, the U.S., France, or wherever."

Yet again, panic prodded me. I decided to steer the conversation back to the table in front of us.

I told Jin-Young that this "new old" "aged" kimchi was excellent. Twenty-four hours after arriving in the country, I'd snuffled my face back into Korea's sweaty red barrel and come up grinning. I'd never tasted kimchi like it, so deep, so sour, so tender. So "eat me." This kimchi spoke to me, it had stories, it probably had a beard, a pipe, and slippers.

"It's the fermentation," she said. "It keeps on living. It makes it more and more sour and very, very tender. Unless you live in the countryside, you can't make kimchi like this today. Where do we have the space to leave something like this for three years? In an apartment block? I don't think so."

In 1996, in a bid to help frustrated city dwellers, a company called WiniaMando started selling the "kimchi fridge." It was designed partly to age kimchi, partly to keep the smell of it contained and away from the milk, cheese, and fruit juices that were much in demand in an increasingly affluent society. A society that was purchasing more and more non-Korean products. Nowadays, big Korean companies like Samsung and LG and many others have their own range of kimchi fridges.

In more recent times, I was told, some Koreans, especially fashionable young women, were going on a kimchi strike and refusing to eat it. Some stated that they couldn't eat "spicy food" and that they "don't like kimchi." The thought seemed anathema to me. Kimchi ran through Korea's veins, like cheese through a Frenchman or maple syrup through a Canadian. What was happening in this country?

Jin-Young got up to pay.

"I insist, you're my guest," she said.

And before I could argue, she had put her shoes back on, pelted her way through the restaurant, purse in hand, and reached the teller at the entrance.

When I caught up with Jin-Young, I noticed there was a woman on a stand in front of the kitchen making fresh *pajeon,* the pancake that we had eaten along with the kimchi. As it cooked, she added spring onion and a kind of flower.

"It's called *doragi* [도라지]," Jin-Young said. "Bellflower. It makes us feel cool inside during the summer months." It seemed there was always a reason for things when it came to Korean food. A reason that didn't always appear obvious to the outsider. Who knew that flowers could cool you down? Certainly not me.

Jin-Young and I walked out of the restaurant. A light breeze ruffled her long, tea-dyed hair. She had it tied into a ponytail.

"So," she said, "where are you going on this food trip of yours?"

"Everywhere I can," I said. "But not Daegu. I hear the food is absolutely awful in Daegu."

Jin-Young looked at me, her face suddenly colder.

"I'm from Daegu," she said.

I looked at the concrete slabs beneath my feet, hoping one would give way so I could slip out of sight.

"Sorry," I said. "But if it's any consolation, I hear the food is even worse in Daejon."

"My father is from Daejon," she said.

I kicked at the slabs of concrete, but they refused to budge. I was trapped. Then the unexpected happened: Jin-Young laughed.

"I'm just kidding," she said, elbowing my arm. "You're right, the food is terrible in Daegu. I was born there—I should know. Steer well clear of it. I wouldn't eat there if it was the last place on earth."

Irony, self-deprecation, the ability to laugh at oneself and one's country. In Korea? This was new, too, and unexpected. Like the now infamous "Gangnam Style" by Psy, a song that parodied the nouveau riche who called Seoul's affluent Gangnam district home. I loathed "Gangnam Style," but I loved what it signified. Koreans had learned to laugh at themselves.

I began to wonder what this aged-kimchi restaurant represented. It was popular, but it was a relative rarity. Was it a sign of what was to come? Something that once choked the mainstream, but now occupied a tiny niche? I had a thought, and it horrified me: had the Korean food I had known in the nineties survived the country's race to embrace everything new across every imaginable sphere of society? And if it had, how long did it have left?

DO KOREANS DREAM
OF ELECTRIC KIMCHI?

I made my way to Myeong-dong, where I was going to meet a photographer. I stood waiting by the Myeong-dong subway exit, feeling insignificant among the rash of high rises. Opposite me, there was a single five-story building.

On the ground floor was a Tous Les Jours "authentic bakery" and a currency exchange stand. On the floors above were a traditional Chinese medicine clinic, an eye clinic, and a language institute; the top floor looked like a storage area. I could see the telltale goulash of plastic bags and cardboard boxes through the slim, dusty windows. The building was like a multilayered sandwich of Korean life: fake or bad foreign food, money, health, plastic surgery, and education.

I wondered whether the customers in Tous Les Jours really believed they were eating authentic French *pâtisserie*. And in the eye clinic, how many patients would the surgeon make look less Korean today?

At street level, in front of me, impersonators of a K-pop boy-band called EXO, dressed in six-foot-high puppet costumes, were about to perform. Each of the ten EXO replicants wore an enormous head with a backward-facing baseball cap. The stand-ins wobbled in their preposterous costumes on the pedestrianized street as they waited for the music to start from a huge PA system.

Next to me was a group of selfie-stick holders. I looked around—they were everywhere. They held their weapons high above the crowd and looked for the perfect picture, as the people dressed up as puppets pretended to be EXO. EXO—the *real* EXO—was a curious, but successful, K-pop boy-band experiment that started in 2011. The band was unusual in that half its members were Korean and the other half Chinese, and they released songs simultaneously in Korean and Mandarin.

Looking at Korea from this angle, the country had a thin veneer of anything you might call real. An EXO-skin of life. It was far from my aged lunch, steeped in a sour and steadfast tradition, at Kimchi Jjim.

Since that lunch, I'd started to see significance in everything that passed in front of me. And for some reason, as I gawped at EXO and studied the buildings, I was reminded of blade runner Rick Deckard in Philip K. Dick's book *Do Androids Dream of Electric Sheep?* In it, Deckard owned an electric sheep and hunted replicants, or androids, for a living. Electric animals were seen as second-rate, poor substitutes for the rarer, real animals. I remembered a section of the book:

> [Deckard] had never thought of it before, the similarity between an electric animal and an [android]. The electric animal, he pondered, could be considered a subform of the other, a kind of vastly inferior robot. Or, conversely, the android could be regarded as a highly developed, evolved version of the ersatz animal. Both viewpoints repelled him.

As the EXO puppets began miming the song now rattling out of the PA, I wondered if the popularity of Kimchi Jjim was in some way a reaction against this replicant life. A life that, perhaps, seemed a little transient, plastic, and unfulfilling. I wondered: when a society changes so much, so often and so fast, all in the pursuit of success, including the cynical cross-cultural marketing success of a band like EXO, what psychological effect did this have on Koreans? As one Korean American writer put it, "Korea's success . . . could not have happened without [a] collectively warped psyche."

I frowned at my own warped thoughts as the crowd watching the EXO puppets grew ever more animated. Thankfully, Josh, the Canadian photographer, and his Korean partner, Areum, arrived at the subway exit to strike out those thoughts. We walked away from EXO and entered the nearby Namdaemun market. Josh had previously lived in Iksan, the same South Korea city I had lived in, though long after I had left. I wanted to hear how the place had changed. And I wanted to ask Areum the deceptively simple, yet alarmingly difficult, question: What is Korean food?

Namdaemun is a warren, a relic, and a scrum. It is the capital's most popular market, and it dates back to 1414, although you'd never guess that from looking at it today. It was flattened during the Korean War and burned to cinders in 1953. It hobbled on until the city authorities decided to renovate it in 2007.

It was a higgledy-piggledy mess of food, clothes, cookware, bedding, electronics, tourist knick-knacks, and restaurants. The good restaurants, Areum told me, were located down a squash of passageways away from the main shopping area. We veered off the central market and into one of them. It was a narrow grid of people-filled veins. Walking through it at lunchtime was akin to being inside a tube of toothpaste. You didn't so much as walk as have yourself squeezed along with the rest of the cram of humanity.

The squeeze stopped at a restaurant with a line. It sold the same dish as all its neighbors, something called *galchi jorim* (갈치조림).

"*Galchi jorim* is the specialty of this market," said Areum. "And this restaurant is one of the most popular places for it. It's one of the oldest, too, and for me, I think it's the best one."

Galchi jorim is silver hairtail fish braised with soy sauce, spring onions, garlic, red pepper powder, sesame seeds, and sliced radish.

"They put it all in a pot and cover it," she said. "The radish acts as a kind of steamer for the fish. The hairtail sits on top of the radish inside the pot along with the spring onion."

Red, white, yellow, and blue signs, all advertising the same dish, disappeared into the distance down the alley like a neon rainbow tunnel. One sign had a plastic model of the long, slim, silvery, eel-like hairtail fish hanging under the restaurant's sign, and every one of the twenty or more restaurants in the alley sold the same thing. They were all packed with customers, and they all had lines, but Joong Ang restaurant (중앙식당) had the longest.

Outside was an angry stove. Nine dull, battered, metallic bowls filled with *galchi jorim* roiled red like furious pockets of lava. The bowls seemed to be arguing with one another. On one side of the stove there were yet more bowls, stacks of them, five high, ten wide. They seemed to be tapping their fingers, irritably waiting their turn on the volcanic flame ride. On the other side was a grill where sole and horse mackerel, known simply as *saengseon gui* (생선구이, "grilled fish"), sizzled. Yet another gas stove was used to cook a steamed scrambled egg mixture called *gyeram jim* (계란찜) in stone bowls. The bowls bubbled, letting out big yellow burps of air. They oozed as if threatening to flood the stove with fluffy, yellow, steaming egg.

Inside the restaurant, the walls were a patchwork of posters, menus, and advertising. Every table was full; rice steamed, pots bubbled, and diners gobbled. The staff was stretched thin.

We went upstairs to the floor seating part of the restaurant. It was like a Zen massage room compared to the fighting pit downstairs. After disposing of our shoes, we sat on tatami mats at the only vacant low-level table in the restaurant.

I was told that the owners bought their fish every day from Cheong-nyangyi market in Seoul. The fish landed the night before from ports in the southeast of the country at Yeosu and Mokpo, and on Jeju island. Unsurprisingly, the restaurant smelled of fish. It was like being smothered in the comforting embrace of a deep-sea fisherman's sou'wester. A plastic flask of cold water and some stainless-steel beakers arrived, and our order was taken.

As I took out the metal chopsticks stored in an oblong wooden box on the table and handed them out, the side dishes arrived. There was dried seaweed, *kim* (김), sealed inside a plastic bag; a dipping bowl with soy, sesame, and finely chopped green onions, along with another of soy and wasabi; and dishes of kimchi, marinated chiles, salted mackerel, and marinated cucumber.

Despite government campaigns to reduce the intake of salt in South Korea, the average sodium intake for Korean adults is more than twice that recommended by the World Health Organization (WHO). This *galchi jorim* spread had enough salt in it to make a Mormon feel right at home.

"When picking our fish, we make sure to look at its thickness for quality," Mrs. Yoon Chae-Yun, the restaurant owner's daughter, told us as she delivered our food to the table. "You need good anchovies, radish, and rice water to make it properly. We add twenty different ingredients to make *galchi jorim* and it has to be marinated for one full day before we can serve it."

Mrs. Yoon grew up in Gwangju, in the southwest of South Korea, before her family moved to Seoul and her mother, Mrs. Kim Gwe-Rae, opened the restaurant. Despite its distance from the sea, Namdaemun market is known as the best place in South Korea to eat *galchi jorim*.

"Why are there so many *galchi jorim* restaurants on Namdaemun?" I asked.

"They used to have a delivery system to the various market stalls here," said Mrs. Yoon, "so the market traders could eat. Shortly after, a number of office workers found out about it and it became famous on its own. A lot of *galchi jorim* restaurants followed suit to take advantage of its popularity. Recently, we have had many tourists from China and Japan. They like to try this dish here."

Areum explained that you eat morsels of the fish on a spoon with a clump of rice or wrapped in a small sheet of the seaweed with chopsticks. Yes, the *galchi jorim* was salty, but rich, deep, sweet, warming, and incredibly tender. Like a salty, velvety, fish-flavored cotton candy.

Areum was an art student from Suwon, a city east of Seoul. She had studied traditional Korean cooking at Dankook University, but she hadn't lasted long.

"It was boring," she said. "Deathly dull. It was all theory, and we didn't learn to cook at all. We never even went into a kitchen."

Attached to the wall next to us was the kind of toilet tissue dispenser you would normally find on the wall in an airport bathroom. I tugged out a few sheets and wiped at the sweet, brown hot sauce that had dripped down my chin.

"They called them cooking classes, but they were more like a history lesson going way back to kings and queens," she said. "We even learned about how a bowl was made. They were cooking lessons without any cooking."

I wasn't sure that with such an education Areum would feel fully qualified to answer the question I wanted to ask, but I thought I'd give it a go anyhow.

"What is Korean food?" I asked.

Essayists, journalists, bloggers, academics, and barroom philosophers have all looked at this question. And I could already imagine some of the answers whirling around Areum's head as she and Josh debated the question.

They mulled over the fact that a lot of Korean food, like *galchi jorim*, is served with a multitude of side dishes, but so is much Middle Eastern and Japanese food. That many Korean foods are fermented, but so are many Polish and Russian foods. That rice is a staple, but so it is for half the world's cuisines. Stumped, they both resorted to what most people seemed to resort to when asked the same question.

"Kimchi," said Areum. "I can't think of anything else."

It was an incredibly difficult question to answer. What makes any country's food *its* food? The clearest definition I had come across was from Mr. Hwang Gyo-Ik, a Korean food columnist and blogger:

"The core of the identity that makes a Korean food is the food ingredient that is only available in Korea or tastes the best when produced in Korea."

While kimchi is distinctively Korean, the methods of cooking—or fermenting—it are not specifically Korean and can be found all around the world, particularly in countries that experience severe winters, like China, Japan, Russia, and Poland.

South Koreans consume almost 2.2 million tons of kimchi per year. However, the country can't make enough of it to feed the national addiction. It has to import an additional 260,000 tons per year. And most of that comes from China. Chinese-made kimchi does not appear in Korean supermarkets, but is commonly served in restaurants.

"Yeah, I read about that in a little newspaper some kids I teach read," said Josh. "We discussed it together. They were pretty surprised to read it."

So much Chinese kimchi is imported that one newspaper headline suggested South Korea was losing its "kimchi sovereignty." The dispute has a precedent. In 1996, Japan wanted to call its own version of kimchi the similar sounding *"kimuchi."* The Koreans didn't like that. They took the issue to the WHO, and, in 2001, a WHO committee agreed that the Korean recipe would be the international standard for kimchi.

"Chinese kimchi?" said Areum. "In Korean restaurants? In Korea? No. That's not possible."

"Yeah, it's true," Josh said. "A lot of the kimchi in restaurants in Korea is imported from China. That's what it said in the newspaper."

"No way," said Areum. "No one would dare sell foreign kimchi in Korea. It's . . . just . . . not . . . possible."

Confusion crossed her face. I imagined a kimchi-making factory in some chemically infected horror show of a Chinese village, churning out batch after batch of machine-made kimchi for Korean consumption. Should the situation continue, my imagination raged, kimchi—Korean-made kimchi— would become exotic and expensive. Like the real animals in Philip K. Dick's novel.

When the kimchi department in South Korea's Ministry of Agriculture discovered the high volume of Chinese kimchi infiltrating the country, they sought to have manufacturers list the origins of all the ingredients used to make it. The government is currently chewing over whether to force restaurants to list the origins of everything they serve.

So, what was Korean in Korean food in Korea today? It was hard for anyone to know. Could I fall in love again? Could I fall in love, if this time love was with an imitation? A replicant? If the real animal was too rare? And I was back with Philip K. Dick as I wondered: *Do Koreans dream of electric kimchi?*

"The ingredients are really important," Mrs. Kim (a well-known kimchi cook) explained in an interview with the BBC from her kimchi lab, "not to mention the water, the temperature, and also the humidity. It's Korea where those elements exist, so the kimchi made in Korea is full of very healthy enzymes. In China, the ingredients are different, and the environment is different as well, so you don't get the same enzymes. Korean kimchi and Chinese kimchi are two totally different things."

To understand the importance of kimchi to Koreans, you must first realize that many Koreans think a meal is incomplete without kimchi. They believe it can fight off illness, that it defended the nation against the 2002 SARS epidemic. There's even a museum dedicated to kimchi, boasting hundreds of varieties of kimchi in the Insadong district of Seoul.

The lengths to which Koreans will go to get their kimchi knows no bounds. In the midnineties, I had Korean colleagues who were terrified of traveling abroad for any length of time in case they couldn't source kimchi. Like addicted squirrels, they'd fill an extra suitcase with it, along with packets and packets of instant noodles. Because, you know, just in case there's nothing to eat . . . "out there."

In 2008, scientists at the Korea Food Research Institute designed "space kimchi" for Korea's first astronaut as she blasted off in a Russian-made rocket for her ten-day mission to the International Space Station. Ten days in the off-world colony was simply too long for a Korean to be without kimchi. Science to the rescue.

Lastly, you must realize that kimchi *is* Korea. Pretenders from China, Japan, and elsewhere are a threat, an insult, an affront to an entire nation, although perhaps not to budget-conscious restaurant owners. It is not possible that kimchi called kimchi, or even *kimuchi*, could originate from anywhere other than Korea. Kimchi's *appellation d'origine contrôlée* is Korea's birthright.

I asked Josh about where I used to live, the city of Iksan, where I first learned to love kimchi. He'd lived there as recently as 2010.

"Just wait until you get downtown," he said. "You won't recognize a thing."

His words sent an excited shiver through me. I was excited for the change, but fearful of the rampant reconstruction he warned me I would witness once I got there.

4

NEO-KOREA

I n 2002, over the sixteen-foot-high old stone walls of the diplomatic district in Seoul's Jung district, a war of sorts played out. Congdu restaurant had not long ago opened behind the British Embassy. It occupied the space between the residences of the British and United States ambassadors.

I was at Congdu to have dinner with Fiona Bae, a Korean businesswoman and good friend of a colleague of mine, the former BBC correspondent in Seoul. Andy had recommended the restaurant. When it came to experiencing Korean food, the chefs at Congdu had a way of making sure the nearby foreign missions had no diplomatic immunity.

"The embassy complained about the smell," Fiona said.

Fiona liked food and she worked to promote it. She had her own PR company and the government employed her to help publicize food. So did Vivian Han, the brains behind Congdu.

"It was the smell of the fish grilling that annoyed them at the embassy," said Fiona. "The chefs used to grill the fish in a space outside the kitchen, but they called the authorities."

"Who did?" I asked. "The British ambassador?"

I imagined the poor, privileged consul sniffing the air around his or her musty office and pestering a local serf to remedy the issue: *"Could you please sort out that awful stench? The natives are cooking up their horrendous stink again."*

"Good grief, no," replied Fiona. "It was the staff at the embassy. The Korean staff. They're the ones who complained that it was too smelly for them. It was the Koreans. Imagine . . ."

I was beginning to warm to this new Korea, the humor, the irony. I had visions of these sensitive Koreans, infected with uppity foreign ways, sitting at their computers with clothespins on their noses, distraught at the foul odor of their native cuisine. Their delicate constitutions probably couldn't stomach kimchi, either.

A potent cocktail of pickled radish, fish, pepper, and garlic stirs the Seoul air like the smog blanketing other cities. Although, with well over three million vehicles in the capital, Seoul regularly boasts smog, too. The streets of Korea are filled with this unsubtle scent and it emanates from the unsubtle food, a pong I didn't fully realize I loved until I'd left it.

While Andy had recommended Congdu, he had also warned me about having any contact with the government.

"For God's sake," he said, "don't speak to the government. They won't let you near a *galbi* house. They will be shoving you in front of Royal Court cuisine and Michelin-starred mincers and feeding you with a shovel loaded to the brim with nationalistic propaganda nonsense."

Both Fiona and Vivian were close to the government. I was wary, but arrived at Congdu with an open mind. I'd been told there were only four or five restaurants like this in Korea today and that Congdu was the first modern Korean restaurant in Seoul.

From the outside, the traditional tiled roof indicated that the restaurant was Korean, but it didn't look like a Korean restaurant inside. It was more Scandinavian minimal than Korean maximal. Where there should have been a TV playing sports or soap operas, there was chamber music.

Where there should have been fluorescent lighting, there were painted walls, dim lights, terra-cotta pots, and white drapes with neat folds.

I sat down at a starched-white-cotton-covered window table. This, too, made me apprehensive: I had never been inside a Korean restaurant with a tablecloth made of anything other than thin, absorbent paper. The waiters wore uniforms and spoke good English; they served with a smile and explained the food to me. Congdu looked about as far from my idea of a Korean restaurant as was possible for me to imagine.

A dish arrived, as wide as an Elizabethan collar with a pit the size of a thimble in the middle of it—that was for the soup—accompanied by a small bowl of rice and another of cold water. This soup didn't look Korean to me. Fiona explained.

"Put the rice in the cold water," she said. "It helps cool the saltiness of the crab."

There was a sweetness to the soup. It reminded me of a deep sweetness I had tasted in Việt Nam, but it wasn't a sugar sweetness and it wasn't artificial.

"It's the crab shell," said Fiona. "That's all they need to make the sweetness of the broth. They don't add any sugar at all."

Korean soups, to my mind, were akin to entering a boxing ring. Red pepper arrived as a right hook, garlic a blow to the torso, bean paste, gochujang, clams, and tiny salty shrimp the final glorious knockout combination. This soup was nothing of the sort. Where Korean food normally attacked me, this soup stroked me. It was subtle, for a start; none of the tastes overwhelmed. It was deep and complex and, beyond that, it was the smallest soup I'd ever seen in Korea.

"The soy crab has a unique taste," said Vivian. She had joined Fiona and me for a chat. A former fashion designer, she wore a beige throw and had her wavy hair tied back. "This crab stew is from an old recipe book."

Vivian's family were originally from Pyongyang, the capital of North Korea. Her family had escaped North Korea during the Korean War.

"We use very old recipe books," she said, "recipes that most people in

Korea don't know. For this soup, we put *gochujang* and *doenjang* in it. It tastes really good with the seaweed."

Vivian used a particular kind of seaweed found only on the west coast of Korea. It has a finer texture than regular kelp and is more bitter. Due to her family's heritage, Vivian said she'd always felt more of a culinary connection with North Korea than with South.

"North Korean people like very simple but elegant-tasting soups," she said, "and we are very picky people. We make three different kinds of broth—pork, beef, and chicken—and then we combine them. If we don't have the three kinds of meat, we just make the pork broth, as that's the most important one."

Cooking knowledge had been passed down orally in Vivian's family. There were never any recipes.

"We never measured things," she said.

The crab soup was astounding, as was every course that followed. From the ornate assortment of variously aged kimchi, a fish carpaccio with caviar, three different petri dishes of different ages of soy sauce (three-, ten- and fifteen-year-old) to a single pine-and-soju-steamed prawn dramatically sizzled by the waitress for all of thirty seconds on a hot stone covered by a bamboo basket. It was steamed in the same soju we were drinking, a premium tipple from Andong, which was like a smooth, cold, grainy vodka. I could almost see a Siberian ice floe glide before my eyes as I drained the glass. There was no hint of the vicious chemicals common in soju's street-corner supermarket edition.

"This is a special kind of shrimp," said Vivian as the waitress served the soju-sozzled shrimp. "We can only catch this kind of shrimp near Dokdo Island. After it's caught, it's frozen very rapidly. We don't really cook it as such, we just heat this stone and we put pine leaves and the forty-one percent soju in the basket to flavor it."

Dokdo is a group of rocks in what the Koreans call the East Sea, what the Japanese call the Sea of Japan. The rocks are a matter of ongoing dispute between Japan and South Korea. Dokdo is South Korean territory, but the Japanese say they want it. North Korea also claims sovereignty. Whatever you do when you visit Korea, don't talk about Dokdo, and do not refer to the East Sea as the Sea of Japan. They're both nationalistic touchpapers.

I'd long wondered why Korea's collective dander rose so aggressively at the mention of Dokdo, known as the Liancourt Rocks in English. There are no mineral deposits, no gas, no oil, and no habitation, beyond a South Korean Police Guard house. As far as I could tell, Dokdo was simply rocks. There is a saying commonly heard in Korea that "Korea is a shrimp caught between two whales"—the whales in the sandwich being China and Japan. And after I spoke with Vivian, and tasted the succulent white ocean flesh of this sea creature, I wondered whether the Dokdo fracas wasn't really a territorial battle over a bunch of rocks at all. I reckoned that the crafty Koreans might merely want to keep the hands of those pesky Japanese colonialists off their delicious shrimp.

Vivian said she'd always been told that salt was the most important ingredient in Korean cooking.

"That's what my grandpa always said," she continued. "If you use bad salt, you're going to ruin your bean paste, soy sauce, kimchi, everything. My family would go all over North Korea to find the best salt."

After growing up in the United States, England, and France, Vivian eventually relocated to South Korea. Like her family before her, she now traveled all around South Korea to find the best bean paste, kimchi, soy sauce, and other traditional ingredients.

"Everything we serve is Korean," Vivian said. "Our chef has to learn the old traditional ways, but he also has to learn 'high technique' and what's going on outside Korea. The food business is very trendy. I was in the fashion business before this, and things change even faster with food than they do with fashion."

As I already had the most basic answer to the question "What is Korean food?," I now wanted to know the answer to another question: "What is neo-Korean food?"

"I use only traditional ingredients," she said. "The only thing we add is our chef's imagination to make our own sauces and to make our food more modern. Sometimes I would really like to use butter or make bread, but we just want to use things that are from our land. That's the difference with us and other restaurants like us in Seoul."

Vivian told me about a group of mysterious Korean sages known as the "grand masters." They were a small band of revered chefs in Korea. Think samurai, but with a kitchen knife and a bag of chiles. And not Japanese in any way whatsoever. They each specialized in one or two traditional Korean foods, whether it be kimchi, soy sauce, or *doenjang*. To qualify as a grand master, they had to make one of these things from an ancient Korean recipe book for twenty years.

"These old people," said Vivian, "they don't write down their recipes and they don't ordinarily give out their recipes."

Around 30 percent of Congdu's customers were foreigners and the rest were Korean. How, I wondered, could Vivian convince Koreans to come and spend so much to eat her Korean food when the fluorescent-light version, with the added bonus of baseball or a soap opera on TV, was so much cheaper?

"The Koreans are the hardest customers to convince to eat here," she said. "We look down on our own food. But I want to show them that you can create something excellent. That you don't have to look down upon it, that you can be proud of it and know that it's truly Korean."

Both Vivian and Fiona agreed that attitudes toward food were changing in Korea.

"When Korean people go abroad, they take their kimchi, instant noodles, and soju," said Fiona. "And at home they only eat *doenjang-jjigae, kimchi-jjigae,* but they're starting to change a little bit, to experiment, although there's still that shame. You know, if a Korean invites you into their home, they won't serve you *cheonggukjang*."

Cheonggukjang (청국장) is a stinker of a soup. It is made of fermented soybean paste, and unlike *doenjang*, it is fermented in air and fermented far quicker. It also includes whole soybeans, not just crushed beans like *doenjang* does. Bowing down before a bowl of *cheonggukjang* has been compared to sticking your head into rotting garbage.

"They'll never serve it to you," said Vivian, "because it's so smelly. Even though they love it, they don't want to show it to you. Even kimchi—sometimes they don't want to show it to foreign people. That's why I started my own restaurant. We're still not very confident about what food we have. But I think that old attitude, that total shame of Korean food, is changing these days, changing quite dramatically."

I suggested that there was a certain irony attached to the fact that Koreans would seek approval of their food from Americans and Britons and other foreigners. These were nations of people far removed from Korea with little understanding of Korean food.

"When I was living abroad, my family had to show people our food," said Vivian, "to share our culture as foreigners would share their culture with us. And we saw that people liked it, and that we could give them a history of this food and they really loved to hear it and to taste the food. I'm very proud of our North Korean kimchi. I'm very happy that my parents gave me that confidence in our food. Now I have that attitude, you know, 'If you don't like it, too bad for you, because you're missing out.'"

If Vivian was any indication of the future, maybe Koreans were indeed becoming more French. The food at Congdu didn't look or taste Korean. Or rather, it didn't look or taste the way I expected Korean food to look or taste. To me, Korean food arrived with a thud. Like a doorstopper novel with a mind-bending Louis Wain front cover and a warped cinema within. Vivian's food was none of that. It fluttered onto my table like a butterfly. A bit like the fruit cake pizza, but with an important distinction: "Everything we serve is Korean," Vivian assured me. This was Korean food, and there were no electric sheep or electric kimchi inside her restaurant.

5

SEOLLEONGTANG

Jongno is at once familiar and foreign . . . Although it's in the center of Seoul, it always seems like a street on the fringes of the city. At the same time, it feels the most authentically Seoul.

—*Young-ha Kim,* Your Republic Is Calling You

The taxi's meter started at 3,000 won as a *SimCity*-like GPS system in the center of the dashboard pointed the way to Jongno; the radio was a giggle of K-pop. The driver wore tight white cotton gloves. As he stopped at a light, a woman crossed. She wore a short black miniskirt, clutched a small briefcase in one hand, and tugged at a cigarette with the other.

As I watched her totter in front of the crush of cars, I remembered a woman I hadn't seen in more than twenty years. Jin had been a Korean student in England with a militant attachment to miniskirts and smoking. In the depths of a British winter, it was something I had found difficult to comprehend.

"I'll wear them until I die," she had said. "And I'll smoke until I die, too. They can shoot me, I don't care."

Long hair and skirts eight inches or more above the knee were banned under Park Chung-hee's presidency during the sixties and seventies. In the eighties, when Jin was a teenager, and well into the nineties, mini-skirts were still frowned upon by conservative Korea. Cigarettes, too: smoking was for men; "good girls" didn't smoke, and they certainly didn't smoke in public. During Jin's teens, the miniskirt and the cigarette were two of the only tools of rebellion available to her.

There was something romantic about the woman walking across the street. Once, she would have been seen as a rebel, but not anymore. The fashions she wore were the norm today; no one looked twice or made rude comments. And, for the most part, women felt free to smoke in public places. Women were still fighting for their rights, but there was a female president, a Ministry of Gender Equality and Family, and more and more women in the workplace. Female rebellion had moved beyond a pack of smokes and short skirts.

The taxi slipped into gear and gunned onward until I reached the vicinity of Imun Seolleongtang (이문 설농탕). *Seolleongtang* is an ox-bone soup from Seoul. It consists of fatty, tender slivers of well-boiled beef and liver in a ox-bone stock and comes with a side bowl of rice. I'd quietly asked people who had lived for some time in Seoul about this dish. And all roads led to this door, this shiny new door.

Imun Seolleongtang originally opened at the beginning of the twen-tieth century, but moved to its current location in 2011. The restaurant was called Imun because that was the name of the old road and the old city gate in this area. On the wall at the entrance was a picture of the old place. It looked like a storybook house. It was unfathomable to imagine such a thing had stood where I was standing just four years ago. The old building had survived wars, colonialism, and martial law, but not Korean progress. The new place was surrounded by modern, mirror-glass monstrosities.

On each table inside the restaurant there was a selection of salt, pepper, kimchi, and chopped red chiles. Cut-up leeks were stored inside stainless-steel tubs and sets of pincers and scissors peeked out of the kimchi vats. The main choices at Imun were two versions of *seolleong-tang*: one was 8,000 won, the other 10,000 won. The only difference was that the more expensive one had more meat. Also on offer were the less popular *doganitang* (도가니탕), which is a cartilage soup, and *suyuk* (수육), which is boiled pork. I didn't need to order, my soup just arrived. My order was pinned to a clipboard, which was then placed upon my table.

Seolleongtang is a freak among Korean soups. It comes entirely un-salted, there is no red pepper, and the soup is a cloudy color. It almost looks like milk with chopped spring onions bobbing about on top. *Seol-leongtang* is pure boiled bone water; there's no subtlety in the cooking. It's that rolling boil that triggers the milky complexion—simmering just doesn't give the same result. You'll also find this basic long-boiled soup in the Korean-style wonton soup called *manduguk* (만두국) or many other soup-based Korean dishes.

While it is the stock that is the foundation of *seolleongtang*, the stars that make this dish shine come from the nuts and bolts on the table. The kimchi in the school canteen–style buckets on the table has plenty enough salt in it already without adding more from the salt cellar. I dragged at the kimchi and clipped it into my soup. The red tentacles dripped a glossy fire of soy, sesame, and chile, then I added some leeks. You can add rice to the soup; some like it with noodles. Whichever way you take it, a slug or two of *seolleongtang* will return feeling to even the most weary of veins. This soup is a pure power-up food.

"It's just regular *seolleongtang*," said the waitress. "It's nothing special."

I looked at her, incredulous. This was a restaurant with a history going back over a hundred years, one that had always used the same recipe, a Seoul institution, but to her, this place was "nothing special." I asked her why, if it was nothing special, was it the most popular *seolleongtang* restaurant in Seoul, the one everyone recommended to me?

"I don't really know," she said. She looked genuinely confused, as if she had never considered the question before. "The chefs have worked here for at least a couple of decades . . . They boil the bones all night long, every night. It takes one day to make [the *seolleongtang*] and we sell over two hundred bowls a day. But I'm not part of the family who owns this place, I just run the floor. I'm not sure why this place is more popular."

She did, however, know a little of the history of the dish and had an idea as to why Seoulites liked it so much.

"People started making *seolleongtang* after the Chosŏn dynasty," she said. "That's a little over one hundred years ago. I think people like it because it's indicative of how life was all of those years ago, when we used to sit around the fire to keep warm. It's really good soup to have in winter."

Maybe it was cognitive suggestion, but I imagined myself as a *yangban*, one of the traditional rulers in Korea, dressed in white, with a long gray beard, supping soup around a wood fire on a scrap of land in central Seoul a century ago. We'd let the beef bone broth seep through us, recite poetry, speak wise thoughts, slap each other's backs, and get utterly annihilated on soju.

This clean, pure soup was like a brick in an old wall, sturdy and reliable, but it didn't like to boast about its presence too much.

"We stick the lot into the pot to make the soup," she said. "All parts of the cow—the head, the intestines, the lot."

I was served a beaker of cold barley water. On the right-hand side of the restaurant was a wall of sliding wooden and glass doors. Laminated reviews tiled the opposite walls alongside a flat-screen TV. A phone rang every few minutes at the front desk. A slim, gray-haired man in a tight black shirt, glasses, and black trousers took the orders and operated the cash register.

"I think we're popular because the price is right," the waitress said. "I'm not sure it goes any deeper than that. No one misses the old place.

The people who own these kind of places, they all would prefer to have a newer place. No one wants to be stuck in some old building or a shed."

Imun had gotten lucky with this location. There was no space in this part of Seoul; the restaurant was like a cornered animal, surrounded by behemoths, all filled with hungry office workers.

"Ten years ago, this used to be a famous private language school and university preparation school area," she said. "Now it's all gone. The private schools moved to Noryangjin, then they moved to Gangnam, south of the river. Gangnam's flooded with them now. The schools just follow the money."

Inside Imun, suits, ties, and perms dominated. It was predominantly an older crowd, roughly 90 percent old, 10 percent young. There were workers who rushed over their lunch, while the retired lingered a little longer.

"Old people come regardless," she said, "even though we are quite far from the subway."

Old men wiped their brows and necks like they'd been under a car all morning, and they coughed as the chile-infused kimchi battled its way through their creaking soju-soaked systems. I paid my tab and took a piece of gum from the basket at the reception. Outside the restaurant were fig trees and a wooden deck. *Seolleongtang,* I thought, *what a wonderful name.* It seemed to work in English just as well as it worked in Korean. It sounded like a soup with a farewell card slipped inside it—a "so long, see you later"-*tang*—and in a way it was, for I was about to leave Seoul.

I thought more about the Korean language later that day when I met Charles Montgomery. He was an American, a professor at Seoul's Dongguk University who wrote about Korean literature in translation.

"Korean is an incredibly flexible language," said Charles as we sipped coffee inside a Paris Baguette outpost in Itaewon. "I have a Korean American friend who grew up in the Bay area, and whenever he comes here, he has to learn a whole new vocabulary."

Thinking of *seolleongtang,* I asked Charles how the language manifested itself in food in modern-day Korea.

"The Korean language is brilliant for making portmanteau words," he said. "New words crop up all the time. You can take chicken and the Korean word for beer, *maekju* (맥주), and you have *chi-maek* (치맥) in one second. Look around—you'll see *chi-maek* is everywhere."

Chi-maek, a perennial favorite of Koreans. So much so that the number of fried chicken outlets in South Korea outnumbered the number of McDonald's outlets worldwide.

"If Korea ever gets subcultures," said Charles, "they're going to be able to create entire new languages on the turn of a dime."

Subcultures, food subcultures—I realized this was what I had seen in Seoul. There were those striving for the innovative at Bar Sanchez, others who were digging deep into the past to create neo-Korean Congdu. There were those who made special what used to be normal—Hanok Jib Kimchi Jjim. And then there were those who'd been doing the same thing since almost the dawn of time—Imun Seolleongtang. I wondered, were these innovators not the metaphorical miniskirt-wearing, cigarette-smoking women of the modern Korean kitchen?

1.5 DAK GALBI

I thought that no matter how many hills and brooks you crossed, the whole world was Korea and everyone in it was Korean.

—*Park Wan-suh,* Who Ate Up All the Shinga?

A synthesized trumpet announced the train as it stopped beside platform one at Yongsan Station in Seoul. It was empty, the chairs inside the carriage automatically swiveled around to face the opposite direction, and then the doors opened. Yongsan Station connects the capital to the country's eastern seaboard, and the fastest trains can make the journey in about an hour.

I was standing at a small cabin called Mom's Snack. It sold hot dogs, coffees, teas, and soft drinks along with the seaweed rice rolls called *kimbap* (김밥), hot-red-pepper-sauce-covered rice cakes called *tteokbokki* (떡볶이), and fish sticks in a fishy soup called *odeng guk* (오댕국).

I picked up a fish stick from the steaming tub at the front of the cabin and turned to look at the train. A group of woman hikers filed onto it. They had matching dyed-black, tight-knit perms, matching red jackets, and matching knapsacks, and they each wore black trousers and sneakers. They were ready for a day of brisk exercise in the mountains surrounding Seoul. The government had recently launched a $10 million "slow hiking" campaign. The aim was to encourage the mountain-loving Koreans to slow down and enjoy a walk instead of yomping across ranges at the speed of a conquering army.

I turned back to the snack cabin. An old man in a sport coat came and stood next to me. A fridge purred next to an array of rice cookers, flasks, instant noodle packets, an electric stove, microwave, and sink. The old man picked up a paper cup and helped himself to a ladleful of broth from the stainless-steel fish stick container. Steam rose like fish fairy dust and obscured the old man's face. Two minutes after the train arrived, the trumpet sounded again and it departed.

"Where are you going?" the old man said to me in Korean.

What Korean language I had gleaned twenty years ago had slowly been percolating back into my conscious memory. I had enough Korean to order food, the two different numbering systems were there, and I could say "please" and "thank you," and ask for directions. I could still read Hangul, the twenty-four characters in which Korean is usually written, and I could still swear, if required, and I knew enough to know when someone was asking me where *I* was going.

"Chuncheon," I said.

Two women arrived and sat down at a small table inside Mom's Snack. They shared *tteokboki* and coffee. I nibbled at my fish stick as the old man slurped at his broth. One of the women took two sheets from the toilet paper holder hanging on the wall next to her and used them to dab her heavily made-up face.

"Ah . . . *Chuncheon*," the old man said. "*Chuncheon* dak galbi . . . *Mashida.*"

Each stopping point on my journey had a target attached to it, and some had more than one target. Chuncheon was to be a quick stop and *dak galbi* (닭갈비) was the bull's-eye. Some people I'd talked to in Seoul said *dak galbi* was the only reason anyone went to Chuncheon and that it was indeed *mashida,* "delicious."

Dak galbi is a mixed chicken dish. It is cooked on a large round hot plate built into the table, comes with cabbage, rice cakes, onions, coarsely chopped leeks, and sweet potatoes, and is layered in a hot, slightly sweet sauce made of red pepper paste, soy sauce, and turmeric. Chuncheon was known as the home of *dak galbi.* There was an entire street filled with *dak galbi* restaurants. As a result, Koreans touted the city as the best place in all of Korea to eat *dak galbi.*

I ate *dak galbi* almost every weekend when I lived in Korea. *Dak galbi* is special, it's a violence, a mess, a mistake that works. It's like a building site where everything Korean that's edible got dumped inside, turned upside down, rattled about, and thrown into your face. I adored it, and I wanted it again.

An American I had eaten *pajeon* with at Gwangjang market in Seoul some days earlier had asked me if I was worried about the trip ahead. "I mean, you're all alone," he said. "And there's the language barrier." I told him I wasn't worried at all. However, as I stood there on platform one, fish stick in hand, waiting for my train, about to set sail around Korea, I suddenly felt a creeping uncertainty.

The conversation with the old man had brought my lack of Korean into sharp focus. I knew that Seoul was a linguistic island, that it was filled with far more English speakers than the rest of the country. If I wasn't worried when the American asked me that question, I was as the train arrived. There was no going back, and much of this trip would be entirely down to chance. The train stopped, the chairs swiveled, the doors opened. I entered and sat down in my assigned seat. Two minutes later, just like the one before it, my train departed exactly on time.

From the fourteenth-floor living room window, Chuncheon sagged in a thin but persistent drizzle. From up there, the city was an undulating mix of childlike mortar building blocks and low mountains. Chuncheon is the capital of Gangwon, Korea's most northeastern province. The city is shaped like a sombrero: the peak in the hat is a green hill with very few buildings on it, and the city is built around the peak. The mountain resembled a neolithic temple, one worshipped by office blocks, apartment buildings, markets, and shopping malls.

I turned my gaze back to the living room. There was an upright piano to my right; a fluffy toy sat on top of it. This was Hyun-Ae's brand-new apartment. She was the young woman from whom I was renting a room.

"So," I said, as the rain dappled the window behind me. "What's there to do in Chuncheon on a drizzly afternoon?"

Hyun-Ae looked at the floor next to the piano. I wasn't sure that she'd heard my question. A tumbleweed gently blew through the space between us. I thought I heard an owl hoot somewhere in the distance.

"There's a river," she said, "and a lake."

Behind Hyun-Ae was a bookcase filled with Korean novels and art monographs. Pages rustled as the tumbleweed bounced by.

"The lake feeds Seoul," she said. "The Chinese like to go to the lake."

I could almost visualize the cogs turning inside her brain. She was searching for the right thing to say, for anything to say.

"The Chinese like to go to *dak galbi* street," she said.

Finally, the tumbleweed rolled to a halt.

"Yes," I said. "I've heard about *dak galbi* street."

"I want to go there, to *dak galbi* street," I said. "Is it easy to get there from here?"

Not knowing how to get to *dak galbi* street was one thing, but I had another dilemma. I didn't know anyone in Chuncheon, and I knew that *dak galbi* was not something you ate alone. It's a dish for two or more people. I'd never seen anyone eat *dak galbi* alone.

"It's not far," said Hyun-Ae. "But . . ."

A look almost of pain spread across her face. Pain accentuated by a pebble-dash of circular, transparent Band-Aids stuck to her cheeks and forehead. Some kind of health thing maybe? It felt rude to ask.

"But . . . ," she said again. It was more of a sigh than a word. "But it's not good," she finished.

Her sigh deflated. It was as if she were telepathically passing on her feelings about the street to me. I received them like an unwanted baton.

"Only the Chinese go to *dak galbi* street," she said, "and the tourists."

She gazed out across Chuncheon. From this great height, as we looked out, I could almost imagine we were steering a galleon across Hyun-Ae's city on a course in search of good *dak galbi*.

"No one from Chuncheon eats *dak galbi* there," she said. "The taste is not good."

Dak galbi street was out—I needed a Plan B, and I didn't have one. In truth, I barely had a Plan A. I'd been scratching around for a dinner date in Chuncheon with no luck. Every contact of a contact I had called up was out of town, didn't reply, or simply had no interest in meeting a complete stranger.

"Where do you go?" I said.

She looked into the distance, frowned ever so slightly, clenched her teeth, tilted her head to one side, and breathed in so that she made a sharp sucking sound. It was the sort of sound you might make if you were in a car, someone else was driving, and you were sure you were about to hit the back of something really big and unforgivingly solid. In those circumstances, it's the sound of fear without screaming. In Korea, it's the sound of thinking. And it's a sequence of movements and sounds that lasts all of one second. Yet it's a sequence so common in Korea that you could almost classify it as a national trait.

"The one I like," she said, exhaling, "is called 1.5."

Drizzle shrouded the lake; the river wasn't visible and the surrounding hills, including the sombrero peak, seemed lost in the gloaming. 1.5 was better than zero, I thought, and it looked like it was a zero kind of a day.

"I can take you," said Hyun-Ae. "If you want?"

I needed a dinner partner, and what's more, I wanted and needed an insider to learn about this place. To find out why Chuncheon was famous for *dak galbi*. And to taste the best rendition the city had to offer. I accepted the invitation and she wrote down the name of the restaurant in Korean.

1.5 닭갈비

"Show it to any taxi driver," she said. "They all know it."

I arranged to meet her in a few hours' time, but before that she wanted to show me the way to an area of downtown with some good coffee shops. We walked through a small street market. A line of old women sat on the pavement with their produce laid out in front of them.

We stopped at one of them. The woman's knees were hunched up to her chin. She looked to be in her eighties. Rivulets of skin wrinkled her face like a shriveled sack. In front of her was a flattened white plastic bag, and upon it were some spring onions. There must have been fewer than thirty of the long thin green stems on her bag. She had washed and pre-cut them for her customers.

"These women earn very, very little," said Hyun-Ae. "That's why I buy small things from them here."

The old lady searched for a plastic bag to put the onions into, but Hyun-Ae held out her own bag, insisting she didn't need another.

"They grow these things on their own," said Hyun-Ae. "Most of them have a small plot of land."

These women were widowers and selling what they could grow was their way to supplement any meager savings they might have along with the paltry state pension. Life was tough for many of the elderly in South Korea.

"Nearly half of elderly South Koreans have incomes of less than fifty percent of the median wage, the worst record among industrialized nations."

The existence of so many fried chicken fast-food joints in South Korea can be partially explained by the same phenomenon. It was often old people who ran them, as fried chicken is seen as an easy business to get into and profitable enough to help boost an otherwise meager income.

"What's this?" I asked Hyun-Ae.

At my feet was an odd-looking cluster of brown lumps the size of bricks. There were five of them tied together with a piece of red ribbon. They looked like blocks of furrowed fudge, but unlike fudge, these didn't look edible.

"It's *meju* [메주]," said Hyun-Ae. "It's a kind of fermented soybean cake. We use it to make *doenjang-jjigae*."

Hyun-Ae's face crumpled at the thought of it. *Meju* is also used to make the hot red pepper paste *gochujang*, and a Korean soy sauce called *ganjang* (간장) and many, many other things.

"Very few people use this nowadays in the home," she said. "Maybe only the restaurants, because it has a terrible smell when you cook it."

Meju is made by soaking and boiling soybeans in late autumn. The result is molded into bricks and hung in a warm place to ferment over the winter. The bricks are then boiled in brine; this is where the stink begins. The *meju* separates: the liquid is *ganjang*, and the residue is *doenjang*. The thought of the cooking process brought back bad memories for Hyun-Ae.

"I can still remember my mother cooking with this," she said. "It was really, really awful. Now we just buy the sauce from a shop."

Hyun-Ae went home, and I walked toward the center of Chuncheon. A sign on a lamppost near the central market was emblazoned with the city's designated English slogan word—"Romantic Chuncheon." It looked anything but.

In their rush to develop the country, the town planners and the architects had never considered differentiating between cities and regions by design or by appearance. A government attempt to use the English language to belatedly do the job for the planners had also failed. Sometimes spectacularly.

Every Korean city name had a designated English adjective, noun, or phrase attached to it. The express intention was to make each city sound different from every other Korean city. The result was the opposite of the intention.

There was the grammatically awkward "Charm Jinju" to describe the small city in the south, "Just Sangju" to describe a city in Gyeongbuk, "Pine City Gangneung," "Season your life with Sunchang," "Wonderfull [sic] Samcheok"—the list went on. And on.

It was still raining when I arrived at 1.5 Dak Galbi. Hyun-Ae texted me to tell me that she would be two minutes late, the traffic was bad.

A *dak galbi* truck whizzed by. A couple of school girls in matching red baseball jackets walked toward me. They had matching bob haircuts and matching half-a-hundredweight backpacks, too. They were a younger mirror image of the older women who had boarded the train earlier that day. I'd read how Korean parents would spend as much as $700 on *randoseru* backpacks imported from Japan. It was so that their kids could have the best and be seen to have the best by the other parents at the school gate. Even if the rhetoric inside the school and from the government was often vehemently anti-Japan, a Japanese backpack was a desirable import. These two girls were out of school and on their way to private school. Before going home to do homework until after midnight. And up to start all over again at six A.M. Hyun-Ae arrived.

1.5 Dak Galbi occupied the ground floor of a modern four-story block on a corner in downtown Chuncheon. Bright yellow, blue, and red signs of backlit neon Hangul characters hovered above the glass-doored entrance. A framed menu pinned to the wall listed four items: *dak galbi, dak nae-jang* (닭내장, chicken tripe), *udon sari* (우동 사리, an extra order of udon noodles), and *bokkeumbap* (볶음밥, fried rice).

"I've been coming to this family's *dak galbi* ever since I was a young girl," said Hyun-Ae. "It wasn't always in this location, but the food has always stayed the same."

1.5 Dak Galbi had been operating since 1989. The parents had passed the restaurant on to their children, who now worked the kitchen. We were joined by Hyun-Ae's husband, who was nine years older than her and ran an IT company.

The restaurant was filled with about thirty tables, each with a round, black hot plate in the center, heated by an invisible gas supply. We sat down at an empty table. As soon as we ordered, the hot plate was lit.

Dak galbi is a "cook and wrap" dish. It comes with a minimal array of only essential side dishes. There was a bowl with murky red water and cubed lumps of radish inside.

"This is *mul kimchi* [물김치]," Hyun-Ae said, referring to the cold, watery, vinegary bowl on the table next to me.

The rest of the spread was made up of a rectangular dish filled with lettuce and sesame leaves. Another smaller dish was divided into two; on one side there were raw garlic cloves and on the other there was a squeeze of *gochujang*. This red pepper paste is all shoulder pads and bluster. It has a power flavor, the loudest, most obnoxious drunk at the table. In recent years it has become a hit with chefs in New York precisely because of its argumentative taste.

A *dak galbi* hot plate is a furnace. The waiter returned and deposited a bucket of chicken, vegetables, rice cakes, sweet potatoes, and noodles upon the furnace; it bubbled, blazed, sizzled, and seared. We each put on a red apron as if we were donning a spacesuit in preparation for lift-off. The waiter stirred the mix with two large spatulas. They looked more like the kind of tools you would use to strip wallpaper.

"I don't know who first came up with the idea for this dish," said Hyun-Ae. "It was a very long time ago."

She apologized that her husband could not speak any English. I apologized for my Korean. He scanned the table; something was missing.

"Where is the kimchi?" he asked the waiter.

It wasn't an oversight, the waiter told us. He explained that they didn't serve it automatically anymore as not enough people ate it and they ended up throwing too much of it away. The waiter fussed back to the open kitchen area on one side of the restaurant and came back with a small bowl of kimchi.

"He feels a meal is not a meal if there is no kimchi," said Hyun-Ae, echoing that oft-repeated Korean sentence.

Koreans often get hammered for this by foreigners. That they are inflexible, unadventurous, stuck in their ways, and stuck in their food. I had long since come to agree with the Koreans, as I was addicted to kimchi. But the availability of kimchi was an issue for me whenever I was outside of Korea.

In 2010, the price of cabbage soared by 400 percent and Koreans cried foul when restaurants started to charge extra for kimchi. The president temporarily lifted all tariffs on foreign cabbages to alleviate the national pain.

I sympathized. I lived in Rwanda for four years, a mostly kimchi-less country, and one day I spotted a group of four Korean women in a butchery. They were easy to identify, as they had the Korean uniform on: heavy white makeup, matching tennis outfits, sun visors. They were expat wives, I deduced, as Rwanda didn't see a whole lot of Korean tourists. I approached them and, after the usual pleasantries, politely asked them if they happened to know someone who might be able to supply me with a little bit of kimchi. Of course, I knew there was no way they would not have any. And I knew they wouldn't understand the meaning of "a little bit." They were astounded at my request and only too happy to comply with my needs. I ended up getting more kimchi than I could have ever consumed during the rest of my stay in central Africa.

"I don't like kimchi," said Hyun-Ae. "I can eat *kimchi-jjigae* and rice fried with kimchi, but not like that."

She looked at the dish next to her husband and winced as he devoured shred after shred of red goodness. He was oblivious to her winces—he only had eyes for his kimchi and his smartphone.

I almost felt sorry for Hyun-Ae. It didn't sound like an affectation, like the young people Jin-Young had told me about in the kimchi restaurant in Seoul. However, times were a-changin'. Studies showed that kimchi consumption was down. By 2015, and for the first time ever, coffee was the most consumed food and beverage item in the Land of the (so-called) Morning Calm.

According to the *Korea Times*, "The average Korean drinks coffee 12.2 times per week or 1.74 times a day. Meanwhile, kimchi is consumed 11.9 times per week, coming in second to coffee."

The waiter gave the *dak galbi* a final slap with the spatulas and signaled that it was ready for consumption. The hot plate was a savannah of sizzling, slippy red. I picked up a lettuce leaf, and put a sesame leaf and a small clove of garlic inside it. I'd long ago learned to go easy on raw garlic. Too much, and you will suffer terrible indigestion. I plucked a piece of chicken and some leeks from the devastation in front of us, wrapped it all up in the lettuce leaf, and popped it into my mouth.

It had been twenty years since I had tasted this dish. The *gochujang* jolted the memories back with an electric pepper shock. It was everything I remembered and more. Storks swam, rainbows flipped, and cats crowed. It was all wrong, but all so right. When Korea gets things really, really wrong, they get things so, so right. That was *dak galbi*. The mess that shouldn't work. I dug in. I would gladly let Korea's jackboot to the taste buds stamp on me until my skull split open.

Meanwhile, Hyun-Ae's husband remained engrossed in his phone. He ignored dinner.

"Stock prices," said Hyun-Ae, noticing that I had observed him deep in concentration, tapping at the large screen.

"Do you do stock prices?" she said.

"No, I don't," I said. "No money for stocks. No money for much of anything, to be honest."

"We are creative people here in Chuncheon," she said. "Creative at making money and creative with food. Creative with everything, really."

"Creative with food?" I asked. "In what way? How many other dishes is the city famous for?"

"We have *makguksu* [막국수]," she said.

This was a buckwheat noodle dish served cold, similar in some ways to a North Korean *naengmyeon* (냉면). Gangwon province was well known for its different *makguksu* dishes. Chuncheon even had its own *makguksu* noodle festival once per year. However, I had my eyes on a different *makguksu* on my next stop on this journey around Korea.

"And *doenjang-jjigae*," she said.

This was one of Korea's most basic soups. Like a powered-up version of miso, it is found everywhere and is so cheap that a slang term utilizing it had even evolved.

A *"doenjang* girl" or "bean paste girl" was a somewhat derogatory term used to describe a young woman who eats *doenjang-jjigae* and little else. That way, the slang definition went, she could save money to buy Gucci handbags, exotic perfumes, designer clothes, expensive jewelery, and high-end makeup and pay the cost of her surgeon's fees and other necessities that form part of being a modern Korean woman. Psy ridiculed *doenjang* girls in "Gangnam Style."

However, I didn't think *doenjang-jjigae* was a Chuncheon dish. It was more of a general dish with no known origin. Like a traditional song passed down orally through the generations, its beginnings lost in the ether.

"Chuncheon has many rivers," Hyun-Ae said. "We eat some river fish, like cherry salmon, as sashimi here. It has a very different taste from regular sashimi. We're also well known for our beef. Korean beef is very good from this area, but it is expensive. How many famous dishes come from your hometown?"

Ouch. Touché.

I had nothing.

It was a fair point, and unreasonable to expect a relatively small Korean city to be some well of culinary creativity. Perhaps my expectations reflected the high regard in which I held Korean food. Thinking about my own roots, I'd never expect even to be asked that question. However, I'm British, and this as Korea, and I knew that Korean food was strictly and proudly regional.

"Food in England," she said, "is very expensive and it's not at all delicious. I had 'afternoon tea' on Oxford Street in your London and it cost me $120."

I have no idea where she got charged that much for tea, but I'd clearly been taking my tea in London in somewhat more basic establishments.

"I looked at the history of your country," she said. "Great Britain has made a lot of wars."

Touché encore.

Hyun-Ae prepared a wrap of chicken and raw chile for her husband. I noticed that she was careful to slot a piece of kimchi in there. He opened wide and she popped it into his mouth.

"I like my town," she said. "I prefer Seoul, but my husband's job is here. I will live and die here."

Hyun-Ae and her husband were well traveled. They had been to France, Britain, Italy, and Vietnam, among other places. She was learning to cook both foreign and Korean food at cooking school, and she wanted to open a foreign-style bakery.

"That is my dream," she said. "To make desserts and breads like the ones I've eaten in France and Italy. Such wonderful breads. I want to make breads like that and to learn painting. I went to the Da Vinci museum in Italy . . . Ahhhhh . . . it was like a dream. I can't explain the feeling I had."

Maybe Chuncheon was "Romantic Chuncheon" after all. Her silent husband ordered a second bottle of soju.

"In Korea we drink and eat a lot," Hyun-Ae said, pouring him and me another shot. "Especially the men."

She said this with an ever-so-slight sigh, as if it was a burden she had to bear.

"About the name of this restaurant," I said, "why do they call it 1.5?"

Hyun-Ae did the approaching-a-car-accident, clenching-teeth, tilting-head, sucking-in thing again.

"I don't know for sure," she said, "but I think that maybe it started as a way of telling customers that they served 1.5 times more than the other restaurants selling the same dish."

"It's a size thing, then," I said.

"Yes," said Hyun-Ae. "That's our style."

We all clinked glasses. We'd finished the *dak galbi* and I was full, but Hyun-Ae's husband wanted rice.

"A meal is not a meal without rice," he said. Or kimchi, I thought.

The waiter returned with his wallpaper-stripping tools. He wore white gloves and gouged at the hot plate with the spatulas. The base was black, shiny, and congealed, and peeled off easily. I was surprised at how solid it was and how it came up in one piece. It looked like a wobbly, deflated black rubber inner tube. With the hot plate now clean, he added some rice and danced with it using the two spatulas. After a minute, he told us it was ready to eat.

"I love the old buildings in Europe," Hyun-Ae said.

"What about the old buildings in Korea?" I asked.

Much as she liked the old buildings, their destruction was a sacrifice she was willing to make.

"The landowners want to make money," she said, "to build apartments. I don't want to lose the old *hanok*s, but I can understand the owners. Korea is a very small country and we have to use our land wisely. In the old *hanok*s, the kitchen and the toilet were beside the building, and it was very hard for the women because they had to cook outside, even in the winter."

"But it wasn't so hard for the men?" I asked.

"Oh, it was hard for the men, too," she said. "They had to go outside to use the bathroom."

I sensed that Hyun-Ae was restless. She seemed thoughtful.

"Maybe," she said, "no one will want to come to Korea if we destroy all the old buildings."

"I've been told there are not that many left to destroy," I said. "I don't think it'll really make that much of a difference."

"It's sad that we have to make buildings and apartments," she said. "They are so expensive to buy in Korea. We will have to build more to bring the price down."

Two men in work overalls who had shouted and smashed their way through their dinner on the floor seating side of 1.5 struggled to put their shoes back on. They were wobbly, soju wobbly, and the floor around them was awash with empty green bottles. When they finally managed to extricate themselves and pay the bill, three waitresses stepped in to clean up the detritus. They were done in seconds.

When we arrived back at Hyun-Ae's apartment building, the couple waited at the elevator. I scratched at the wall looking for a button to call it. There were no buttons to press. Hyun-Ae and her husband stood stock-still and stared at me.

"It knows," said Hyun-Ae.

And she looked up at the elevator lights above the door. I could see the numbers changing; the elevator was coming down, and quickly. The elevator "knew" we were there. I thought about the train at Yongsan Station in Seoul, the efficiency and speed of it. And of Hyun-Ae's fridge: she could connect to it from her phone via the Internet. This was really "important" and "useful" for reasons I couldn't quite fathom. I suddenly felt old and quaint, like the village idiot in medieval England. The elevator arrived, the doors opened. We stepped in and zoomed skyward. It knew which floor we were going to.

"I've never seen this before," I said. "It's . . . amazing. And very fast."

"We Koreans," said Hyun-Ae, "we like to be quick."

BUCKWHEAT PILGRIMAGE

I t smells like burning dead bodies," said the first woman.

"It smells like hell," said the other one.

I'd bumped into sisters Yoo-Jin and Min-Ju earlier that day. They worked in tourism, and it was their day off. They screwed up their faces in mock disgust.

I sat down in a chair at the entrance of the hotel in Gangneung. I'd arrived by bus that morning. Gangneung, a seaside city in Gangwon province, is just over sixty miles east of Chuncheon. I looked down at my purchases; there were two of them and they were each a foot and a half long.

"They're gifts," I said. "One is for an old friend and one is for my wife."

"Do you love your wife?" asked Yoo-Jin, the slimmer of the two. She pointed at the packages, sealed in plastic and tied closed with a red ribbon.

I first noticed the squid for sale on the early evening walk back to my hotel. The stand-alone shed was as bright and blinding as a phosphorus bomb. A squid sun with its own gravitational pull. Rows of the withered alien beings hung on laundry lines surrounding the blast zone. Like dried-up radio antennae dredged from the seabed, the dangling squid broadcast good eats.

The vendor had ushered me under his hanging gallery and into his shop. He cooked a small dried squid for me on a powerful electric grill. Black flakes of charred squid littered the plastic-covered table where the grill was. It was like the debris of a grilled-squid hairdresser.

"He grilled a sample for me to try," I said to the sisters. I passed them the bag containing the leftovers. It was the sample bag from which the smell emanated. They each took a nibble.

Gangneung dried squid is a local speciality, and the quiet coastal village area where I was staying was lined with squid dryers. The hapless corpses, dried stiff in the sea breeze, hung on laundry lines outside shops, houses, and between the trunks of pine trees.

My two dried whole squid remained sealed in their bags. There was only the faintest whiff emanating from the packages, but the sisters had a point. I'd have to carry these monsters around with me for the best part of six weeks. In my suitcase. With my clothes. I questioned the wisdom of my purchase. My wife loved dried squid and I liked it, too, but only if it's grilled very crispy, even blackened, and dipped in chile sauce.

"That's why it smells like death," Yoo-Jin said.

I felt she was embarrassed by the smell. That she didn't really find it that repulsive herself, but wanted to be seen to find it repulsive. In a sense, she wanted to empathize with what she thought I must think. Like Vivian had told me about the stink of *cheonggukjang*, the fermented soybean dish. There was no way Yoo-Jin or her sister would ever have offered dried squid to me, let alone *cheonggukjang*.

"We prefer it with a small dish of *gochujang* and mayonnaise," said Yoo-Jin as she tore into a morsel of the charred sample. "Half *gochujang*, half mayonnaise, split down the middle, like a red-and-white sauce flag."

They were in their midthirties. I told them of the first time I encountered dried squid, one afternoon in a movie theater in Iksan, in southwest

Korea. There were four or five couples watching the film. Each couple had a dried squid and were feeding each other the tentacles. The stench was overpowering, so I moved seats, but I couldn't escape the foul odor.

"But I very quickly grew to like it," I said. "That's partly why I came here. To buy it from the source."

It was the wrong season to visit a seaside town. The shore looked depressed. A clutch of tourists, a couple of lovers, and a small group of students all battled against the buffeting wind coming in off the East Sea. Crabs, fish, urchins, squirts, and squid heaved inside blue aquarium tanks outside the long stretch of restaurants along the beach.

There were three things I wanted to try in Gangneung: a tofu dish, a cold noodle specialty, and what some call Korea's hottest bowl of noodles. All three dishes were natives of Gangneung and were impossible to find done well anywhere else in Korea.

I'd enjoyed the first on my list earlier that day.

Sundubu-jjigae (순두부찌개) is one of the most common staple dishes in Korea. It is a fiery tofu stew with pork, clams, and fermented vegetables, and it bubbles volcanic at your table. The Gangneung rendition of *sundubu-jjigae* is quite different. It is not fiery at all. It is not even a *jjigae,* or "stew." It is simply *sundubu* (순두부), silky, unprocessed tofu, and unlike in other parts of Korea, in Gangneung the tofu is made with sea water. It has the appearance and consistency of cottage cheese or very white, very runny scrambled eggs.

On the Gangneung coast, just south of Gyeongpo Beach, there is a village called Chodang. One part of the village is filled with *sundubu* restaurants. It's a village within a village and it's called, appropriately enough, *sundubu* village. There are ten or more restaurants in the village, but no choice when it comes to ordering: there's just one thing—tofu— served one way, the right way.

My order at Yechon restaurant (예촌) came with seven small side dishes, a bowl of rice, and one small bowl of soy sauce mixed with sesame seeds, chopped spring onion, and red pepper flakes. In another small bowl was *biji* (비지), the residue left after soy milk is pressed to form silken tofu. In some countries *biji* is used to feed pigs.

Mrs. Kwon Ye-Ji was from Gangneung and opened her restaurant in 2013. She was embarrassed.

"It's not famous yet," she said. I looked around; the walls had only menus on them, no photos of TV stars. It was almost as if she felt her restaurant was not worthy of my attention, as it had not yet been featured on TV.

"I've never eaten *sundubu* like this," I said. "What makes Gangneung *sundubu* so different?"

"We use something called *gansu* [간수]," she said. "It's a bitter solution that remains after salt is made. When the salt has crystallized out of sea water or brine, we use this to make tofu. It helps make the tofu thicker, helps it hold its shape better."

The tofu shone like the back of an alabaster polar bear trudging across a glacier. Steam from the tofu rose like wind-whipped snow.

"We use salt water to make the soft tofu," she said, "and this makes the soup richer and more flavorful."

"But," I said, "is it made the same anywhere else in Korea?"

"No," she said. "You can only find it in this area of Gangneung. In Chodang-dong."

Both the *biji* and the tofu bedded down well with the soy sauce dip. And the kimchi, salted dried anchovies, seaweed, and other simple side dishes that came with the *sundubu*. It was like no *sundubu* I had ever seen or tasted before, and I'd eaten plenty—*sundubu-jjigae* had always been a lunch of choice when I lived in Korea. This tofu was almost fluid in consistency. Salty, smooth on the tongue, and nutty.

"A long time ago," Mrs. Kwon said, "people used to hand-make tofu like this, but these days they only buy it from the factory or grocery stores. Nothing is handmade anymore."

I'd failed at finding the second stop on my agenda: a renowned thirty-year-old *makguksu* (막국수, chilled buckwheat noodle) restaurant on the outskirts of Gangneung. It had been replaced by a demolition site that was to be part of the Gangneung Olympic Park, one of the venues for the 2018 Winter Olympics in South Korea. The athletes, and me, would have to eat *makguksu* elsewhere. I knew this, because I'd just walked the three miles there to find that out and the three miles back after I realized it no longer existed. I was hungry when I bumped into Min-Ju and Yoo-Jin.

"Oh, you should have told us you were looking for that restaurant," said Min-Ju, the younger of the two sisters. "It closed over a year ago."

"Did it move?" asked Yoo-Jin. There was confusion. And then they both shrugged. "It closed."

Yoo-Jin and Min-Ju were marooned in Gangneung due to family commitments. Both were married; one had moved to Gangneung from Seoul and the other from New Zealand, where she had a successful *dak galbi* restaurant. They had to come to Gangneung "for a year or two" to help their aging parents with their tourism business.

They offered to take me for *makguksu* in a quiet area dotted with pine trees a few miles away. The trees rustled like dry newspaper in the night breeze. The upper branches resembled ostrich feathers under the moon and the pine needles pricked the air. All around us, fish were being plucked from aquariums and brought to low tables, baby octopi writhed on chopping boards, and sea squirts squirted their last.

"It's not the season for *makguksu*," said Min-Ju. "People will start eating it again at the end of next month, when it's hotter."

Makguksu is a popular summertime dish. It's very cooling, but spicy, and it's known as a speciality throughout Gangwon province. There's even a *makguksu* museum in Chuncheon, and the dish is celebrated with a festival in the summer.

We entered Semil Mak Guksu restaurant (세밀막국수). It was filled with new Formica tables. There were ten of them in the main restaurant and at least two other smaller, private rooms opposite the open kitchen at the entrance.

We sat down on the floor. Min-Ju served us all warm barley water from a kettle on the table. Mournful piano music played; the restaurant was empty.

The kitchen was stacked high with bowls and kettles and the fridge was full of booze. There was a freezer next to it, and pictures of doughnuts, cookies, milk bottles, and muffins were pasted onto the walls. Upon the window, an impenetrable English phrase was stenciled: FLOWER HOUSE YOU WILL BE IN MY HEART.

"I don't like *makguksu*," said Yoo-Jin. "My husband does, but I prefer *naengmyeon*."

Naengmyeon is a cold buckwheat noodle soup. Sometimes it is served dry, with no broth, and called *bibim naeng myeon* (비빔 냉면). But it is always cold and slightly vinegary, with a clean and pure taste. It is a Korean noodle gazpacho, very popular in the summer. The North Korean capital, Pyongyang, is the home of *naengmyeon,* and it is a close relation to *makguksu,* but held in higher esteem. I planned to try the North Korean original later on in my journey.

"The only good *naengmyeon* are in Seoul or Busan," said Yoo-Jin.

"And Pyongyang," I said.

"Well, yes," said Yoo-Jin. "That's what everyone says, but we can't go there."

The owner of Semil Mak Guksu, Mrs. Park Hee-Yeon, came over to take our order. She was originally from Kyungnam in Busan, in the southeasternmost corner of Korea, and had opened this restaurant in 2010.

Yoo-Jin ordered *bibim makguksu* (비빔 막국수), the dry version of the *makguksu*. I felt sorry for her. Something to love, or at least respect, about Korean people is that they will do things, eat things, go places they might not really want to themselves, just to please you or help you, to show you something of their country and their culture. It's an endearing quality, but can result in a little guilt on my part on occasion.

The *makguksu* arrived in a large, deep, metal bowl. Several stalks of watercress and half a boiled egg slumped upon a spoonful of *gochujang* atop the cold buckwheat noodles. The soup formed a moat around the mountain of noodles in the middle. Mrs. Park explained that she didn't use any MSG and that she made her own *maeshil chung* (매실청, sweet plum syrup) to add a sweet spark to her food.

The broth is made from a vat of vinegary radish kimchi called *dongchimi* (동치미). Finely chopped dried seaweed and roasted sesame seeds floated atop the moat surrounding the noodles. Against the black surface, the seeds glinted like rusty emeralds in a dimly lit mine.

The two side dishes were pickled mustard greens and finely sliced pickled radish, and on the table were plastic bottles of vinegar and mustard vinegar. There was also a bowl of sugar.

I stirred the dish and slurped up the noodles; a lick of fire battled the coldness. As I devoured the contents of my bowl, the seaweed and sesame seeds stuck to the sides. It was as if the tide was going out on my soup as I ate, and sesame and seaweed were the tide mark. I half expected to find some driftwood in there. I liked the *makguksu*, but cold noodles, much like cold borscht, are an acquired taste, and I wasn't sure I'd hit it up again anytime soon.

Yoo-Jin had a generous smile, a dark brown bob, and wore almost no makeup. I should have read the signs when I first met her. For a woman, wearing no makeup in Korea is akin to walking naked through the streets.

I remembered the rebellious woman I knew in England. Jin, the miniskirt-wearing, cigarette-smoking, wannabe fashion designer. Not only did she wear the clothes she felt she couldn't wear in Korea, but she didn't wear makeup, either.

"I don't wear makeup here," Jin had told me in England. "In Korea, it's more makeup, more, more, more. If I didn't wear loads of makeup in Seoul, people would think I was mad. It's like a uniform you have to wear."

It would be fair to say that there are many makeup overwearers in Korea. But there are many under-wearers, too. The differentiation can act as a hint about someone's background. "Korean Koreans" tend to wear more makeup. Koreans who have lived or studied abroad might be inclined to wear less. The Korean diaspora look altogether different. And don't think makeup use is only an issue for women. According to one survey, Korean men in Korea use on average thirteen different cosmetic products, making them "among the most appearance-conscious males around the world."

I slurped at my *makguksu*. Like much Korean food, it is a thing of beauty when it arrives, so pretty you almost don't want to disturb it, but disturb it you must. I could understand why so many Koreans took photographs of their food. I asked Yoo-Jin about her favorite food, and without hesitating she thumbed through her smartphone and showed me pictures of the dishes she liked. She paused to look at her dinner; she'd eaten half and looked ready to quit.

"My favorite food is the most simple food," she said as she passed me her phone and rattled one more time around her bowl like a timpani drummer. "Just a grilled mackerel with side dishes and a bowl of rice. That's what I like, not the stuff in Gangneung."

Her sister, Min-Ju, was a fan of the live baby octopus dish called *sannakji* (산낙지). It's an appetizer really, or late-night drinking food. The tentacles are cut and seasoned with sesame seeds and sesame oil. The tentacles quiver, squirm, and snake their way across your plate and wriggle down your throat; occasionally, a sucker will latch onto your esophagus on the way down. It's a challenging snack.

"In Busan, there's this alley on Jagalchi market that sells *gomjangee* [꼼장어]," she said. "It's a kind of eel, but it's still alive. It's very scary as they cut it up and grill it while it's still moving and you eat it like that. I couldn't finish it when I went there."

"But you can eat *sannakji*?" I said.

"Oh, yes," she said. "No problem with it. It's delicious."

"She's only been to Busan once," said Yoo-Jin. "What does she know."

"Twice," said Min-Ju. "I've been there twice. I'd move there, if I could."

My miniskirt-wearing, cigarette-smoking, makeup-rejecting friend of yore had told me, "If you move to Korea, only go to Seoul or Busan. Don't go anywhere else."

"But surely the real Korea is outside of those places?" I had replied.

"Yes, but you don't want to go there."

"You mean I don't want to see the real Korea?" I said.

"No, you don't. No one does," she said. "It's bloody boring."

The sisters were clearly unhappy to have found themselves in Gang-neung.

"We don't like living here," Yoo-Jin said, unprompted.

"What do you do for fun in Gangneung?" I asked.

There was silence, and they both put their heads down, embarrassed. It looked like they were in confession.

"Swimming," said Yoo-Jin.

"In that cold?" I said. It was eight degrees Celsius today. "Do you seriously go swimming in that?"

More silence.

"I go drinking," said Yoo-Jin. "With my husband. We go into town, not here. When I finish work, I go drinking. That's what I do."

"You both look very sad," I said.

More silence.

"Like the characters of a Korean soap opera."

Laughter.

"Korean TV dramas are miserable," said Yoo-Jin. "Death, divorce, cancer. I have no idea why they are so popular."

Yoo-Jin and Min-Ju were looking forward to the end of their year in the purgatory of Gangneung.

"One thing I really miss in Seoul is *sundae* [순대]," said Yoo-Jin, referring to the Korean blood sausage packed with noodles. It's a common snack and drinking food.

"But *galchi jorim* [갈치조림] is the dish I miss the most," Yoo-Jin said, referring to the braised silver hairtail dish I had shared with Areum and Josh at Namdaemun market.

Like unhappy people all over the world, the two sisters talked less about where they were and more about where they wanted to be—Seoul or Busan, not here, not Gangneung—and the things they would do and eat if they were in those places.

Gangneung was not only well known among Koreans for tofu; it was renowned for buckwheat, too. The entire province harvested the stuff by the ton. It's what was used to make the many noodle dishes in this part of Korea.

"What do you plan to eat tomorrow?" asked Yoo-Jin.

I told them the name of another noodle place, but they didn't know it. They weren't local enough or interested enough in the city. I showed them pictures of what looked like a pretty rundown shed somewhere in the center of Gangneung.

"No, I've never seen that place," said Yoo-Jin. "It looks very old. Do you want us to come with you?" she asked.

"No," I said. I wanted to make this visit alone. It felt like it would be a pilgrimage.

The entrance to Gangneung market (강릉중앙시장) in the center of Gangneung was almost entirely lined with *ajummas*, with their tight black perms and padded jackets with fat money belts strapped across their groins. They sat on cushions on top of oil cans on the pavement, behind neat stacks of dried fish tied together with yellow ribbon. Hanging above them were more dried fish swaying from a red-painted iron bar with hooks.

It was inside the covered market that I found Mrs. Rhee. She was selling simple *maemil jeonbyeong* (메밀전병), buckwheat crepes filled with kimchi. A basin filled with buckwheat batter dripped next to two iron griddles on a long table to one side of her stall. On the other, there were two huge brown covered plastic buckets of kimchi. Above her, on proud display, was a six-foot-by-three-foot banner with a photo of a famous person inserting Mrs. Rhee's food into his mouth. A TV star's note of commendation. I looked down the alley, and all the stalls had different notes from different TV stars.

In the space behind her stall was a fitted kitchen and a buckwheat grinder. Knives stood blade down in a white box nailed to the back wall, and ladles and sieves hung from hooks next to a thick pair of red rubber gloves above a central sink.

There was just one table for customers to eat at. Most diners, I deduced, bought the snack and walked off with it. I sat down and looked out at the market. Opposite was a garlic, sesame seed, soy sauce, and chile powder seller, and next to that was a ginseng stall. They were each a craggy shambles of ingredients, polystyrene boxes, cardboard, jars, and bags.

Mrs. Rhee spread the crepe batter across the griddle. It quickly bubbled and bound into a light pancake. She filled it with kimchi, rolled it, cut it into four pieces, put it in a polystyrene tray, and placed it on the stainless steel table in front of me along with some disposable wooden chopsticks. The crepe glistened slightly under the fluorescent lights.

She turned on the fan next to me and the toilet paper roll hanging from the stairs began to waft. I took a bite of the *maemil jeonbyeong;* it was soft, spicy, and light. For all intents and purposes, it was a kimchi sandwich. I could see why customers would just grab this and go, or perhaps eat it at the front of the stall. A two-minute snack that evolved entirely as a result of local ingredients. It was a Gangneung original.

The center of the market boasted a coffee shop called Coffee Harrar. It stood upon a raised wooden deck, apart from the remarkable squash of stalls. It was as if the deck announced that the common market, at ground level, was not quite good enough for it. It was a good vantage point, stationed as it was at the crossroads of the market. I sat down, ordered a coffee, and observed.

The market was almost entirely populated by women, be they buyers, sellers, or workers. The dried-goods stalls were a jumble of sacks, boxes, sheeting, bottles, and polystyrene. The entire market looked like it was run by a community of compulsive hoarders. An old lady shuffled about her mess. She occasionally scratched at her perm, and wondered where she put that box of dried chiles in 1975. How did she find anything?

Next to a seaweed stall was a pigs'-head seller, just pigs' heads, no other heads and no other bits of pig. Next to her was a beef butcher selling "LA Kalbi," thinly sliced cross-cut short ribs.

Then there was the smell, or the three smells, to be exact—they're always there. The trilogy of much Korean cooking might well be soy sauce, red pepper paste, and brown bean paste, but the triptych of the Korean market is the warm, roasted nuttiness of sesame seeds; the deep, comforting, rich, fruity, winter warming jujube; and the sour vinegar strains of kimchi. They're the most unlikely band of hitmakers, but they play the same symphony in every market in Korea. Yes, there's garlic and onions and fish and meat and all the pastes and sauces a Korean kitchen could ever dream of, but when it comes to the smell of a Korean market, they are all backing singers to this three-piece main act: sesame, jujube, and kimchi.

In the center of the "crossroads" were two motorbikes and two metal carts. Traders used them to move stuff around the market. The men rode the motorbikes and the women pushed the carts.

At a bright pink stall a young woman in a pink thermal jacket sold sweet, crispy fried chicken. She stood in front of the stall, her arms folded, cracking her gum. It echoed rhythmically along the alleyway like a pair of stilettos walking under a bridge.

A slim woman with a striped shopping bag talked into a white smartphone. Her hair was dyed brown and tied back with a red bandanna; she had a serious face. Some women ran. Someone was always running for something in Korea, and normally it was women doing the running.

Apparently, South Koreans spend very little time in the kitchen these days. In a 2015 survey looking at how the world cooks across twenty-two countries, the Koreans were at the bottom when it came to amount of time spent in the kitchen.

As I looked at the women running by one after another—as if they were all part of some unfathomable, demented relay race—I wondered if all that time they didn't spend in the kitchen was the time they spent running to buy food from the market and in takeout restaurants. Or maybe it was market field day.

A more practical reason was that Korean food was good, cheap, and easily available, and much of it was very hard, and in many cases too stinky, to cook at home. Buying out was practical.

A group of three women trotted by wearing hiking gear. Bright, expensive hiking gear, and those long visor hats so beloved by Korean and Japanese women. I was reminded of something Hyun-Ae had said to me in Chuncheon:

"You could spot a Korean in the Himalayas," she had said, "because of the clothes."

It sounded like a running joke shared among Koreans. Another example of how Koreans had learned to laugh at themselves. Although there was a serious side to the sartorial choices of Koreans. So renowned had Koreans become for their eye-catching bright sportswear that Korean tourism operators had begun advising tourists to tone it down when they traveled overseas. Europeans, the Korean tourists were advised, found it odd to see people in hiking gear outside the Houses of Parliament, the Eiffel Tower, or the Colosseum. In Europe, those clothes were only worn in the mountains. They were brightly colored so that should the wearer get lost or become injured, he or she would be more easily visible to a rescue party. On the city streets of Europe, Korean tourists had become so visible that they had become something of a magnet for pickpockets.

The man in the corner shop was distraught. He led me by the hand from his pokey hole, jammed with instant noodles, drinks, and cigarettes. I'd shown him a photograph of my intended destination on my phone, but he didn't know it. This part of Gangneung was less of a market and more of a pedestrian zone with glitzy shops, flashy lights, and pumping music.

He stopped two passersby; they looked at the photo, but they didn't know it, either. I opened my arms in a "What can you do?" expression. He bowed and repeated, *"Mien-hamnida, mien-hamnida* [미안합니다].*"* "Sorry, sorry." He gave me some gum. I thought he might cry.

But I knew I was close.

I set off alone, guided only by the vague sense of "it's probably over that way somewhere."

Without very specific directions or a guide, even if you can read Hangul, places and things are not always easy to find in Korea. Signposts and landmarks change. A street-naming system as such didn't exist until 2014, and even then it seemed to have sowed almost universal confusion among Koreans and foreigners alike. Meanwhile, restaurants moved or closed daily.

If I tell you this restaurant is located down a narrow alley between Starbucks and Nature Republic on a main street running through Gangneung city, I've no guarantee that those two landmarks will still exist to guide you there by the time this book is published. But I'm hopeful that the restaurant will still be there, as it's a Gangneung institution. And I was a little surprised that no one I had asked in Gangneung knew about it.

I'd found pictures of Geum-Ak Kalguksu (금악칼국수) on the Internet. It looked like an old, well-worn leather shoe; a bit tattered, wrinkled, well loved, and comfortable. A relic by Korean standards, but a glittering jewel to my eyes. It was, I told myself, places like this that were the fonts of food goodness in Korea. It wasn't just the food I was after. I wanted the creaking, collapsing splendor that surrounded it, too.

I found the alleyway with Starbucks on my left, Nature Republic on my right, and I followed the narrow passage. Very soon I was walking alongside an old stone wall behind the shiny, tall, glass buildings of the main street. There were two trees behind the wall. One boasted cherry blossoms that looked like popcorn. I approached the door that I'd traveled a very long way to eat behind.

The roofed gateway into the small courtyard looked different from the photo I had seen. It was new—they had changed it. How dare they? I shrugged. I wasn't that surprised—everything was new in Korea. However, I was relieved to see that, as soon as I crossed the threshold, it was Gangneung, Korea, 1975, all over again. Or it was as imagined by me.

The courtyard was concrete. There was a jostle of upside-down, empty brown plastic vats huddled to my left; to my right were bins covered with a blue tarp and some plants in tubs next to them. The space between led to an opened room, part of the restaurant. It was a mess.

Boxes, bowls, baskets, bags, packets, a fridge, two clocks, exposed wiring, and a rickety fan. An old woman with a hunched back and a frizzy perm led me to one of the four or five cabins that formed the center of the room. The entrance to the cabin was a sliding wooden door. It was about three feet high and very narrow and the only window in the door was a pane of glass at the bottom. As such, it was all a bit Alice in Wonderland. I took off my shoes and crouched and squeezed my way into the rabbit hole.

I found myself inside a six-by-nine-foot cell. There were two floor tables, a stack of flat cushions, and a fan. I sat down at a table. The under-floor heating, the *ondol,* warmed the floor. There were red aprons hanging from a nail in a corner and a plastic box of tissues on the table. The walls and roof had once been white, but now every inch of space was covered in graffiti. There were heart shapes, manga-like figures, and portraits, but the majority was Hangul and date stamped. I was surprised at the lack of penises, or anything rude—no breasts or vaginas, either. It was, I thought, incredibly civilized graffiti.

As the name of the restaurant suggested, the menu was minimal. This was a good sign. Most diners came here for *kalguksu* (칼국수). *Kalguksu* means "knife noodles." The idea is that the noodles are hewn by the hand of a knife-wielding chef, and in some places, they still are, but in others, a machine now takes the strain.

Five minutes after taking my order, the hunchback woman returned with a tray. On it was a small dish of kimchi, a tumbler of water, and the *kalguksu*. The soup was blood red; funnels of steam rose from it and wavered in the light let in by the opened door. Rough-cut, slimy, thick buckwheat noodles poked through a surface speckled with seaweed and sesame seeds. It was like looking down at a child's ruddy drawing of a map of a topsy-turvy world. I felt sure I could see Africa in that bowl and the mainland United States. Mushrooms and spring onions peeped out from New York and Johannesburg. I tasted: it was a thick, fiery soup, and it dripped delicious violence.

Two women entered my cell and occupied the table next to me. They looked embarrassed to be in a room with a foreigner. As if they had to say something just because I was foreign. I said hello in Korean.

"This restaurant," one of them told me in painful, faltering English, "makes the soup from beef broth, but other restaurants use crab or clams." This was, apparently, the defining difference at Geum-Ak Kalguksu.

They bowed, motioned for me to enjoy my meal, and continued speaking in low voices together. I clattered on with my metal chopsticks against the metal bowl. As I bent down to delve deep inside, I could feel the blades of the chile-infused steam open the pores in my face. *Some people pay ten times the price of this soup for the same treatment at a spa,* I thought as I wrestled the noodles between the chopsticks and took a bite, *only here I get lunch thrown in.* As such, it seemed like a bargain.

There was a subtle firmness to the noodles that elicited a pleasing click as I bit through the bundle. The flotsam and jetsam of seaweed and sesame that mingled with the buckwheat strands stroked me with strains of nut and salt. Arriving at the rear was the inevitable, the loudest, brashest brute at the party, that reassuring hundredweight red chile brick to the taste buds. The soup itself was a loud dustup between the satisfying heat of the chiles and the deep beef-bone heartiness; the mushrooms were mere fluffy onlookers. It was a sensation. I drained the bowl. Not a spot of gruel, sesame seed, or fleck of seaweed remained. Satiated, and a little spent, I leaned back against the graffiti.

A pilgrimage this was. I'd traveled considerably farther than the ninety-three miles of the more famous pilgrimage of the Route of Santiago de Compostela, but it felt no less significant a journey to my hungry soul. If I had seen the light, it was that this place and this soup were a sign of what was to come. I'd known it ever since I'd seen the photograph of the place years before my arrival here and the writer had said as much:

> The room took me back to my childhood growing up in Korea in the 1970s . . . It looks just like the room my siblings and I used to sleep in behind my mom's beauty salon . . . [the] spicy broth . . . tastes like 1975, too . . . For W6000 I got to taste my childhood again. I think for that price, it was a bargain.

Even though I am not Korean, I knew exactly what the writer meant. Places like this were special in Korea today, and I knew now that I would have to seek them out. They were not going to greet me upon arrival, on the street corner, opposite the hotel, next to the bus station, or at the side of the road. I'd wanted Korean food to stay static, but the main street had moved on.

THE WHOLE HEAD OF A COW

There were two restaurants on the ground floor of Gangneung bus station. One was stock Korean and the other was mock Western. There were nine tables and one customer inside Han Il Snack restaurant, and there were fifteen tables and no empty seats inside Mom's Touch Chicken & Burger.

The immediate question that arose as I surveyed the two eateries was, whose mom provided the touch? This was of particular concern to me as I read the stenciled description upon the restaurant window:

> Everyone enjoyed eating chicken. For both internal nutrition
> and taste of chicken. Mom's touch with the whole family.

Taxing English aside, there was a more important question: Why did Koreans prefer Mom's Touch? How could this happen? Had Korea really sunk this low? So low that a low-rent, low-grade, subpar, mock Mickey D's could plant a knockout blow on a low-rent, low-grade, subpar conventional Korean joint without so much as breaking a sweat?

I walked inside the Korean restaurant. A large, practical white-on-red board listed eighteen bus station standards. Noodle dishes like *udong, kalguksu, ramyun,* and *naengmyeon* together with *kimbap* seaweed rice rolls and *manduu* (만두) dumplings. I picked at a plate of *kimbap* and looked across the station at Mom's Touch.

Bright menus covered the main window, vivid photographs showed enormous burgers, and servicemen sat in groups and sunk their teeth into double cheeseburgers, quarter pounders, and imitation Big Macs. Hordes of students lined up to order. It was hideous.

I looked around Han Il Snack. It was quiet, although the TV was on. A soap opera played, a woman moping at someone's hospital bed while a cello wept. The only other customer in Han Il Snack put his chopsticks down, picked up his cane, and limped out. I looked at Mom's Touch again and I remembered something Fiona had told me in Seoul.

"Most young people in Korea don't like kimchi," she said. "They prefer Western food."

I sighed, wiped my face with a couple of sheets of toilet paper, and walked out. I boarded a bus going south to the city of Andong (안동) and sat on the back seat. The journey would take three hours.

I was reading a book by the popular modern novelist Young-ha Kim. The book was called *I Have the Right to Destroy Myself.* It was a cheery story about a woman who wanted to kill herself. I looked up from my book; the soldier who was clambering aboard the Universe Space Luxury bus looked like he'd spent the night exercising his own right to destroy himself. And by the looks of things, I reckoned he'd very nearly succeeded.

He lumbered up the bus like a blubbery, wheezing walrus. He lurched and snorted his way over the backs of seats. His mad eyes rolling upon a turbulent sea of soju, he flung his bulk into the seat next to me. He slumped low, farted, closed his eyes, and proceeded to snore. He reeked of cheap soju. It crawled from under his camouflage uniform and formed a throbbing plume around him. He was a time bomb.

Outside, a man with a fridge wrapped in cardboard was trying to load it into the baggage space under the bus, but it was too big. His fridge would have to take a different route south. From the raised height of the back seat, I could see the phones of the other passengers. They held them at head height with their left hands and tapped with their right.

The bus lunged out of Gangneung. The soldier fell forward and back again as the bus maneuvred. We entered a long tunnel; the roof lights flashed past like a flip book. The strobelike effect must have felt like the repetitive beating of a hammer to the messed-up military man. He spat on the floor, farted some more, and eventually resumed snoring and dribbling. Andong was a long way away, and there was a free seat two rows in front of me. I took it.

If it hadn't been for a pee stop, things might have worked out fine. However, next to a muddy river with some ducks, the bus stopped to allow a woman to run off the bus to relieve herself. She was impressively quick, ran back onto the bus, bowed apologetically at everyone, and sat down. The bus lurched, swayed, vibrated, and bounced onward once more. The soldier blinked back to life at the sudden movement. He looked utterly bewildered, and it was then that the time bomb stopped ticking and the inevitable happened.

A jet containing the contents of his all-nighter sprayed the back seat, his boots, the floor, the dozing soldier in front of him who had, rather unfortunately, set his seat into a reclining position. The rear of the bus was covered in gloop. After a couple of encores, presumably to paint the areas of the bus he'd previously missed, the gross slob went back to sleep. Occasionally he shuffled his feet; they looked like two fat, black, laced-up spatulas as he paddled back and forth through the sauté.

The soldier next to him took out his wallet; some coins fell out and landed in the mire. He looked down at them forlornly, then looked at the annihilated wreck. He looked down again, but he knew the coins were lost to the contents of the slumbering soldier's stomach. I thought I saw the metal dissolve. Miraculously, the reclining soldier who'd received the splash of undigested kimchi remained fast asleep throughout. The unavoidable stench of puked-up soju and kimchi was like a hair in the throat. It just wouldn't go away, and it made me feel sick. As the sun came out and entered the bus, the puke gently cooked—no one, during any of this, said anything. The Koreans were beyond British in their restraint. Someone quietly opened a window.

We entered Andong. A large battalion of apartments had set up camp outside the city center and looked poised to invade. I waited to see what the slob would do. As the bus engine juddered to a halt and the brakes hissed, the soldier awoke, startled and disoriented. He looked at the puke and frowned as if to say, Who the hell puked on me? And then he staggered off the bus. The bus driver trekked to the back to view the aftermath. The perfume of the night before had reached him as he was driving. He shook his head and rubbed the back of his neck.

"*Aish,*" he said. ("Shit." Not that you needed a translation.)

The soldier had left his military cap on the back seat. It, too, had puke on it, the driver saw. He left it there and followed me off the bus.

There was a certain poetry to the journey. Like me, the soju-sozzled soldier disembarked in Andong. Andong is the home of soju—"the capital of the Korean spirit," so the slogan at the bus station told me. Not just any soju, either, but ancient, premium soju. In his own way, the soldier was just bringing the spirit back home with him.

I hopped on a city bus. It had blue seats and blue "hold-on" bars and an LED sign that told me the name of each stop and the direction we were going. The bus was crammed with old people. They wore thick-soled slip-on shoes, had blotchy faces and gray scalps that peeked out from under their dyed-black hair. As we sped toward a bridge over the Nakdong River, I saw an old couple planting seeds on a scrap of dirt. Their land was sandwiched between their tiny old house and a gargantuan apartment complex, and I thought of the spring onion sellers in Chuncheon.

An old woman, one of ten on the bus, sat in front of me; her skin looked like a ginseng root. She had three strong, yellow, plastic-knit sacks of rice, each was marked with its weight: 20 kilograms. She dragged the sacks one by one so they were closer to the exit door. She knew that buses didn't hang around at bus stops in Korea and she'd have to offload quickly if she didn't want to lose a sack or two.

The bus stopped and the doors opened. A group of ten young Koreans stood waiting at the bus stop. I expected them to help the old woman, but none of them moved. They barely looked up from their smartphones to check the bus number. I got up and helped the old lady shift the sacks of rice. She nodded a thank-you and smiled. The door closed and the bus continued. Twenty years ago in Korea, it would have been unthinkable for no one to help an old woman off a bus.

I arrived at my stop, the soju museum. It was the first of three mistakes I made in Andong. The museum was small and filled with glass cabinets. Inside each were plastic food items on tables with signs in Korean and English—"Sacrificial Table," "Feast for Queen Elizabeth II in 1999," "The King's Dinner Table," "Drinking Table for Each Season"— together with explanations of how soju is traditionally made. The guard, in his gray uniform and gray cap, stood by the door and tapped his fingers, urging me to leave.

The second mistake was perhaps less a mistake and more of a disappointment. There were six or seven restaurants on one side of the street all selling the same thing—Andong bibimbap (안동비빔밥). It was a mixed rice dish, a cousin of its far more famous relative in Jeonju. The main difference in Andong was the inclusion of fish, not beef. Like most places that get popular in Korea, or elsewhere, for that matter, there was no love in here. It was all function, no soul. I thought I would get closer to Korean food the farther I got from Seoul, but the opposite was true in this establishment. I felt like I was getting farther away from what I knew Korea had to offer. This wasn't pure and simple nostalgia on my part. There was a genuine sense of loss of a great cuisine, of the eating experiences I knew this country could offer. The one thing I never expected on this trip was to have to hunt out the exceptional—I had expected to trip over it at every turn. This felt fake, this felt lazy. I enjoyed the food, but food without love is only fuel, and I wanted more than that.

The third mistake I made in Andong was going to the wrong market. I went to the big central one, Andong Gu market (안동그시장), which stayed open into the night and is home to *jjimdak* alley. Just as Chuncheon has a *dak galbi* street and Gangneung a *sundubu* village, Andong has a *jjimdak* alley. *Jjimdak* (찜닭) is a broiled chicken, vegetable, and noodle dish, particular to Andong.

Every restaurant on *jjimdak* alley served the same thing, though some were more popular than others, and the ones with the TV celebs on their advertising seemed to be doing best. I avoided them and picked one of the others at random. Mom was out front broiling at two weighty woks, while her son was in control at the eight tables inside. He could speak a little English.

"Are you alone?" he asked.

"Yes," I said. "Will that be a problem?"

"No," he said, "but *jjimdak* is usually for two or more people."

I thought about *dak galbi* in Chuncheon, of Hyun-Ae and her husband. I'd never eaten *jjimdak* before, but I'd eaten *dak galbi* a ton of times.

"You should just order a half portion," he said. "That should be enough."

I took a floor seat in the corner. The fridge was stacked with soju, water, beer, cider, and Pepsi. There was a menu on the wall next to me, and at the far end of the room, there was a row of aprons hanging from wall pegs. There was a cheap painting of a field filled with sunflowers on another wall, while next to it was a glass frame with three wooden masks inside with the inscription HAHOA MASKS OF KOREA in English. Andong is known for its traditional masks. Behind the cash area at the entrance was a washing up sink. A reassuring toilet paper roll hung off the wall above it, and a large silver rice cooker sat on the restaurant floor.

A cooking show played on the flat-screen TV on one wall. It was a Saturday night. My table was low and wooden and the floor had the standard vinyl cover.

The side dishes arrived first. Make that singular, one side dish—just pickled cubes of radish. The son placed two large empty metal bowls on the table. For a moment I thought he might bring a pet dog out and feed it from them. Alas, no.

"This one is to eat out of," he said, pointing at the smaller of the two. "And this one is for the bones and tissues."

I took out a spoon and two metal chopsticks from the box on the table.

A couple sat at the table opposite me. She took photos with a large camera. I noticed that she was very studious, but her partner looked annoyed. He clearly wanted to eat. Another couple was engrossed in the TV show.

My *jjimdak* arrived, and the steam rose from it like morning mist. My eyes streamed and the other customers were a blur to me. *Jjimdak* is a fiery mix of transparent noodles, fried and then broiled chicken, potato, carrots, seaweed, leeks, cabbage, soy sauce, ginger, and sugar. The idea is to combine the taste of fried chicken with that of broiled chicken. It starts off sweet and quickly gets hot, a deep-spice hot hit. The glass noodles retained the temperature very well. Too well. I burned the roof of my mouth and struggled to get the mess down. The metallic plate didn't help disperse the heat, and the noodles were cumbersome to handle, long and clingy. It was like drawing water from a well just to pull them up and drop them into the small metal bowl.

My eyes watered, but it wasn't just me. The food photographer waved a hand over her mouth and her partner rubbed his eyes with a damp cloth. *Jjimdak* brought out the sweats. The potato was barely cooked— the carrot, too. I didn't know if this was how it was meant to be.

Is *jjimdak* an endurance test? Well, it had me beat on volume, but not on taste. Of that there was plenty, but it ripped out my tongue and flung it into the alley outside, where it sought the comforting balm of ice in the fish section of the market. There was too much going on in *jjimdak*. It was an orgy, and a pretty messy bacchanalian one at that.

The son could see that I'd reached the end. My stomach was telling me to stop, although the Koreans in the house weren't done yet. They ate with their mouths open and clicked, chomped, and chewed their way ever onward. It was like listening to a small flock of odd birds.

"Really," said the son, "*jjimdak* isn't a dish for just one person. I could put the remains in a box for you."

"No," I said. "I'm full, thanks. I couldn't eat anything more."

I'd barely eaten a third of what had landed on my table. There was enough left for a nuclear family and the nuclear family's pets and one or two of the neighbors and their pets, too.

Outside the door, *jjimdak* alley was thriving. I wondered how the hell the mother-son pair managed to coax customers into their restaurant.

"It depends on luck, primarily," the son said. "If you treat customers well, they will continue to come back."

And then, after these three mistakes, things went right—very, very right.

Sin market is a five-minute walk from Andong market. There are no tourist trinkets, no lines of Chinese waiting to eat something they'd read about or been told to eat, and no *jjimdak*.

At one end of the only restaurant alley inside the white-tile-floored covered market was a string of dog meat stew, or *boshintang* (보신탕), restaurants. Moving along there were pork restaurants, some fish outlets, and, lastly, a place selling *seonji gukbap* (선지국밥). I'd never heard of this dish before. It was the only place serving it on the market, and it was the only place with a line outside. The smell hit me like an enthusiastic teenager screaming for the concert hall to open, running to be first to the front of the stage. I took my place in the line; I was one of twenty, all men.

The white tiles beneath my feet were wet. A student zipped past me on an electric bicycle. On my left were a dried skate seller, an octopus vendor, and a shellfish stall. Large mussels flexed in a red bucket, dried skate doused in sesame seeds were draped across a stall, and cone-shaped clams gurgled in a bucket on the floor. A customer arrived; she seemed interested in the octopus. A trader packed up an order of dried fish, wrapped it in plastic, and stuck it into a bag as the line edged forward.

The customer bargained at the octopus stall as the vendor picked up a twelve-inch-long knife. They haggled and the customer made a telephone call. She nodded as she spoke and then she clipped closed her phone.

"Ee ship man won," the seller said—200,000 won. The customer nodded.

The vendor put the tentacles inside a plastic bag, the customer glugged from her bottle of barley water, handed over the cash, and moved next door to the skate trader.

At my feet, black rubber hoses delivered water to blue aquariums of live fish and crustaceans and buckets of sea cucumbers and sea squirts, and black plastic bags hung at head height from weighty meat hooks.

The line had progressed and lengthened as I watched the octopus buyer. By the time she was done at the skate stall, it was my turn to enter the restaurant. I sat at one of the six tables stuffed inside. There was a huge stainless-steel fridge at one end of the room. On the wall was a poster showing the named and numbered cuts of meat on a cow. The restaurant was full of middle-aged men, none of whom talked and none of whom drank. Perhaps they were here to seek a cure for the previous night, before they started drinking again. The broth permeated the restaurant, carnivorous and sweet. The men coughed and wiped their heads. It sounded like a doctor's office during a flu epidemic.

There was no need to order, as there was only one dish. *Seonji gukbap* came with four side dishes, rice, and a small dish of minced garlic and chile powder, just in case it wasn't already potent enough. I could see the sliced chiles winking at me from the browny depths below.

Mrs. Kim Song Hee had worked in this restaurant for the past five years. Her mother had run the restaurant before her in a different location, and her grandmother had run it before *her* in yet another location. In Korean, *seonji gukbap* is commonly referred to as a "hangover stew with clotted cow's blood." It's an attractive-sounding proposition. Mrs. Kim told me more.

"I use the cow's head," said the forty-nine-year-old woman. She had studied cooking to master's level at a university in Korea. "You need the whole head of a cow, the blood, and the meat to make the stock. I add ginger and radish and let it cook for between five and eight hours."

Mrs. Kim had stark black, penciled eyebrows and heavy whitening makeup. She had two vats of soup on the go inside the kitchen. The broth turned like a furious, roiling sea and it swathed the cramped, packed restaurant with sword swipes of mighty spicy meat mist.

"I cook the vegetables separately out there," she said, pointing to a vegetable vat containing leeks and chiles in front of her restaurant.

"I add *gochu* powder to the beef stock," she said, referring to the red pepper powder. She pointed to the two vast vats I had stood next to outside while I waited in line. "You see, this one is for tomorrow."

A server in Mrs. Kim's restaurant heaved a bucket of fresh stock from the outside vat.

"If we're running low on soup in the kitchen," Mrs. Kim said, "we take some fresh from the stock outside. We get busy, so this happens a lot."

The server poured the extra stock into the kitchen cauldron, and the kitchen purred in appreciation.

"It'll be ready for the five A.M. start," she said. "That's when I'll mix the vegetables with the beef stock, and that's when our soup is ready."

I was curious to know if this was a local dish.

"Yes, it's local," said Mrs. Kim. "Everything I cook is bought locally, from the cow's head to the vegetables."

Mrs. Kim's mother handled the cash—7,000 won per person—and directed operations. Mrs. Kim's father wore white gloves as he sorted the fine cuts of fatty beef from the cuts with tendons and prepared each black bowl for the next customer.

"But is it a local dish?" I said. "Does it come from Andong?"

"I grew up with it," she said. "That's local. That's all I know."

The cow's-head soup was a relief. Korean markets all look alike: they have flags on the roof, the same stalls selling the same things. It was as if the market was delivered as a Korean market kit. For some reason I thought of the crappy soju museum and the crappy city slogans. I didn't care if *seonji gukbap* was an Andong-specific dish or not, as this was what I'd come back to Korea to eat. This was what I was looking for. The honest guts of Korean food, of the country, not some loveless replicant claptrap.

I got up to leave. A woman pushed a cart down the alleyway in front of Mrs. Kim's restaurant. She had four large plastic crates filled with leeks. She deposited them at the side of the restaurant. Mrs. Kim replaced the lid on her soup vat.

"The delivery for tomorrow's soup," she said, nodding at the cart. The bulky woman pushed the cart back from wherever it had come. Mrs. Kim left the leek delivery there. She would deal with it when the midday rush was over.

I looked up above the stalls in the market. There was a photograph above the octopus stall. It was in soft focus and it looked fake. There were three people in it and they were all smiling. A woman with a black perm was holding up a large octopus and showing it to a gorgeous young couple. The soft focus of the photograph jarred with the hard focus of Sin market.

Legend has it that when Queen Elizabeth II visited Korea in 1999, she asked to be taken to the most Korean place in Korea, and so she was taken to Andong. I hope that she got to visit Mrs. Kim's and not bibimbap street or *jjimdak* alley.

I boarded another bus. I was heading deeper and farther south, toward the edge of Korea.

IT'S OUR TIME NOW

Before sunrise the squid boats came into the brightly lit docks.
The squid, thrown in heaps on the docks, moved about, tangled
together. A few squirted black ink.
   — *Young-ha Kim,* I Have the Right to Destroy Myself

Before returning to Korea, I had coined a two-bit theory. I thought the country had raced ahead, but the food had stayed the same. I had been wrong—I knew that now. The food was changing with the people and not just now, of course—it had always been changing. One of Korea's core ingredients, red pepper, an item you see on the street in sacks and strewn across sidewalks to dry, was a foreign import that arrived a very long time ago.

"Red pepper, the base of almost every Korean meal, was introduced from Japan at the end of the 16th century. Korean peasants used the peppers to heat their food and themselves during Korea's brutal winters. Red peppers rapidly caught on."

Jjimdak, which was thought to be a recent invention in Andong, was a dish that relied heavily upon this red pepper. Supposedly, its creation was a reaction against the boom in fried chicken outlets in South Korea that had rocketed during the financial crisis of the late nineties.

Imports of cheese were up year on year. Once thought of as quite disgusting by pretty much every Korean I've ever known, cheese was now cool. It was added to everything from dak galbi to kimbap and even instant noodles. It won't be long before, as with coffee, Koreans begin to demand quality European cheeses as opposed to the low-quality cheese that makes up most of the current imports.

And now, a little over seven hundred years since alcohol first arrived in Andong via Mongol invaders and the Koreans first concocted soju, the alcoholic content in soju has been reduced from 21 to 14 percent—its lowest-ever level—to attract female drinkers, because it is women who drive change in everything in Korea. Get the women, goes the theory, and the men will follow. From K-pop to beer to food to fashion, Korean women are the trendsetters. In addition, very few people cooked in the home, fast food was a massive industry, and the family unit was disintegrating. As a result, rapid change would appear to have delivered a mix of both the good and the bad and the potentially proto-fantastical.

Perhaps this was part of the reason the kalguksu cabin in Gangneung had felt like a pilgrimage and why Mrs. Kim's cow's-head soup was like a last supper. These were anchors to a past that wasn't fading from view so much as being blindfolded, shot, and slung into a shallow grave.

It was with these thoughts that I got off a bus at Busan's Express Bus

Terminal. I descended the stairs into the subway and headed toward the center of the southern port of Korea's second largest city.

It was a Sunday. Opposite me on the subway was a woman in her sixties. She wore fishnet gloves, shiny black boots, black trousers, a black coat, and black-rimmed glasses, and, of course, she had a tight black perm. Her ghostly white makeup masked smoker's wrinkles. She looked like a Goth retiree. A man sitting next to her wore a charcoal-striped black suit, shiny black shoes, a bowler hat, a gold watch, white cuffs with gold cufflinks, and a red-and-white-striped tie. I felt like a tramp.

Then an *ajumma* got in. She wore a shiny pink jacket, Day-Glo leggings, and sneakers, and as she elbowed me out of the way, I noticed something I'd seen a lot of on this journey. Next to the elderly Goth and the man in the bowler hat, there was a line of old people sitting, standing, muttering, waiting. There were so very many old people in Korea.

As I ascended the steps into the air of the city at my stop, I started to think about what this megalopolis had to offer. Eight of the ten tallest buildings in South Korea emerged from Busan soil. The eighty-story, 984-foot-tall, awkwardly named Haeundae We've the Zenith Tower A in Busan, was the country's tallest residential property. Busan was also very well known for its seafood.

The central part of the city is shaped like a broken bowl that's snapped in the middle. At the bottom of the bowl, by the port, taxis crept over zebra crossings, nudging inches forward, anticipating a sluggish green light. High above, on the lip of the bowl, on the steep hillside of old Busan, rooftops of blue and yellow blinked along with the red and green of water tanks. As it started to rain, the water galloped down the steep sides of the bowl, turning the roads into channels, conduits, and tributaries heading toward drains. The rain was like the people: it moved faster than any rain I'd ever seen anywhere else.

I'd arranged to meet Mr. Bang at his office. He had an import/export company on the eighth floor of a faceless, gray building at the bottom of that bowl, at sea level, in downtown Busan.

As I waited for him in his office, I could hear a vendor in a truck outside. He was selling bean sprouts, *namul* (나물). The looped spiel from his loudspeaker battled with pneumatic drills and a truck sucking the drains clean from the eight-lane highway eight floors below. As the rain shower stopped, cherry blossoms flittered past the window like flecks of pink snow.

Mr. Bang moved to Busan from nearby Geoje Island in the 1960s. After university, he worked for the Customs Office for thirty years before starting his own company. He was sixty-seven years old, a worldly man who had traveled to the United States, throughout Europe, and across Asia. We had a mutual acquaintance, a former British ambassador to South Korea.

"When I first came to Busan, there were just these middle-sized buildings," he said, gesturing into the distance on the other side of the window. "Nothing like what we have today. There were about a million people living in Busan back then. Now we have just under four million. There were no apartments blocks before, and no air conditioners. Some people want to keep the old buildings as kind of historical places, but the majority do not. Everyone wants new."

An assistant tapped the thin door. Mr. Bang said "Enter" in English, and a young woman in a black pencil skirt entered. She bowed and placed two paper cups of coffee onto the small glass-topped table that separated Mr. Bang and me. Coffee, for someone of Mr. Bang's generation, came from a packet. It was instant, powdered, sweet, creamy, and quite awful.

"Lovely," I said. "Thank you."

"I used to live in a small house on Geoje Island," he said. "Now, like everyone else in Korea, I want to live in 'advanced systems.' The American way of life seemed like a dream when I was a boy. I thought New York City was like paradise."

"And now?" I asked.

"Well, no," he said. "It's not paradise, is it? They have boys shooting children in classrooms. No, it's no paradise. No such thing exists on earth."

I'd arranged to meet Mr. Bang because I wanted to know what life had been like back in the 1950s; what food he had eaten, what food he missed from those days, and had things changed for the better, for the worse?

"We lived on rice at that time," he said. "Gradually, when we worked with American soldiers, they brought their food and our tastes changed a bit. We learned about beefsteak and Spam, of course."

Spam is the most unlikely luxury item in South Korea. Supermarkets and shopping malls stock gift sets of the stuff in neat boxes, wrapped in ribbons. *Budejigae* (부대찌개), or army stew, is a popular winter dish. The first Korean American fusion food, it is an implausible mix of instant noodles, Spam, baked beans, pork belly, hot dogs, garlic, kimchi, and *gochujang*. It is a dish born of a time when Spam, baked beans, and hot dogs were alien items to Korean chefs, and alien back then meant exotic and prized. That legacy continues today.

"Food in Busan back then was traditional Korean food," said Mr. Bang. "We are developing into 'advanced food' now. When I moved here, in comparison with my hometown, there was, of course, so much more variety."

He repeatedly apologized for his poor English, but it was excellent. I think he wanted to be praised for it, and it was clear that he took great pleasure in speaking it.

"As a small boy I used to catch fish," he said. "I used to fish with a fishing rod that I made myself out of bamboo with a line. At that time, we all caught our own fish, just small fish, sea squirts, and sea cucumbers. We could pick them up with a net or by hand. I'd slice them there and then on the rocks by the beach and eat them. Fresh, raw sashimi like that is very healthy and absolutely delicious. A lot of seafood these days is polluted because of fish farming. The chemicals accumulate in the stomach of the fish and harm our health."

Mr. Bang had relatives who still lived on the island. They worked mostly as government officers while others farmed barley. However, life on the island had radically altered since his childhood.

"Geoje Island was a village when I was a boy," he said. "Now they build container ships, oil tankers, and oil rigs there. That small fishing village has been completely transformed. There were only two roads before. Now there are four-lane highways."

His office was sparsely furnished. There were framed photographs of Mr. Bang meeting various ambassadors, including my acquaintance, some framed certificates, a calendar, and, in one corner, a fist-size gray rock. It sat on an oval plinth in a dish filled with some tiny gray stones that looked like they had been combed.

"What is it?" I said.

"It's a rock from a local mountain," he said. "I moved the mountain to my office. I find it calming to look at the rock inside my office."

"That sounds almost poetic," I said. I'd had the semblance of a poem buzzing around my brain throughout this trip. An urge to write poetry was something I had not had since I was sixteen years old. "Do you like poetry, Mr. Bang?"

"Indeed, I do," he said. "Traditional Korean poems are very rhythmical, but common poetry is not rhythmical at all. I still love to listen to poetry; it makes me feel good. I can feel it, but I cannot define that feeling. It's something to do with the music of the language. It's always short, but very meaningful."

As I listened to Mr. Bang, I thought about the content of my poem. It was about men of Mr. Bang's age, but not men like him. He was a success, whereas many others of his generation were not, but I put poetic interests aside and turned back to food.

"But how," I said, "has food changed in Busan since you were a boy? Beyond the influence of American soldiers and Spam?"

"To make a long story short," he said (he would use this phrase many times throughout our conversations in Busan), "in the 1960s, my country was very poor. Many North Koreans came to Busan after the war, and some of them got hired as cooks by restaurants. They tried to make their North Korean food, you know, their *naengmyeon*. It's very famous in North Korea."

Mr. Bang seemed distracted. As if all this talk of food were making him hungry. He glanced at his watch.

"Have you ever tried *milmyeon*?" he said.

"No," I said.

He stood up.

"Come on," he said. "It's lunchtime. I know a good place—let's go."

I'd eaten *naengmyeon* once before, in Jeonju, many years ago. I'd found it an interesting dish, but not one I had immediately fallen in love with. A cold, vinegary noodle soup was a step too far for me at that time. I wasn't sure I could ever really like a cold noodle soup. Similar to the *makguksu* in Gangneung, it was a little too out there for me. Like the confused free jazz explorations of an otherwise ordinary pop group.

Unless you knew it was there, or you could read Hangul, or had a local to take you, you would never find Hwan Cho Milmyeon restaurant (환조밀면). It was hidden down a blind alley off one of the roads surrounding the household goods–stuffed Gukje market in downtown Busan.

There was a sign on the main street, but it was nestled among the plethora of neon green, yellow, white, and red Hangul plastered just above head height along the busy, shop-strewn street. Hwan Cho Milmyeon had been operating for thirty-five years. In Korea, this meant it was ancient, veritably Stone Age.

"Ever since the end of the war, a lot of people in the south like *naengmyeon*," said Mr. Bang. "*Naengmyeon* made by North Korean people is much more delicious. South Koreans didn't like it much before then. They didn't even know about it before the war. But *milmyeon* is a little bit different."

Inside the restaurant, the TV was on, playing a lunchtime news bulletin, and there was a huge photo of Hawaii spread across one wall. The floor was festooned with jars and great plastic jugs of soy sauce. There were ten tables; we sat down at one of them.

There was no room for coats on the wooden coatrack hanging from the wall in front of me. Five red net sacks filled with dried leaves, bracken, and jujube hung suspended in the place of coats. There were two items on the menu: *milmyeon* (밀면) and the slightly more expensive *milbibim* (밀비빔). Mr. Bang explained that the first was "wet" and the second was "dry" and spicy. We ordered the wet one.

"More tasty," he said.

Milmyeon consists of the cold, vinegary soup, a stack of noodles, fatty pork, cucumber, a splodge of *gochujang*, and half a boiled egg, and it looked very similar to *makguksu*. On the table were a kettle filled with hot chicken stock to drink like tea, a stainless-steel pot of mustard with a spoon in it, and a plastic dispenser of vinegar. The only other accoutrement was a small side dish of pickled, finely sliced, sweet radish.

"When the North Koreans arrived here, they tried to re-create their food," said Mr. Bang. "But, they could only find wheat flour here. That was the flour the Americans brought with them. There was no buckwheat as they had in the north, so they had to adapt."

Mr. Bang directed me to add a spoonful of mustard and a splash of vinegar to the *milmyeon*.

"*Milmyeon* noodles are softer than the buckwheat ones they use for *naengmyeon*," Mr. Bang said. "They're chewier, too."

It was a cold day, and there was only one other customer in the restaurant. I was assured that this restaurant would be packed in a month's time as the summer heat began to arrive. The other customer was reading a newspaper. He grunted, hawked, burped, and farted his way through his lunch. Mr. Bang seemed completely unfazed by this symphony of the stomach coming from the nearby table.

"So, *milmyeon* is not really North Korean food," I said. "It's an approximation of it that started through necessity in Busan?"

"That's about right," said Mr. Bang. "North Korean cooks are very creative."

Verdant-leaved plants occupied one corner of the restaurant next to a tree in a pot and vats of ginseng. A clock hung from a wall; the pendulum below it swayed. Next to it was a cage with two birds inside. They argued incessantly, and as their chirps rose and fell in intensity, Mr. Bang chimed in by slurping noisily at his noodles.

The stubborn flour noodles stuck together; we cut them in our metal bowls with scissors from the table. The soup's cutting chile heat was cooled by the temperature of the soup and sharpened by the vinegar, but the soup was big, too big for me to finish any more than two-thirds of it.

"But now," Mr. Bang said as a cluster of reddened noodles disappeared down his gullet, "*milmyeon* is known as a local dish, as it's unique to Busan. It's funny how these things quickly catch on and kind of attach themselves to a place."

Inside the birdcage was a fake nest. The birds were both white, but one had ruddy-colored feathers on its head and back and the other had black. They squabbled nonstop. I reasoned that they would never be able to lay an egg in their fake nest. Or maybe they were just unhappy with their fate, stuck together for a lifetime inside their Korean cage.

Mr. Lee Kyung-geun ran the *milmyeon* restaurant with his wife, and they were both originally from Busan.

"We've been in this location for just four years," he said. "We used to have a different place in Busan, and we've been serving this dish for thirty-five years."

He told us that his mother used to have a restaurant and that he had helped her run the business ever since he was eighteen years old, right after he finished school. His mother had since passed away.

"What makes a good *milmyeon*?" I asked.

"We cook it the traditional way," he said, "with our hands, and the broth is made in-house. We try to follow the traditional way of cooking, and we don't allow anyone in our kitchen except for me and my wife. We haven't even told our adult kids any of the recipes. I feel confident when the food is made by my hands and no one else's."

There were two entrance doors to Hwan Cho Milmyeon: the one we had taken from the main road and the less obvious one at the back of the restaurant, which came from a market alleyway. We left the restaurant by this exit. The alleyway was long and narrow. We passed a children's toy shop inside it, and as we reached the open air and the market, I saw a large inflatable yellow sign with the name of the restaurant on it. It wobbled in the breeze.

I looked down at my feet. Stuck upon the alleyway asphalt, with heavy-duty green duct tape, was another sign for the restaurant. Every which way I looked, the word 밀면 was now visible. This restaurant wasn't hidden at all; it was all in the seeing, in observing my surroundings, looking for the unexpected in the normal, deciphering the code among the uniformity of the Korean landscape and knowing that *milmyeon* was a thing. A delicious thing.

As we stood there clicking on the butterscotch sweets Mr. Lee had given us when we paid for our *milmyeon,* I told Mr. Bang that I planned to eat at Jagalchi market (자갈치시장), Busan's largest fish market.

"A long time ago," he said, "just after the war, Jagalchi was a small pebble beach. People sold long, silver fish there, but I never saw it like that. When I came to Busan, there were already buildings down there, but that's how the market got its name, as *jagalchi* means 'selling fish on pebbles.'"

A couple walked past us in the crowd. They wore matching red hoodies with two small white pointy ears and big yellow eyes embroidered into the hoods. The couple wanted to look the same. I thought they looked like clowns at a children's birthday party. Mr. Bang didn't seem to notice them.

"Try one of the eel restaurants," he said. "That's a very local dish. You won't find it on the rest of your journey. It's actually a hagfish, not an eel, but it looks just like an eel."

I remembered the sisters I met in Gangneung. Min-Ju had found the eel, or hagfish, in the market in Busan so disgusting that she couldn't eat it. Mr. Bang didn't seem to have any of those fears for me. I wondered if Min-Ju's disgust was more based upon fear that I would see what Koreans really ate and how they ate it.

Every now and then, walking the streets of Busan, I would hit a cloud of the triptych: jujube or sesame or sour kimchi. All these smells on the Korean streets were like waymarkers for blind people; dried squid, hazelnut coffee, fried chicken, stale soju. They let you know where you were, and they brought life to the streets. The streets of Busan by night were cloaked in the smells of Korea: from chestnut sellers, sweet potatoes roasting in brown tubs, a kettle simmering on a brazier made of an upturned converted hydraulic oil can, a stall selling fried, greasy, sweet cakes called *hotteok* (호떡) next to a stand with fish paste sticks steaming in front of a bubbling vat of lava-like, thick, gloppy *tteokbokki*. Shops spread out onto the sidewalk and the street. They poked at you just enough so that you took notice, maybe enough for you to buy something, or maybe just enough to get annoyed at the inconvenience to your walk.

A market should look dog-eared. Like a newspaper left on the train: thumbed, creased, passed around a few too many times, the crossword half finished, a Hitler moustache doodled upon a photograph of a loathed politician, a telephone number scrawled in the margin. Jagalchi market next to Busan's Port of Nampo was just such a market.

A pandemonium of multicolored buckets surrounded old woman vendors. It was as if someone had just cracked open a game of seafood eight-ball across the market floor. The old women, like macabre pet shop managers, knifed, gutted, and tossed abalone, clams, sea squirts, sea cucumbers, giant mussels, scallops, cockles, baby octopus, fish eggs, and large and small prawns. They writhed and wriggled across the wet baize. The octopus section of the market was like an Area 51 mortuary. The vendor was fenced in by opened polystyrene boxes, a mess of buckets, umbrellas, and portable floodlights, her trade laid out upon an icy slab. A fat woman sold man-sized lengths of glossy green kelp that looked like massive mounds of unspooled cassette tape. A rubber-clad gnome marshaled a line of dead silver fish. She sat with her head down, her face invisible under her film director's visor. The long, slim fish cascaded over her stall like Rapunzel's hair. A man at a stall next to her scaled fish like he was filing his nails.

An unceasing herd of noisy customers passed in front of the stalls. The vendors isolated the most pliant looking from the pack. Traders squabbled over lost trade, swiping paws at each other and exchanging cutting barbs. It was into this warren that I went in search of dinner.

The shed-style restaurant section was at the far end of Jagalchi market. It consisted of a row of fifty or more simple plywood-and-plastic-sheeting structures surrounded by gurgling seafood. It was unlike the rest of the market; it had a hunted look, it was too rough for modern, thrusting, twenty-first-century Korea. It was a part of the past the authorities had not yet gotten around to destroying. For me, it was love at first sight.

This section of Jagalchi market was also home to the single-most aggressive women in all Korea. How to choose? Go to the full shed, the empty, the small, the grimy, the spick, the span, the this, the that? All had signs in Korean, some Japanese, and a few Chinese, too—none had English. I tried to block out the hail of shouting and shoving on all sides, but it was like trying to ignore the really annoying kid at school who always wanted the last word. I plumped for the almost-empty shed where a chef worked alone. It was the one place I had not been hassled to enter.

Koreans will often tell you that they are the "Italians of the east"—passionate, aggressive, and highly demonstrative on occasion. Busanites believed they were more Italian than any other Koreans.

I walked the short aisle from the alleyway toward the shed. To my left were a series of buckets filled with live seafood. There were five small aquariums. Fish, abalone, octopus, sea squirts, and crustaceans wriggled.

In a white aquarium, under a tank of abalone, were the hagfish. A network of hoses fed water around this miniature aquatic zoo. On my right were buckets, vats, umbrellas, sacks, bottles, basins and bags and bins of kipple. The shed chef's joy was apparent as I entered. I heard the curses of the spurned in the sheds I had rejected outside.

I sat down on a wooden bench covered with beige vinyl. A red-and-white blanket had been taped over the vinyl. I planted my elbows on the worn table and looked up at the menu posted at head height on a metal grill that formed the window at the end of the shed. On the other side of the grill was the harbor and auction space. From three A.M. every day, seafood was sold here and delivered across the country. The menu had eight items, each illustrated with a photograph and the name in Hangul: sashimi (회), hagfish (꼼장어), whale meat (고래고기), abalone (전복), baby octopus (낙지), conchi clams (멍게소라), sea squirt and sea cucumber (멍게해삼), and sea penis (개불).

As so often happens in Korea, it was the Korean who began. She was in her twenties, alone, but the table was set for two and she was the only other customer.

She put her book down and looked at me.

"Can I help you with you order?" she said in English.

"It's okay," I said. "I know what I want to eat."

The elderly lady—and sole employee—who cooked, cleaned, and waited upon customers in the shed wore glasses and had three gold teeth. They glinted under the fluorescent light as she smiled at me, waiting upon my choice.

"What would you like?" she said in Korean.

"I'd like the hagfish, please," I said in Korean.

The chef looked perplexed and shook her head. The young woman at the other table shook her head, too. Then the two of them proceeded to have a conversation about my dinner.

"She says you shouldn't order this dish," the young woman said. "It's too spicy. And . . . it's a little gruesome."

Her name was Soo-Jin. She was an elementary school English teacher and she came from the nearby city of Ulsan. She was in Busan for the weekend. Her husband had business to attend to and would be joining her later.

"It's fine," I said. "Please don't worry about me. I'm very keen to try it."

A little resigned, the chef returned to her kitchen-cum-zoo and began delving through her buckets for my dinner. Soo-Jin invited me to join her.

"I only teach the grammar," she said. "That's why my speaking is so bad."

It wasn't bad at all—it was good. On this trip, I had noticed how the English of the nation had improved dramatically. It was still some way behind other countries, but in terms of English, the Korea of today was in another league compared to twenty years ago. There was a telephone number to call twenty-four hours a day that offered free translation in a number of languages. My fears of having trouble communicating had been, for the most part, unfounded. Largely through luck and meeting people like Soo-Jin, I'd yet to need the phone service.

Soo-Jin was a rather prim looking twenty-eight-year-old. She was cold and had a blanket on her lap. She suggested we order the food together, as she was a regular at the shed. She told me that the old lady chef was called Mrs. Kang and that she'd done well enough from her shed to send her son to university in England some years ago.

"I don't remember the name of the city he lived in," said Mrs. Kang as she brought us an appetizer of some chopped-up sea squirt and sea cucumber in a small basket. The just-cut orange flesh of the squirt pulsated.

"He kept telling me where it was," she said, "but I don't remember it."

I found it odd that a mother could send her son to a foreign country and know so little of where he actually lived.

"Korean mothers," said Soo-Jin. "It's just study, study, study. They don't care about the little details, like where he lived."

"Please," said Soo-Jin. "Eat."

I didn't need any invitation. I was not a big fan of sea cucumber; it's a texture food, tough like a tendon with crunchy, strong, briny bursts of sea inside. To me, it was a bit like chewing through an underwater sea cable. However, sea squirt was a different story. I'd been waiting to eat sea squirt, or *mongeh* (멍게), again for twenty years. It came with a *chojang* (초장) dipping sauce made of vinegar, sugar, *gochujang*, and sesame seeds. I took a morsel and bit into it; the tantalizing, tender, buttery orange flesh was filled with ocean, and it performed seaweed-covered backflips inside my mouth. If you've never had the opportunity to eat it, imagine eating a soft mango filled entirely with sea. That's what eating *mongeh* is like.

I'd heard Koreans describe it as looking like a creature covered in acne. Admittedly, it wasn't the prettiest beast, but the taste was sensational. Maybe it was a little less refined than an oyster, but it was as deep, maybe even better than a sea urchin. Not that I am comparing like with like here, but I have often wondered why this simple sea creature has never caught on in the West.

Mrs. Kang prepared fish on a wooden slab at the entrance to her shed. She grilled to order on a briquette burner on the floor. Next to it, the air-conditioning unit that stood in a corner was wrapped in a plastic sheet, awaiting the arrival of summer.

On the wall behind her was a tatty collage of posters. It looked like the back wall of a school classroom at the end of the school year. The posters had Photoshopped images of sophisticated models. These elegant men and women advertised some of Korea's roughest alcoholic beverages. Soo-Jin saw me eye the advertising.

"Soju and *mongeh*," she said. "It's a marriage, you know." And she ordered a bottle.

The floor was strewn with empty soju bottles. There must have been thirty of them. I thought about the vomiting soldier.

"Why do you come here?" I asked as we clinked glasses. "Isn't it a little rough and old-fashioned?"

"She reminds me of my mother," Soo-Jin said, looking at Mrs. Kang, who was preparing a tray for us. "That's why I come here."

Mrs. Kang brought four dishes to us. There was raw carrot and raw onion on one, raw garlic and raw chile on another, and a small bowl of *doenjang-guk,* the miso-like soup made of bean paste that accompanied many dishes in Korea. And there was a "sweet sauce." These were for the main event, the hagfish. The small steaming bowl of mussels that followed was to nibble on while we waited.

Mrs. Kang opened the shed at about ten A.M. every day and closed at ten or eleven P.M., depending on when her customers wanted to leave.

"I'll stay open a little longer if the customers are not finished," she said. "I don't mind."

"And what if they're blind drunk?" I asked, pointing at the floor.

She shrugged.

"It's normal in Busan," she said. "Men drink."

Mrs. Kang took off the first and second Thursday of every month. The market as a whole took the last day of the month off. The government had created a rule whereby all supermarkets and the like had to close once per month. The aim was to encourage people to buy from the small traders on the streets. As the nation became more and more gentrified and more and more used to buying from supermarkets, fewer and fewer people frequented the traders along the alley from Mrs. Kang's. And fewer and fewer people ate at places like Mrs. Kang's.

"My son tells me to slow down now," said Mrs. Kang. "But I enjoy it too much. What would I do stuck at home all day? Besides, I like meeting people. I like it when strangers become regular customers."

"That's the name of her restaurant," said Soo-jin. "'Regular Customers' [단골횟집] in Korean."

Mrs. Kang wore a red apron and a neckerchief and blue Wellington boots with thick white soles.

"The hardest thing," she said, "is sometimes it can be very boring when there are no customers."

I asked her about the whale meat on the menu. The deliberate killing of whales for meat is banned in Korea, but plenty of restaurants sell it. The Korean coast guard allows "the sale of meat from incidental catches: whales that are caught in nets designed to capture other types of fish."

A whale, I thought, is a pretty large thing to call an "incidental catch."

"I get some Russians and Japanese coming here," she said. "They like whale meat more than the others."

Soo-Jin asked Mrs. Kang to bring out another dish. The chef hauled a creature out from the aquarium under her cutting station.

"Sea penis," said Soo-Jin. "That's what we call it. It's *gaebul* [개불] in Korean." It is more appropriately referred to as a marine spoon worm in English.

It was a long tube, and indeed, it looked like a penis. Mrs. Kang cut it up and added it to the basket of sea squirt and sea cucumber. They were dark brown in color, and the cut-up pieces wriggled slightly as the nerve endings twitched off their last glimmers of life. I tried a slice: it was crunchy, but it had no real taste.

"We eat it for the texture," said Soo-Jin. "Some men eat it for other reasons."

And we clinked glasses again.

Mrs. Kang wrestled the hagfish from the aquarium and locked them inside a fish grilling basket. She grilled them like that, still alive, inside the shed, as if doing it within our eyesight would make us confident that what we had chosen to eat was the freshest possible. The hagfish convulsed violently as they sizzled on the grill. This kind of fish is not commonly eaten in Korea. It was the Japanese who harvested it when they colonized Korea. They used the skin to make shoes and discarded the meat. Hungry Busanites gathered the meat, spiced it up, and ate it, and a Busan dish was born.

"This hagfish," Soo-Jin said, "is probably the spiciest dish in Busan."

Mrs. Kang placed a light-green gas burner on the Formica table. The tabletop was marked with the scratches of plates, burners, keys, and coins. Mrs. Kang poured soju onto a tray covered with aluminum foil and an alcoholic fog enveloped the shed. She added sliced onions and cabbage and poured over some *gochujang*. Then she picked up the blackened grill basket, scraped the hagfish off, bundled it onto the cooking tray, and used a red spatula to mix the lot together.

Soo-Jin told me she'd been coming to Mrs. Kang's for years. However, it had become much more popular after Mrs. Kang had appeared on TV. Soo-Jin pointed to a poster behind me. The inevitable stamp of approval: Mrs. Kang on a TV show. The TV certificate of excellence, it seemed, extended even to the most basic, run-down, and shabby of shacks.

"Was it a soap opera star who came to eat here?" I asked.

"No," said Soo-Jin. "It wasn't for a soap opera. Mrs. Kang was in a local news report about the market."

A Korean rice cake seller strolled in front of the stall. He shouted and cranked an old-style football fan rattle to announce his presence. He had a large polystyrene box of snacks slung over his shoulder. The box was entirely covered in peeling brown masking tape. Mrs. Kang shook her head at me, as if to say, don't look at him, don't buy anything. She brought us a plastic basket of lettuce and sesame leaves, pointed to the foil-covered tray upon the cooker, and motioned for us to eat. It was ready. The rice cake seller continued on his way along the seafood strip.

Soo-Jin and I clinked glasses again and emptied the shots.

"Men in Korea drink too much," said Soo-Jin as I held up my glass for her to refill. "All the time drinking and falling over. But us twentysomethings of today, we don't really drink the same way."

I took my chopsticks and dabbed at the red, soju-soaked hagfish and wrapped a morsel inside a lettuce leaf. The bean paste sauce that accompanied the hagfish was *ssamjang* (쌈장), a mixture of doenjang, garlic, and sesame. Unlike the name of the fish might suggest, these hags were anything but tough. The fish were hot, but tender, like explosive little bullets that unfurled upon the tongue and prodded it with a soothing chile needle.

"It's changing slowly," Soo-Jin said as she munched through her first wrap. "I think we'll always drink heavily. But we're not like the old ajoshis."

Soo-Jin waved her hand behind her as if directing her thoughts to what was happening beyond the fiberboard wall. I could hear them through the other side of the shed in the next stall. Clinking, drinking, shouting, and eating. A glorious racket from the past coming from a parallel hagfish shed. It was a universe that sat uneasily in the Korea of the present day on this side of the fiberboard.

"I feel sorry for them," she said. "They're out of sync with Korea today. Korea has changed so much, and I think they feel lost. Their time is over—it's our time now, and we're so different. Look at me—I'm twenty-eight, no kids, and my husband and I go away every weekend we can."

"You don't feel the necessity to visit the in-laws or your own parents every weekend?" I asked.

Most married Koreans I knew, back in the day, lived with their in-laws, and those who didn't felt duty-bound to visit them at least once a week, and it was impossible to escape that duty.

"No, not anymore," she said. "I mean, at least not on a formal, dutiful, weekend-after-weekend basis. We share with our family, we do so many things together, we still do all of that. But we also make time for us, for our couple."

The hagfish sizzled, the foil blackened, the soju bottle emptied, and we ordered another. This part of the market felt a bit like the traditional Korean family. Its time was almost over.

Mrs. Kang told Soo-Jin to turn off the gas.

"How is it?" said Soo-Jin. "Not too spicy for you?"

"No, not too spicy," I said. "And it's not salty at all."

"That's where the ssamjang comes in," she said, tapping at the small dish smeared with bean paste. "Compared to some of the other shops along here, Mrs. Kang's is not at all spicy. She says she doesn't like it too spicy. So she just cooks it the way she likes it."

Mrs. Kang pulled out a bag of Shin Ramyun (신라면). Given the choice, 100 percent of Koreans will choose Shin Ramyun when looking over the instant noodle shelf at the local supermarket. It's the spiciest—and best—instant noodle. Mrs. Kang cooked them in a saucepan of boiling water on the briquette burner she'd used to cook the hagfish. Then she stirred the noodles into the leftovers and added some steamed rice.

It was reminiscent of the end to the *dak galbi* dinner I'd had in Chuncheon. But this time, it was instant noodles, not just rice. Once Mrs. Kang was satisfied that she'd stirred it enough, she sprinkled some chopped-up *kim* (김, dried seaweed) on top, put it back onto the tabletop grill, lit the gas again, and ordered us to eat.

Behind Soo-Jin there was a toilet paper roll hanging on a holder. She tore off a few sheets and asked me to wipe the dripping noodles from my face.

"The younger generation in Korea are more about enjoying life," said Soo-Jin. "It's not like before. It's healthier."

At the end of the night, I got out of a taxi atop one of Busan's surrounding hills. I closed the rear door of the yellow cab. My apartment was up a steep set of steps. Cherry blossoms shuffled over a drain cover. Maybe it was the soju, but the scene made me think of the poetry again.

A huge advertisement of a smiling man in bright-colored hiking gear loomed large above a seven-lane highway in downtown Busan. He held his hands in the "ace in the hole" position as he stood in front of a superimposed image of the Eiffel Tower. I wondered if the advertiser was deliberately countering the Korean tourist company's guidance on what fashions to don when traveling overseas.

A strip of blue paint upon the road denoted the bus lane. A taxi driver parked his car on it, got out of his cab, and jogged in place on the spot.

His hair was slick and dyed jet black, and it stayed perfectly still as he jogged. He looked about the same age as Mr. Bang.

Now I wanted to hear what the thirtysomething generation thought about their country. Not just about the food, but the country, how it was changing.

I was on this street, near a subway exit, to meet Min-Hee. She came from Busan, was married to an American journalist friend, and was in her thirties. She arrived dressed all in black, with a diamond tattoo visible just below her neckline. We sat in big armchairs on the ground floor of Coffee Mr. Dutch in central Busan and ordered four-dollar coffees.

"I sometimes miss the old days," Min-Hee said. "There was more humanity back then. Back in those days I could remember thirty or forty phone numbers. Now I can't even remember my mother's or my husband's. You don't have to remember anything anymore, or know anything—it was more real back then."

"Even with all the spitting," I asked, "and aggression?"

"It's true, we were like barbarians back then," she said. "We're much more civilized these days. It's the Chinese who look ridiculous now."

I described Mrs. Kang's shed and told Min-Hee I had found it surprisingly hard to find that kind of place in Korea.

"That whole row of restaurants in Jagalchi," I said, "how can they survive?"

"I don't think they'll be there for much longer," said Min-Hee. "And the people will miss it when it's gone."

We sipped at our coffees. It was good coffee, a galactic mile away from Mr. Bang's instant coffee packet.

"But it's not just the place," I said. "It's a culture. A way of eating that is very Korean, and I get the feeling it's almost like an endangered species."

"It's true," she said. "There are these rough, old *ajummas*. They make good, simple, unpretentious food out in the open. They'll say 'eat more,' they'll give you more. There's kindness in among the roughness. Even though they're dirt poor. It's not just the places or even the food—it's the people, too. It's a way of doing things that is disappearing."

We'd arranged to go eat at the opposite end of the Busan dining spectrum from Mrs. Kang's. Chris Tharp, Min-Hee's husband, had lived in Busan for almost a decade and suggested we make for the hills to eat another Busan specialty.

The bus creaked and juddered up the steep gradient. The road was twisting and the brakes screeched as the driver navigated hairpin bend after hairpin bend. We were heading into the misty green above Busan to a village called Geumseong.

We'd climbed these mountains to eat *heugyeomso bulgogi* (흑염소불고기, black goat). Min-Hee suggested we eat at a place called Sa Gye Chol Jjib (사 계 절 집), or "Four Seasons House" in English. For their economic survival, the villagers in the mountains relied upon people coming to eat their black goats. The village is built around a stream that runs between the road and the restaurant. The bed of the stream had a concrete bottom. We crossed a small bridge lined with potted succulents, herbs, and flowers to enter the restaurant, which was little more than a series of small, basic rooms. They surrounded a central courtyard, which had a cheap, vinyl-covered raised platform on which people could smoke and sleep off their food. It was the Korean equivalent of an after-dinner opium parlor.

The meat, the locals said, was low in fat, good for your health, and very tender. However, the smell was off-putting to many. That was why they grilled it and added onion, soy sauce, and sesame to make it Korean *bulgogi*-style.

Four cut logs leaned against the wall; this was the wood for the barbecue to grill the goat. Outside the kitchen area, a bundle of just-picked greens lay upon the cracked concrete floor. Dirt dropped from the pale roots. A waitress, with her trousers tucked inside thick, colorful socks, ushered us into one of the small rooms. She quickly covered the single low table with a thin plastic sheet, like a diaper for the table.

Apart from the calendar and clock on the wall, the room was entirely unadorned. Flowery wallpaper licked the edges of the vinyl floor, which itself curled up like a lip around the perimeter of the room.

Min-Hee ordered Geumjeong Sanseong *makgeolli,* an alcoholic drink made from rice, wheat, and mountain spring water.

"This is the one you find everywhere in the mountains around Busan," said Chris as I held up a brown bowl for him to fill. Chris told me how he first learned about Korean food.

"I had very little experience with Korean food back in the States," he said. "I'd tried some just a few times and didn't even know what I was eating. I arrived here eager to dive in."

The ultra-minimal look of the restaurant had the effect of giving the food a certain amount of gravitas. There was nothing else to focus on. A room like this could only ever be about food. Food and conversation. I imagined some people could even find a room like this threatening. Chris remembered something similar in the United States.

"I used to visit Koreatown in LA," said Chris, "but it was kind of intimidating. I lived within minutes of the largest Korean neighborhood outside of Korea, but I never ate there. Part of it was the language barrier. So many of the signs were in Hangul only, as if to suggest that they only really wanted Korean customers. Another factor was the sheer size of the place: Where do I even begin? This was before the days of food blogs that illuminate those hidden, previously hard-to-break-into treasures."

Our black goat lunch started to arrive, and I could see that it was going to be big. There were mushrooms, kelp, minari (a kind of Korean cilantro), an acorn jelly, and another kind of kelp, a sweeter one, like samphire. There were some sweetened nuts, chiles, *doenjang,* garlic, and pickled onion. I marveled at the packed table. I'd often thought Korean restaurants didn't deserve Korean food, that they were too dull and in no way matched the food. I was wrong: drab worked. The food was the star.

"I suppose there was a fear of standing out, too, that kept me out of

Koreatown in LA," said Chris. "Rolling in alone to a restaurant or district where you're the only white guy takes a bit of balls. I wasn't sure if I would be welcomed. Once I moved to the actual country, however, I was forced to shed any such hang-ups if I wanted to really eat well."

Two kinds of *chwinamul* (취나물, or wild green plants) arrived: one was dried with sesame and the other one was fresh. There was soy sauce, a salad, and a large *pajeon* with spring onions and squid.

"My ignorance with regard to the cuisine actually excited me when I got here," said Chris, "because I knew nearly everything would be new and exciting. Food was a kind of key into Korea for me."

I knew what he meant. I'd been there, I'd held that key, too, opened that door, and gotten hopelessly, happily, deliciously lost. Plate after plate of grilled, marinated black goat started to arrive until the table was full. There was no space even for my notebook. By now, there were almost twenty plates on the table and the room throbbed with sweet barbecue, soy, and sesame.

Mrs. Lee Suk-Ja opened this restaurant in 2010. She explained how she started it.

"This area is surrounded by old fortresses," she said. "Lots of people come to walk and the most popular drink is *makgeolli*. We tried to find something to eat with the *makgeolli*, but there were only goats on our land. However, it worked, and this area became famous for its black goat and *makgeolli* combination. Right now, we can't keep up with the demand, so we have to get our goats from Geoje Island or other places. The goat meat grilled over charcoal is the most popular dish, and it goes best with the Sanseong *makgeolli*."

A restaurant opened and found a modicum of success, the copycats followed, and before you knew it the whole area was known for a particular dish. However, this village felt like a real village—albeit one entirely reliant upon the bleating black beasts that lived on, in, and around the organic farms in the mountains here.

It was very tender meat, marinated in the same sauce you'd add to beef to make bulgogi and grilled quickly. The goat was sweet and nutty.

"We like to eat, and we like to watch people eat," said Min-Hee.

She glanced at me. I really do not think I am a pretty sight at the best of times, and certainly not when eating. I was attempting to pick up a piece of the acorn jelly. It was covered in leaves, carrot, and seaweed. It was soft and easy to cut with the metal chopsticks but difficult to raise into an eating position before it fell.

"Hence *mok-bang*?" I asked, finally able to taste the soft flutter of acorn jelly.

Mok-bang (먹방) is a peculiarly Korean phenomenon. *Mok-bang* means "dinner broadcast," and "*mok-bang*ers" are people who eat lots of food, film themselves eating that food, and broadcast it live on the Internet. They are known as "broadcast jockeys" or BJs. Some of them are stars who have hundreds of thousands of viewers, advertising deals, and endorsement contracts and receive donations from viewers and fans. Some earn far more from eating live on the Internet than they do from their day jobs. One, who went by the name of BJ the Diva, quit her day job to *mok-bang* full-time. She earned nearly $10,000 per month until she retired when the pressure to perform, and eat vast amounts of food on a daily basis, became too much for her (and her apartment building's sewage system, presumably).

"We're a sick society in many ways," said Min-Hee. "We're not positive and we work too hard. We developed so fast, in such a short period, we don't actually enjoy ourselves apart from drinking and eating."

We were making big inroads into the table. I imagined BJ the Diva plowing through what the three of us had already eaten. Our dinner would hardly have rated as a snack for a broadcast jockey with her stamina. Min-Hee had more tales of Korea's sick, or at least somewhat odd, society.

"There's this baby," she said. "He's mixed. He has a white father and a Korean mother. Photos of the baby were used somewhere, in some advertising thing, and now this baby has fans. People write to the baby and they blog about the baby."

"Baby fans is a thing." Chris sighed. "It's entirely innocent, but it is a thing in Korea."

"Like I said," said Min-Hee, "we're a sick, sick society."

I found it quite beguiling, alarming, and cute all at the same time. At the end of the meal, rice and a small, earthy *doenjang-guk* arrived.

If there was one dish that comes anywhere close to taking a long, hot soak inside the soul of Korea, *doenjang-guk* is it. Sipping it is like tasting the windswept mountainside, a crusty hut with a dripping outside tap, fermented vegetable–filled basins piled up at the back. There's a dog tied up, barking, while inside the hut people are laughing and drinking. *Doenjang-guk* is the definitive taste of Korea. It's always there, nudging you, not punching you like its sometimes more difficult to get to know and less friendly neighboring soups do. *Doenjang-guk* is the quintessential taste of Korea, and it always comes with rice.

In the near distance we could hear music. A CD was playing in the kitchen. It was all turgid, sugar-coated, pump-action melodies.

"I don't like K-pop," said Min-Hee. "Can you even call them musicians? Dancers, maybe. Singers at a stretch, but musicians? No. Most of the young generation like K-pop. It's this whole model look they aspire to. It's total show business, but they're just part of a factory."

A factory that, if you believed Korea's state propaganda machine, was taking over the world. *Hallyu* (한류), or "Korean wave," started with a government cash injection of $50 million. The investment clearly paid off, as by 2013, South Korea earned $5 billion from K-pop exports; the government wants to double that by 2017.

One of the benefits of the popularity of K-pop and Korean soap operas throughout Asia is that it has helped give Korean women confidence because of how they are now perceived in other Asian countries. As Min-Hee told me, Korean women today are seen as the beauty standard in the region. Even if, in the majority of cases, that perception is the result of an afternoon spent lying on the surgeon's operating table.

"The first time I felt how different we Korean women are seen was in Sumatra," said Min-Hee. "When I went there, I had all these women wanting to touch me, see my skin, take photos of me with them. This fascination with this image of Korean beauty all comes from the soap operas and from K-pop."

I went back to Mrs. Kang's den late one afternoon. I ate sea squirts and drank soju.

If Koreans' dreams were filled with electric kimchi and the people were losing touch with where they came from on a culinary level, the hagfish stalls represented everything pre-electric, pre-transistor to me. Perhaps this life was more from Korea's valve era.

There was a golf driving range on one side of hagfish alley, the dock on the other, and the eating sheds were squeezed between the two. Out at sea, tugboats surrounded by old car tires chugged amid the salty fug. Bigger boats hummed farther out. A drunken roar went up from a nearby hagfish shed. It was probably from a drinking game. Above me, hard white balls hit the dark green nets of the floodlit driving range. Higher still and farther away, mist stroked the tops of the apartment blocks that crept up the mountainside around the city. The neon fluorescence was already out. Like this, Busan looked like a down-home, Day-Glo Monaco.

"Now you're a regular customer," said Mrs. Kang. She put the squirming basket on my table and pointed at the restaurant sign, 단골횟집. I remembered what Soo-Jin had told me: the name of Mrs. Kang's restaurant meant "Regular Customers" in English.

On the dock, a group of fifty or more down-and-out *ajoshi*s in thirty-year-old city suits milled among the detritus that seeped from the hagfish sheds: buckets of fish guts, bags of bones, shells, skin, and used briquettes. Water drained from the alley and leaked into the harbor.

A cluster of *ajoshi*s gathered around a pair of men pushing counters across a homemade Chinese checkers board. The men shared soju and chatted. Seagulls scavenged and cried around them. One man smoked as he peed off the harbor wall, and farther along, two men fished. Their nylon lines shot across the horizon as they cast their hopes into the oily film that formed a layer across the Port of Nampo.

I nibbled at the sea squirt. I wanted to savor it, as I knew it was unlikely that I would eat this again when I left Korea.

Two women arrived at the harbor with large cardboard boxes, and the *ajoshi*s stopped what they were doing and gathered around. The women were dressed in red and white and gave out foil-wrapped *kimbap* from the boxes.

Even if they wanted more out of life, or just more life, all doors were closed to this heap of old men on the docks. Like a thrift shop full of stopped radios, their imminent extinction almost seemed like part of a plan.

As Soo-Jin had told me, "Their time is over. It's our time now."

POEM

time is over

we lived our lives fermented red
built concrete vinegar

now we sail in bottles of gathered time
and spit tears into telephone rags

we're the stopped radios
we're deaf
to the cloudless ears of imaginary men

LOW-RISE LEFTOVER

I sat down near the back of the bus. It was 8:50 in the morning and the bus would depart at 8:55. Both the driver and the passengers already aboard were mesmerized by a news report about sea penis harvesting playing on the TV at the front of the bus.

From what I could gather, the sea penis harvest happened at night, close to the shore, in shallow water. The creatures sucked plankton and lived in muddy holes on the sea bed. They could grow up to six inches long and were actually a kind of worm. Not a squirt, not a fish, and not a penis.

The news moved on to a story about an unexplained bandage on the wrist of the supreme leader of the Democratic People's Republic of Korea, Kim Jong-un. The passengers were uninterested and their heads bobbed back to their phones. I pulled the green embroidered curtains back a little to shield me from the sun and the bus dashed out of Busan.

For the first time on this trip, I was going in a westerly direction, back across South Korea, but this time along the southern edge. I was going to Jinju (진주), a small city in South Gyeongsang province. It was almost halfway across Korea, nearly 185 miles south of the capital and home to almost four hundred thousand people.

I watched as the apartments passed me. To the west of Busan is Nakdong River, Korea's longest, at just over 310 miles. It originates in Gangwon province, where I'd eaten *dak galbi, sundubu, makguksu,* and *kalguksu,* and I'd last crossed it in Andong. Crossing the river again was a jarring jolt. High-rise Busan was suddenly behind me, and in front of me were low-rise storage buildings and row after row of plastic-covered greenhouses. No building was higher than two stories; as such, it was an entirely functional landscape. By now, just minutes into the journey, the apartments that scarred Busan's outskirts were a forgotten delirium of distant dominoes. I saw a forest ahead; it was scattered with blossoms. It looked like a child's finger painting: the pink and white splodges peeped from among the greens of the leaves, the grays of the branches, and browns of the tree trunks. Like in any country on this line of latitude, spring was a wash of pink and autumn was filled with warm browns and golds—but even more so than in other places, I thought. I'd always reasoned that Korea's seasons sparkled more brightly because the cities were so uniformly concrete.

My phone rang. The bleating electronic zither snapped me away from the drifting immensity on the other side of the window. I clicked the answer button.

"Where are you?" asked the voice.

"On a bus," I said.

It was Vivian from Congdu.

I was planning to stay in Jinju for a few days to try the city's grilled eels from the Namgang River, for *jijimi* (지짐이), the local version of *pajeon,* and especially for the city's own version of bibimbap, a mixed rice dish with raw beef, called, you guessed it, Jinju bibimbap (진주 비빔밥).

"No, no," she said. "You need to get to Damyang."

"Damyang?" I said.

"You can have eels in Gochang on Sunday," she said.

"Gochang?" I said.

"Yes, we're going to Gochang after Damyang," she said. "They have the best eels in Korea. Then we'll go to Haenam."

"Haenam?" I said.

She went on to explain that "we" also meant me, and that we would visit Haenam and a tea plantation in the middle of nowhere. And that she would drop me off in Jeongeup on Sunday afternoon, from whence I would take a train to the southwestern-most city of Mokpo.

"Get to Damyang by tomorrow night," she said. "I'll pick you up the morning after."

"Okay," I said.

"I'll call you when we're just outside Damyang," she said. "I'll see you at about ten A.M."

Click. The phone went dead.

I was exhausted, and all I had done was pick up my phone. I put it down and looked out of the window again. The forest had gone, replaced by the inevitable trudge of apartment buildings.

Vivian would arrive from China at about six A.M., dump her bags at home, and pack new bags. She'd be on the road again by seven A.M. From Seoul to Damyang was a distance of 155 miles, and with good traffic on her side, the trip would take between three and four hours.

We were going to eat at some choice restaurants in the southwest of the country, the most famous region for Korean food in Korea. And we would meet some of South Korea's "grand masters," the country's very own comic book heroes.

I thought about the last time I had seen Vivian, with Fiona in Seoul, and I remembered something she had told me about the reason she traveled around the country to seek out endangered Korean food items.

"I tell my chef we have to travel a lot all over Korea to meet these people," she said. "Otherwise, it's going to be gone. Because these old people, they don't write down their recipes and they don't give out their recipes."

These recipes would be of little use in a country where few people cooked at home and where most relied on takeout or prepared food. However, in this land of instant everything, it was a legacy that Vivian thought was worth hunting down and preserving. It was a mission I could appreciate and respect.

"There's this one grand master," she said. "She's from Haenam. She learned her recipes from relatives going all the way back to the Chosŏn dynasty. This long dead relative had written down his own secret recipe, but just for his family. I begged and begged her for months and months asking if I could learn about it, and then one day she said, 'Okay, you come down and I'll give you the recipe.'"

It was these recipes, these finds, discovered and rescued from the depths of the Korean countryside, that Vivian adapted and preserved on her own restaurant's menu back in Seoul.

My time in Jinju was going to be shorter than I had previously thought. I picked up the notebook with the list of places where I planned to eat. I had time only for one destination, and it was the last one on the list.

The restaurant looked wrong. It was like a yellowing photograph, a low-rise leftover, a rip in time. It looked as if it were sinking in among the high-rises at a small crossroads in the central market in downtown Jinju.

Cheonhwang restaurant (천황식당) was a *hanok* bungalow. It was opposite a shoe seller and a general store with a buckwheat grinder outside. The store sold dried squid, seaweed, sesame, and other staples. To the right of the restaurant was a ginseng chicken soup restaurant, and to the left was the market.

Tan, beige, and yellow mushrooms lay upon a blue flowery bedsheet on the market street next to Cheonhwang and wrinkled in the heat of the sun. A small white pickup truck trundled by; it was jammed with black net sacks filled with mussels. Another truck went in the opposite direction, this one overflowing with bundles of spring onions. A woman wearing a white sun visor and a padded jacket pushed a cart with oranges and bananas between the two trucks. Above me, the fraying veins of telegraph wires snapped taut along the market alleyway. The wires were quiet. The conversations that once pulsed through the twisted cables now zapped into outer space from antennae on the tops of hotels.

Cheonhwang restaurant opened in 1927. It was like the rock inside Mr. Bang's office: out of place, but calming. Outwardly, it wore the memories of the years that had surrounded it. It had survived Japanese colonization, the Korean War, military dictatorship, and the rocket-propelled development of the nation. It was a tiny, tiled anomaly in among encroaching modernity.

Standing outside, looking at it, amid the rash of sun visors, cars, and beeping trucks, I imagined the walls inside. They seeped the scent of bean paste as a legion of sesame perms doled out Jinju's signature dish and the air pulsated pickled red. I stopped imagining and pushed open the door. It creaked and swung violently as I stepped inside.

There were eight wooden tables, each with a chair, and a side room for private groups. I sat down at what looked like an old school desk. The original dark brown polished tabletop had long been worn away by the friction of elbows, trays, and bowls to reveal the grain beneath. The wooden chair was very small and my knees were squashed between chair and desk. The wall next to me was covered with white tiles. The wooden frames of the sliding windows were a chipped, peeling, grubby white, like a stale, crumbling wedding cake.

The air inside Cheonhwang didn't flicker red, but it shimmered with rice steam and the sound of sharp knives on cutting boards. It resembled a 1970s classroom. I was one of just three customers, and we each sat at our own small wooden table. As in many of the restaurants I'd visited so far, the one-dish menu meant there was no need to order.

Many Korean dishes, like *dak galbi,* bulgogi, and *samgyeopsal,* are impossible to eat alone, unless you are incredibly greedy, exceptionally unself-conscious, and/or have an eating disorder. Those dishes are communal foods. Jinju bibimbap is not one of them—it's a one-bowl-per-person dish. Koreans are only just beginning to get used to eating alone. I thought about this as I waited for my dinner, and I thought about Min-Hee's sick—or, as I preferred to think of it, "endearingly odd"— society.

A number of university studies have found that more and more young people in Korea are eating alone. Students said they ate alone because of a packed schedule. Some "experts" see this societal change as a sign of something more sinister.

"More and more university students lack social skills after growing up in small families and suffering intense competition at school. If people prefer eating alone this may be a sign of psychological problems," said Kim Hye-sook at Ajou University.

A portmanteau Korean term had been coined to describe these feared social outcasts: *honbap*, or "being alone eating," from *hon* meaning "alone" and *bap* meaning "rice" or "eating." Supermarkets had only recently started selling "cooked food in small portions for single people." According to one newspaper, these include "special Chuseok dishes." Chuseok is traditionally a family holiday, a three-day harvest festival celebrated on the fifteenth day of the eighth month of the lunar calendar. Many single Koreans in the Korea of today avoid returning to the nest at this time. The supermarket singles meals are an indicator of this trend.

"Such options allow those who choose to spend the holiday alone to still enjoy some of its atmosphere while getting some quality time to themselves, instead of being held up on congested roads traveling to their hometowns, or being bothered by preaching from relatives."

Dinner at Cheonhwang arrived on a tin tray. There was a small bowl of soup with pork and congealed pigs' blood inside. In a dish were strips of dried, shredded squid sweetened and colored orange with rice syrup; another small bowl held *dongchimi,* radish kimchi with a whole red chile in it. And, of course, there was kimchi: one dish of cabbage kimchi and one of cubed radish kimchi. Then there was the bibimbap.

The large, shiny, stainless-steel bowl was a quarter filled with steamed rice, *yukhoe* (육회, raw meat), mung bean jelly, steamed bracken, dried seaweed, and *gochujang*. It was like a glorious farmer's bucket hauled in from the countryside and dumped at my table.

The *yukhoe*, raw strips of julienned beef, distinguish Jinju bibimbap from other bibimbap in Korea. Other kinds have fish, as in Andong, and some are vegetarian. Jeonju bibimbap has minced beef and North Korean *haeju bibimbap* (해주비빔밥) has pork. But all variations follow the same baby food principle: sling everything in a bowl, stir it up, spice it up, and spoon it down.

I poured a glass of warm barley water from the stainless-steel kettle the waitress brought over, stirred up the bibimbap, and dug in.

There were four framed certificates above the kitchen, along with a clock and an old photograph of Jinju. From my seat, I could see through a small door into the courtyard. Soju bottles filled a stack of green crates against a wall. Three women in black aprons sat on low surfaces chopping garlic, spring onions, and radishes. They were like a band of uninterested session musicians plodding out rent-paying chords, more focused on the gossip they shared than the vegetables they chopped.

There's something reassuring about a spoonful of bibimbap. It's something that's not immediately apparent when the bibimbap first arrives, because it looks sophisticated, like something from a design magazine. You could imagine photographing it, framing the photo-graph, and putting it on prominent display in your kitchen. But once stirred into the gooey rice slop that it must be for you to enjoy eating it, it is less attractive. This is not a dish to pick at. You need a spade. You're mixing delicious Korean cement here, and a well-mixed bibimbap is as comforting as any mom's home-cooked favorite.

In front of the kitchen, right next to the cash register, I noticed an old black telephone. It was a rotary-dial phone, an ancient thing made of Bakelite. It was as if someone had just never gotten rid of it, as if it were a forgotten artifact left over from opening day. I was stunned when the thing actually rang and the chef answered it. In ultra-high-tech Korea, smartphone adopter bar none, with the fastest Internet in the world, fridges that talked to you, elevators that know what floor to take you to, imaginary digital girlfriends, and robot drinking friends, this restaurant, this anomaly in the matrix, still had a working black Bakelite rotary-dial phone.

A band of salarymen, each wearing a name badge, stumbled out of the private room section of the restaurant. The floor inside was shiny and new. One by one the shoes scattered across the floor at the entrance once again filled with feet and were gone. As is the custom in Korea, one man, often the eldest or whoever's turn it was, was left to pay the entire bill. No one goes Dutch in Korea.

I looked up from my almost finished bowl and scoped out Cheonhwang restaurant. It was clear that all was not quite as it had first appeared to me from the outside. Apart from the furniture and the tiled walls, almost everything else inside was new.

I stood and looked inside the private room. It could have been a room in any other Korean restaurant; the walls were beige and bare, an A4-size menu typed on a piece of paper was glued to one wall. There was a clock at the far end and two small, cheap, aluminum-framed sliding windows.

The restaurant was literally a shell of its former self. The guts had long been replaced and all that was left were the furniture, an old phone, and, fortunately, the food.

SLOW KOREA

I left Jinju in Gyeongsangnam province in the morning and headed west by bus. Samjicheon is in neighboring Jeollanam province and was a six-hour trip requiring multiple buses. There were three reasons to visit Samjicheon.

First, it was close to Damyang, where I was going with Vivian. Second, it was one of Korea's designated "slow" villages, and I wanted to see how Koreans did slow. It was something unimaginable to me. Korean women ran like they were being chased by invisible monsters, elevators zoomed, trains zapped, taxi drivers snarled in the face of imminent death with every fare and thundering press of the accelerator. It's not that Koreans didn't do slow; they'd never heard of it.

The last reason to visit Samjicheon was offal. There were few restaurants in Samjicheon, a village with about five hundred residents, but most served offal. I wanted to taste the famous guts of this part of Korea.

I'd arranged to stay in a *hanok*. As I alighted from the local bus, the driver pointed a white-gloved hand toward an alleyway. The *hanok*, he told me, was "just down there." And with that, he powered on down the only through road in Samjicheon. The rumble of the bus soon faded and was replaced by silence. I listened. No, it wasn't quite silence. In the distance, I could hear a road, a big, busy, fast road. It hummed like a transmission tower.

"Slowcity Samjicheon Village," as it is known, is a maze of old, head-height, thick brick walls. In 2007, it was the first village in Asia to gain "slow" status from Cittaslow, an Italian organization affiliated with the Slow Food movement. *Hanok*s hide in among almost two and a half miles of these walls and the village is surrounded by leek, rice, and cabbage fields. It is a glimpse of Korea as it once was.

I dropped my bags in one of the sixteen functional, box-size rooms with on-the-floor sleeping, at the house of Mr. Kim Yeong Bong. The original *hanok* was just over a hundred years old, but the three *hanok*s used to house visitors were new builds. They were gorgeous from the outside, but a little plastic on the inside. My room was bare and had a vinyl-covered the floor. I slid back the slatted wooden door, with paper instead of glass between the slats, and sat on the wooden platform in front of the door facing the garden.

There was a group of strategically placed rocks under a pine tree in among bushes and flowers. The rocks were not alone; sparrows and finches tweeted between the pinky-white buds on the otherwise bare cherry trees. White butterflies flitted around a water pipe next to some large, brown, broken *doenjang* vats. Over the way, a woman with a long ponytail was hanging laundry to dry. At my feet, an ant carried a dead ant toward the metal garden gate. The old wall on either side of the gate was covered in ivy, and lined up against it were three hollowed-out stumps for mashing up garlic, sesame, roots, and nuts.

I lay back on the wooden platform of the *hanok*. The sky was cloudless. This was Korea at its calmest. A place for Zen moments. Koreans seek out these places on weekends, as it's moments like this that more and more people yearn to extend and make more permanent.

In 2001, a mere eight hundred people migrated from the city to the countryside. In 2013, almost sixty thousand people made the move. Most were baby boomers, people in their fifties, but increasing numbers were in their forties, and, unsurprisingly given Korea's ultra-competitiveness and long working hours, they came looking for a slower pace of life.

The calm couldn't last, and sure enough, it soon received bad news. First, in the form of electronic opera music. The dirge emanated from the top of a garbage truck. It was very yin-yang, as if the faux, synthesized sounds of opera were battling to balance out the dirty job of trash collecting. The truth was, both stank. As the truck's tunes circumnavigated the village, a gaggle of Korean tourists arrived. I could see their heads, hats and visors bobbing just above the thick stone wall outside the *hanok*, but I heard them long before I saw them. To make sure I and the whole village heard them, the guide utilized a loudspeaker. She barked a list of facts about the *hanok*s, the stone walls, and the gardens, and the tourists nodded. For thirty minutes I listened as the tour made its way around the village. The loudspeaker grated with the garbage-truck opera and the hum of the distant highway. This was the more common kind of Korean calm: a slightly noisy, reassuringly agitated calm.

I walked into the village. It was six o'clock in the evening, and there was a small market area on one side of the main road. A woman sat on the ground. She had bowed legs and wore the market trader's uniform; black perm, sun visor, track shoes, money belt, and red apron. She was surrounded by fifteen large plastic sacks of enormous red chiles. She sorted, cut, and arranged the drying giants. Next to her were vegetables, roots, fish, seaweed, ginseng, and condiments. Almost every other trader was packed up or tightening down a green tarp over the back of a mini truck, about to drive home.

A waitress in jeans, slippers, and an apron came out of a *manduu* restaurant across the road. She trotted over and collected an empty rectangular tray. It had one metal bowl and three small side dishes on it. It must have been an order of *manduguk*, a beef broth with dumplings and a single beaten egg. Back and forth from market to restaurant she went as she hunted down the lunchtime and afternoon delivery debris. A colleague at the *manduu* restaurant fired up the steamers on the sidewalk, ready for the night trade.

I walked to my dinner destination next to the market. I passed two redundant pay phones. I'd yet to see anyone use one. There are more phones than people in South Korea and most of those phones are smartphones. The country has the highest smartphone-penetration rate in the world. The blue cabins that must have enabled thousands of conversations over the years now looked like sad, mute ghosts.

Gukbap street in Samjicheon village was more of a courtyard than a street. There were seven or eight restaurants in it and they all sold offal. The slow city got the mass transit tourist trade from Korean and Chinese tourist buses. The restaurants were too big to survive by servicing the population of this one small village alone. The restaurants all looked the same; I entered one at random and sat down.

Each item on the imposing menu was written vertically, ended in *gukbap,* and cost 6,000 won. All except one, that is: a dish that cost 7,000 won. Feeling flush, I ordered it. The waitress raised an eyebrow and repeated my order back to me.

"Yes, that's right," I said. "I'd like *modum gukbap* [모듬국밥]."

She had that look of "Well, you asked for it. Don't blame me, I'm just the delivery girl."

What arrived on the hospital ward–style wheelie tray squinted at me as the waitress laid it upon my table. I knew immediately that I'd ordered the wrong thing. This was no restaurant I was sitting in: I'd just arrived at a vivisectionist's potluck.

I looked down at my dinner. Ovaries, intestines, blood, cartilage, guts, and stomach smiled up at me like Carrie on prom night. It was almost as if my dinner were attempting a horrific selfie or begging me to hold the camera up to it, to take a picture as it smiled its blood-soaked grin at me. If this soup had possessed vocal cords, which, by the looks of it, was a distinct possibility, it would have only known how to scream. This soup didn't do pillow talk.

My *modum gukbap* came with three kinds of kimchi, along with raw garlic and raw chile, *doenjang, gochujang,* and a dish of tiny salted shrimp called *saeu* (새우), which are used for seasoning as you would use salt.

I'm not a texture man. Hard-core, visceral offal is the one thing on the Asian table that I've never adapted to, and I have an aversion to gnawing through tough, squeaky, shiny organs. Like a medieval doctor fishing inside a corpse, I poked my chopsticks at dinner until I spotted chunks of *sundae*. There was hope.

Sundae is a blood-stuffed intestine, spiced and mixed with sesame, spring onions, glutinous rice, sometimes kimchi, soybeans, and bean paste, too. *Sundae* was something I could eat. It was a close cousin of the Scottish haggis and the stepsister of a French boudin. The *sundae* was crunchy on the outside, like the crispy skin of a well-grilled sausage, and peppery on the inside, whereas the soup was slightly sweet and deeply meaty. It felt like having a cold in winter, taking the day off work, and snuggling up on the sofa with a warm blanket, a spoonful of codeine, and *The Rockford Files* on repeat. To bypass the offal, I went the Korean baby food route and mixed the soup with the rice. If the chef had trashed the entrails and loaded the soup with *sundae,* I'd have been much happier. In fact, if I'd just ordered precisely that dish—*sundae gukbap* (순대국밥)— for 1,000 won less, I'd have been much happier and ever so slightly richer.

The owner of the *gukbap* place asked me how my corpse was.

"*Mashisoyo* [맛있어요]?" she asked.

I half lied. I said it was *mashida*, delicious, and I paid and scampered out before she could see the abattoir I'd left, minus the soup, the *sundae,* and the rice. I imagined her dejected look reflected off the sheen of a pig's stomach.

I strolled back through slow Samjicheon. The village was devoid of human activity; a dog lolloped down the center of the road, and a breeze funneled its way past a hairdresser, a dry cleaner, and a dilapidated supermarket. I tried to take a positive away from my meal. I'd nibbled at the physical guts, but I hadn't enjoyed them, but what I wanted to get at on this trip was beyond the guts, physical and metaphorical, to the soul, the heart, the center, the essence. I wanted to go deeper into the past, to find out what Korean food was way back when. And Jinju and Samjicheon felt like stopgaps, precursors to something more. What was it that drove Korean food? And in 2015, who was drilling deep into the core of Korean cuisine's being, protecting and nurturing it? I was about to find out.

12

THE BIG KIM

Another day, another tour party, another lecture via loudspeaker. The finches looked bewildered and the ants marched silently by when Vivian called to tell me she was arriving. Moments later, a small minibus screeched up to the gate of the *hanok* and the door opened.

"Get in," said Vivian. "We're going for burgers."

"We" were Mr. Lee, Vivian's chef at Congdu, and Vivian's sister, Kay.

As the *hanok* gate swung behind me and clicked closed, I felt the Korean calm leave me. I left it locked inside that private garden among the rocks and trees and birds. I was heading back into the other Korea.

Burgers were not on my list of regional Korean dishes, and I wondered if I'd get a toy with my meal. The fruit cake pizza seemed like an age ago now, but it sounded like I was heading back into unfamiliar territory.

"How has your trip been so far?" Kay asked.

Kay had worked in New York City and Hong Kong as a fashion designer and only recently returned to Seoul to retire. She had gray hair with blue tints in it. I recounted the dog leg I had traveled and at every tale of breakfast, lunch, or dinner, there was a response:

"Oh, but you should have tried X." "You mean you didn't visit Y?" "But that's not the best place for Z." "You know what you should have tried?" and the occasional, begrudging "Okay. You chose quite well there."

Opinions, glorious, impassioned opinions, rained from people who knew what they were talking about, people who made Korean food and who lived and loved it. You know you're in a good food country when you meet people who express opinions so openly, loudly, and persistently.

"This isn't an exhaustive trip," I said by way of apology. "I want to eat where people eat every day. I don't want the best, I want the normal. I want to see where Korean people are at today, but I want to know where what's going on today comes from, too."

And anyway, I didn't have time; the depth, variety, quality, and seasonal variations required one lifetime at the very least to explore this nation's bounty. I needed several lifetimes.

We pulled up at Damyang Aekkot (담양애꽃). This was no McDonald's, but there was a Mickey D's–size parking lot out front. It didn't look like any kind of burger joint I'd ever seen before. Was I really about to meet The Big Kim, a quarter pounder with kimchi, *gochujang,* and a slab of pickled radish? Or watch some pallid cheeseburger limp my way?

"We've made a reservation," said Vivian. She looked more relaxed outside of Congdu. She had her permed, dyed-brown hair tied back in a bun, and she powered out of the vehicle and into the restaurant to check on our table.

It was a modern restaurant. Koreans mobbed the place—there were hundreds of people eating and hundreds just milling about, lost, waiting their turn, like hungry pilgrims. The entrance resembled the aftermath of a mad panic; discarded shoes and boots covered the floor, their wearers having succumbed to sharp hunger and dashed into the restaurant.

"We're going to eat *tteokgalbi* [떡갈비]," she said as we followed her in and added our shoes to the hysteria. The interior was almost entirely made out of teak. "It's a kind of *galbi* they serve here, but it's made with minced beef and pork and shaped into patties, like small burgers. It comes from here, and this is the most well-known restaurant for it."

Galbi is grilled food. For decades, *galbi* only came in two forms: traditional pork ribs, or *dwaeji galbi* (돼지갈비), and *dak galbi,* the spicy chicken dish I ate in Chuncheon. LA Galbi, which uses thinly cut beef ribs, is the bastardized Korean American version that is also popular in Korea. *Tteokgalbi,* which means "rice cake ribs," is the newest kid on the block. There isn't any rice in it, but the minced pork and beef mixture is shaped to look like a rice cake, or *tteok.* Now *tteokgalbi* is sold all over Korea.

"*Tteokgalbi* started maybe ten years ago," said Kay as we sat down in a partitioned room with one long floor table already laid out with an abundance of side dishes. "Or at least, not many people knew about it ten years ago, but it started to become more well known at that time."

Vivian and her head chef were already dabbing at a side dish here and a side dish there, a slurp of barley water here and a shot of bamboo hooch there. The bamboo drink was called *daeipsul* (대잎술).

"You have to drink it fairly quickly," said Kay.

She held the fat bottle, made out of a bamboo stalk, to pour me a drink.

"The bamboo bottle soaks up the alcohol," said Vivian. "If you leave it too long, the drink vanishes. If you buy a bottle, you have to drink it within one month; otherwise, you'll have to suck the bamboo to retrieve the alcohol."

It had a 15 percent alcohol kick and a soft, smooth, earthy taste. The label said: "Korean traditional bamboo leaf wine."

"It's made from rice and herbs, not just the bamboo," said Vivian.

For a moment I imagined myself as a drunk panda, and I resisted the urge to gnaw at the bamboo bottle. Instead, I surveyed the side dishes. It looked like a D-Day battle plan, rolled out for inspection. In Allied territory, there was some fresh white radish shredded to look like white noodles and sprinkled with black sesame seeds. Next to the radish was a mung bean pancake. I extracted a set of metal chopsticks from their paper envelope and nibbled at a shred of radish as I studied the invasion plans. I was handed a bowl of rice with chopped-up young bamboo shoots inside. Another dish had fresh lotus with a sweet-and-sour pickle. One of the rectangular side dishes had some long, dark green stems on it.

"Garlic leaves from Ulleungdo," said Mr. Lee, the Congdu chef, referring to a popular tourist island seventy-five miles off the east coast. Unlike Vivian and Kay, he didn't speak much English. "There are lot of mountains on Ulleungdo and lots of garlic grows there in the wild. These are quite rare and expensive."

They looked like long, transparent green tea leaves and tasted nutty. The *tteokgalbi* was grilled on a metal hot plate in the center of the table and there was one patty for each of us. They looked like homemade burgers; quite fat in the middle, almost spherical in shape, and dark in color. Their taste was quite bland, their texture very soft. Underneath each *tteokgalbi* was something I didn't recognize.

"It's a *songi* [송이]," said Kay. "A pine mushroom. Real, wild *songi* are very expensive. I doubt this is a wild one."

It tasted of nutty earth and reminded me of mushrooms in southern France, but this one was far softer, like a velvet curtain as opposed to the dark, brutal, delicious rub of a cèpe. *Tteokgalbi* was entirely new to me.

Kay explained how Korean tastes had evolved in recent times.

"In the nineties we started using a lot more Ajinomoto," she said, referring to the original brand of monosodium glutamate, or MSG. Ajinomoto was first sold in Japan in 1909 before it conquered the whole of Asia. "Korean is kind of a natural food and we don't need all that MSG. But that's when food and tastes started to change, when people started using too much of that."

I picked up a shredded cabbage leaf. Kimchi.

"That's aged kimchi," said Vivian.

I thought back to my dinner with Jin-Young in Seoul and of the glorious, saggy, bloody cloth of vinegar-heavy kimchi draped across the table like a wrinkled red octopus.

"What is it with this aged kimchi thing?" I asked. "I've been hearing about it during this whole trip. Kimchi is by its nature aged. Do you need to actually call it aged? Isn't it like saying water is wet? Isn't this just a gimmick?"

"Aged kimchi has been in South Jeolla province since forever," said Vivian. "It only started to spread out across the country about three to five years ago. They like this specific kind of kimchi in South Jeolla, but the kimchi changes taste the farther south you travel."

"I've noticed it's spicier here," I said.

"People in Seoul like simple, clean tastes," said Vivian. "Farther south, like around these parts, they like it hot and spicy."

"There was this trend a while back," said Kay, "for girls in their twenties to say that they didn't like kimchi. It was kind of a pretentious trend."

I remembered Hyun-Ae in Chuncheon and her kimchi-loving husband. It hadn't seemed pretentious to me that she didn't like it, but I *had* found it odd. And I still found it hard to grasp that there existed Koreans who did not like kimchi. What was wrong with them?

"In the south," said Vivian, "they use far more fish sauce and garlic in their kimchi than they do in the north. North Koreans only use a little fish sauce to make their kimchi, and there are far fewer ingredients in the north. They add pork broth to it, but very little red pepper. So North Korean kimchi is not so fishy, and it's not really that spicy, either."

I was in the zone now, in Jeolla, the home of the best Korean food. However, even though I'd lived in this province before, I wasn't sure why Jeolla should be any different from any other province.

"The Jeolla taste is all from the ingredients," said Kay. "They like to pile everything on: garlic, spice, sesame, the lot. It's really very powerful food."

"Salt, too," said Vivian. "Everything has more salt in South Jeolla. In Seoul, we don't keep kimchi too long, as it's not salty enough. We have a far milder palate in Seoul, and it's the same in Pyongyang."

"Koreans believe what you eat cares for your body," said Kay, pointing to a dish of roots, one of which I'd just finished eating. "It's bellflower. It's for your lungs when you're full of phlegm. We make tea from the white bellflower root when we are ill."

"When you're too warm," said Vivian, "you take cold ingredients and dishes to help you."

She ordered a round of *mi-ja* (미자) to finish. It is a tea made from a kind of red fruit called a five-flavor berry, native to northeast Asia and Russia. It was a pinky-red color, and if you can believe it, it tasted bitter, spicy, salty, sweet, and sour all at the same time. It was like the Bee Gees doing disco, rock, folk, psychedelia, and hip-hop all in one Top 10 hit. It was quite delicious, but incomprehensible to my unrefined taste buds.

As we left the restaurant with those five different flavors lapping over the memory of the *tteokgalbi,* I thought about these changing tastes of Korea once more.

Tteokgalbi was a simple adaption of traditional *galbi*. Meat off the bone, minced, seasoned, shaped, and grilled on a hot plate. There was no wrapping with lettuce and sesame leaves in this version, and the side dishes were all different, but the inspiration had come from one Korean dish, not something foreign, and had resulted in the creation of another Korean dish. It was wildly popular.

Maybe I'd been missing something all along with the fruit cake pizza and American *pajeon* in Seoul. Sanchez really was no different from the brains behind *tteokgalbi*; he'd just gone in a less traditional direction. Maybe Korea wasn't just ready for The Big Kim but, like a giant black hole of culinary trends, had consumed it already and moved on. Maybe it was me who was lagging behind.

13

IN THE HAMLET OF YUCHEON-RI

I n the hamlet of Yucheon-ri, in Changpyeong-myeon in the county of Damyang, there is a forest. On the edge of the forest there are small houses with corrugated blue roofs. To one side of the hamlet, hidden by pine trees, is a graveled area about the size of a tennis court. A secret army resides within. Standing to attention, we see them. An earthenware infantry, a thousand strong and 360 years old.

Gisoondo (기순도) is Mrs. Ky's place. She is one of Korea's grand masters. She makes soy sauce and *doenjang,* among other things, and she looked like she'd dressed up to meet me. She wore makeup and a yellow-and-black *hanbok,* the Korean national dress. I think she might have thought I was from a TV station. Regarding the national dress, it would appear that Korean women pulled the sartorial short straw. The *hanbok* is part Queen Victoria, part parachute, designed to cover, not flatter, in attractive, brightly colored silk. The cumulative effect is of an oversized, albeit pretty, sack.

When I'd first heard about the grand masters, they sounded like a band of Marvel comic-book heroes. And in a way, they were just as powerful. This elderly group was tasked with saving Korea's food culture from the evil powers of fried chicken, burgers, and Koreans who'd grown up squealing at the sight of kimchi.

"It's a system set up by the government," Vivian reminded me. "Each master has to make the same menu, or same food, for twenty years. There are grand masters for kimchi, soy sauce, and *doenjang*. All the masters have to follow a recipe book, a few of which are a hundred years old or more."

Master Ky has lived and worked among this army for forty-four years, ever since she got married, and her family has been making soy sauce in Damyang for almost four centuries.

"We haven't always been in this location," said Master Ky, looking up at the pine trees that buffeted in the breeze around her soy sauce lot. "This soy sauce–making area used to be our family's persimmon farm."

The earthenware urns, called *onggi* in Korean, were surrounded by *hanok*-style buildings. These variously served as a shop, a showroom, a warehouse, and a food-processing factory. Below us was the living, breathing army of vats.

"The seed of the soy sauce is inherited," Master Ky said. "The wife of the son originally passed it on from all those years ago. Three hundred and sixty years, to be precise."

She makes soy sauce once per year. In the lunar calendar, that's in November, and in my calendar, that's in December. It takes one month to ferment, so the sauce is ready in January.

"We make the *meju* in December," she said, referring to the fudgelike blocks of crushed soy beans I learned about from Hyun-Ae in Chuncheon. "We put salt on the *meju* during the same month and we begin to make the soy sauce. We only use water, *meju*, and bamboo salt, so it's all natural and nothing extra is added."

The bulk of the soy sauce Koreans buy in shops is a cheaper Japanese-style production-line soy sauce made using chemicals.

"The popular Japanese soy sauces are very quick and cheap to make," she said. "It's different because they use chemicals, but the quality is much lower and it only takes two days to make."

Of the soy sauce Koreans buy, less than 2 percent is made the way Master Ky makes it.

"Can you see?" said Vivian. "This is why I travel all around the country to find the best ingredients, from places like this. Sometimes they're the most expensive ingredients, but it's producers like Master Ky that we should be proud of."

Master Ky led us on a walk through the urns. Close up, I could see that each urn had slightly different markings; some had brown swirls brushed across the sides, or a tight squiggle, like a child's sketch of a snake, around a rim. Some were bigger than others, or wider, had a fatter neck or a narrower bottom. Some were darker brown, some more reddish. Each seemed to have its own character.

"It's a very spiritual day on the day we make soy sauce," Master Ky said. "Some of these soy sauces are over one hundred years old."

She removed the lid of one dull, matte urn and used a gourd-shaped ladle to delve into the tar-black substance inside the vat. She let the fermenting soy sauce drip back into the murk. It formed bubbles on the surface, as if the contents of the urn were gurgling as they grew.

Master Ky told us that she had added another fifty urns to the army earlier that year. Some jars were as old as the soy sauce–making family themselves. The urns can cost around a thousand dollars apiece, but the oldest jars were, Master Ky told me, "priceless."

I smelled burning. Master Ky walked us behind the *hanok*, which served as a shop and tasting room. Three women in shower caps, aprons, and rubber gloves were washing dried bean sprouts to make *meju*, but this didn't explain the smell. Master Ky pointed at a large kiln with a big chimney.

"Salt," she said. "We put mineral salt from the west coast of Korea inside the bamboo and seal it with clay. We burn the salt inside the bamboo nine times to kill any poisonous germs. The purest salt is made this way, and the salt must be pure to stop the soy sauce from spoiling."

Just like wine, soy sauce can go bad before and during fermentation for any number of reasons. Although those reasons are somewhat different in Korea than they might be in Napa Valley or the south of France.

"If a person with the last name Shin [신] works on the sauce in the early stages," said Master Ky without any hint that she was joking, "he or she can spoil it. So can anyone who is going to a funeral. If the preparation of one or all of the ingredients is wrong, then it can go rotten. If it goes rotten, then there cannot be any soy sauce from that year, as the whole lot will be ruined. As for the quality, it really depends on the weather as to how good the soy sauce is. Too much rain can also ruin it."

The earthenware jars, the precious, priceless urns, can also go bad, especially in the summer.

"Each urn has to dry out properly," she said. "We do this in the summertime. If it hasn't completely dried out, then the sauce or the bean paste can go bad."

The urns were like family to the master, and like any child, they needed care and a daily routine.

"We take the lids off in the daytime," she said. "The pores in the earthenware help breathe life into the sauce, while the sun aids the fermentation and kills germs. We also wash the jars from time to time, but when they're fermenting, they do not move."

She said this as if they could move if they wanted to, as if they had a life of their own, that the army could march should it so wish. As we walked among the sentries, I imagined this battalion at the gym all day doing pull-ups, pumping iron, and socking punch bags.

"I am most blessed," said Master Ky. "My son is going to follow the family trade."

He joined us and he told me that he had a PhD in soy sauce making. He showed me how he labeled each urn with the date and time the fermentation began. This helped him check on how each urn was developing. However, Master Ky had a different way of doing things.

"I do it the old way," she said. She walked us to another urn. This one didn't have a label on it. It had two small stones on top of the lid.

"This is the way it's been done for centuries," she said. "I don't need a computer. I know that the jars with seven stones on them are the more precious ones."

Again, I thought of Mr. Bang's rock in Busan. I'd never considered a rock to be calming before, but I was coming around to the idea. Compared to Master Ky's son's labels, I liked the analog rocks. Admittedly, the computer-printed labels were a necessary nod to the twenty-first century, but the stones seemed to me, at that moment, to represent the difference between the generations. The stubborn luddite and the data-driven computer maven.

Inside one of the *hanok*s, Master Ky set out a tasting table for us. Vivian and Kay had been asking questions with me the whole time, and Mr. Lee, the chef, busied himself in the food preparation area. It was like a whisky tasting, but saltier and nonalcoholic. There were three sauces—a five-year-old, a two-year-old, and a one-year-old—in three small bowls, alongside bean pastes: brown bean, red, and, a relatively new invention, another Korean twist on the old, a red bean and "strawberry" paste.

I took a stick of cucumber to dip into and taste the soy sauces. Master Ky cautioned me as I approached the five-year-old. The eldest was shiny, oil black; the two-year-old was a dark brown, like the bark of the pine trees that protected the fermenting urns; and the youngest was a much paler brown, the color of an old, well-used leather briefcase.

"The older it is, the saltier it is," she said. She suggested I take a dab on my finger. The taste was pure salt fire, like a salt lick for a rhinoceros.

The sauces descended in power as they descended in age. They were all earthy and understandably beany. The *doenjang*—the paste that forms the basis of Korea's most soulful food, *doenjang-guk*—was also very salty. But, as with the soup of the same name, eating a dab of *doenjang* is like tasting the earth of this country, touching the source, the center of the earth.

I realized that *doenjang*, beans, is what it all comes back to in Korea. This journey up until this point had been like tracing the Rolling Stones' classic album *Exile on Main Street* back through to John Lee Hooker. But here in Yucheon-ri, I'd reached Muddy Waters and gone further. We'd gone way on back to a train station in Tutwiler, Mississippi, in March 1903, when a man called W. C. Handy saw a "ragged loose-jointed black" playing guitar with a knife as a slide:

> The event was unforgettable. His song, too, struck me instantly . . . the weirdest music I had ever heard.

That's *doenjang* for Koreans. It takes them all the way back. As the blues is to the Rolling Stones, *doenjang* is to Korean food. It's the earth, but not quite the soul. That title is reserved for another ingredient.

The glossier newbie, the strawberry concoction, was sweet and spicy.

"The sweetness offsets the spiciness," said Vivian. "She started making this one about ten years ago. I think it's an interesting adaptation. You see, this is how our cuisine is evolving: through experiments by experts like Master Ky and by us in the kitchens in the restaurants."

She offered me a sweet and crunchy Korean-style cookie made of sesame oil, ginger, egg, rice flour, and rice syrup to offset the saltiness of the soy sauce.

"There was no sugar many years ago," said Master Ky, "so we added rice syrup, but it takes all day to make it. You're constantly cooking and stirring—it's like making marmalade."

Judging by the neat surroundings and the number of workers, Master Ky was doing well for herself. However, her products were only in demand from a small, elite clientele: the high-end restaurant trade, overseas buyers, and Korean food enthusiasts. Korea's average Mrs. Lee was largely ignorant of the pleasures of these ancient Korean soy sauces.

And while Koreans would balk at buying Chinese kimchi or become upset at unknowingly eating it in a restaurant, they would be reluctant to shell out the extra won needed to buy high-end soy sauce or *doenjang* from a Korean grand master.

"There is still this mentality that Korean food is cheap," said Vivian, "and, therefore, not something to be proud of or to spend money on."

14

SET THE CONTROLS
FOR THE HEART OF THE SUN

There was a chill in the early evening air as we arrived at Grand Master Han's. She wore a neon green jacket, the zipper pulled up high, concealing her neck. She made *doenjang*, soy sauce, and the pungent *cheonggukjang* paste. Her gray hair was freshly permed, but unlike the majority of older women in Korea, she did not have it dyed. I always took this as a good sign in people in Korea. It was a sign of confidence: confidence in how they looked, confidence in their age.

Master Han runs her fermentation and vegetable-growing business in the sparsely populated county of Haenam on the southwest coast of mainland Korea. Haenam is fifty-five miles south of Damyang in South Jeolla, or Jeollanam-do, province. This is the end of mainland Korea. Heading south, after her town, there was nothing but sea and islands.

The lot of her "farm" was filled with ceramic soy sauce urns, all old, some ancient. She walked us between the urns and pointed to a large, imposing jar with a faded facade.

"This one is five hundred years old," she said. "The one next to it is two hundred and fifty years old. All the stone you can see here that was used to make the ceramic for the urns came from Haenam."

She stroked the elder urn's belly like it was a prize bull.

"Rich families always kept a big one," she said, "because the soy sauce would taste better from it, and they also put things in them when it was time for a daughter to marry."

Master Han was seventy-six years old, but she looked a lot younger. Her skin was smooth like a pebble with nary a wrinkle and no signs of the surgeon's knife. To ferment the *doenjang,* she covered the *meju* in salt and sealed the urns with plastic. She opened two to show me.

"These are 2012 and 2013," she said. "You see, these are ready now. Try."

She encouraged me to dip a finger in and claw up a taste. That familiar nutty earth flooded through me on a wave of salt. *Doenjang* normally needs one year before it's ready, but it can keep fermenting for up to ten years. However, Master Han assured me that after six months it is "already beginning to have a good taste."

"For the fermentation to work," she said, "you need to have a breeze from the south to the north. Also, you can't have any shadows. And you need sun, you need a lot of sun."

Master Han has over a thousand urns in this space. The urns, she explained, were of different sexes, and different sexes were used to produce different kinds of sauce. The slimmer male produced soy sauce, while the more rotund female made brown bean sauce.

"You see that this jar has a bigger arse?" Master Han said, giggling at the pear-shaped urn next to the more modestly endowed male jar. "Huge arse—that's how you know it's a female."

There was a highway nearby Master Han's place, and traffic hummed by at speed as we talked. The sea breeze drifted through the traffic to her urn-festooned concrete lot. We were surrounded by transmission towers; there was a church spire in the distance, and the ever-present pine trees swayed in the breeze.

"My mother-in-law gave me all the secret recipes," said Master Han. The recipe she used to make *cheonggukjang* is over five hundred years old. She also made vinegar and tons of other things, including, of course, her own *meju*. An ingredient apparently discovered by Genghis Khan's troops in the thirteenth century:

> Genghis Khan's troops carried cooked soybean rations on their horses. The warmth rising from the horses' bodies naturally caused the fermentation of the beans, resulting in a rudimentary form of meju.

Master Han stored her *meju* on a series of bamboo shelves and low, slatted tables. They ran the length of a large greenhouse covered in transparent plastic sheeting. The *meju* looked like cracked crusty bricks of bread. Master Han stored them here for ninety days before they could be used.

Strolling between the seemingly innocuous brown bundles, I realized these simple creations formed the catalyst for Korea's entire cuisine. Each brick was a concentrated block of Korea.

Meju is the basis of *gochujang*, of *doenjang*, of soy sauce, of almost every soup in Korea. *Meju* forms the building bricks of the Korean kitchen, and without *meju* there is no Korean food. *Meju* is the sun, the soul, the star that gave birth to myriad other stars. In the dreams of homesick Koreans, dreams that are crowded with Korean food, it is *meju* that connects them all. Yet, as Hyun-Ae told me in Chuncheon, hardly anyone uses it in the home anymore. It is potent, powerful, stinky stuff. You need space and time to make it, and space and time to utilize it, and twenty-first-century Koreans lack both. In addition, having arrived from Mongolia, this Korean culinary cornerstone wasn't really Korean, but like any immigrant who finds a welcome haven, over the millennia it was now an integral part of its new home.

Master Han had a barley grinder to make flour. Next to the milling room was a fermentation room, and she dried malt on trays outside. In another greenhouse, golden squash, pumpkins, and small yellow melons grew. Over the road was a large warehouse that served as her freezer storage area. It was a vast operation for one elderly woman to be in charge of. Plant pots, flowers, and bonsai trees surrounded her *hanok*-style house. Master Han walked us over to an imposing urn that stood in the courtyard.

"This is 2011," she said. "*Doenjang*."

I tried it. It was sweet, deep, and red and very, very salty. I was back at that rhinoceros salt lick again.

"You mix this with water to make a sauce," she said. "Every day we clean it to make sure no bugs get inside."

Then she pointed to another urn.

"Inside here is my one-hundred-year-old sauce," she said, with a look that warned against touching it, the laser-eyed, mind-melting, soul-destroying stare of one of Korea's grand masters. I felt the power of this comic-book hero.

"We had to replace the old urn because it was damaged," she said. "But the sauce inside this is one hundred years old. It's the base of everything we produce."

An assistant opened the lid, and inside twinkled a nation's heritage, the constellations of Korean food, for centuries born of stinking bricks of *meju*. Inside the giant urn was the living, breathing history of Korean food.

Master Han dug a ladle into the urn of black liquid and poured some into a small dish. She put the dish on top of another urn along with five spoons, and we each tasted a drop.

I want to say that it tasted of dreams. That the sauce ebbed on a pepper gauze, that it breathed jets of sweet, salt, vinegar, that egrets steeped in glimmering gold swooped past us, that upon my swallowing this ancient sauce, the veins of the universe revealed themselves, that they flowed with the space blood of distant planets and that those planets orbited a single telepathic seed of soy found in Master Han's garden.

But nah, that didn't happen.

Much as you might expect from a hundred years of festering, the source of Korean food, the power, the engine, and the guts of Korean food, this soy sauce was an epic, deep, dark, very, very salty, earthy, grumpy, roasted spirit. He was an angry wee shite, and he wanted out.

Every year, Master Han added five-, ten-, and twenty-year-old soy sauce to the urn to top it off. But essentially, the core of what stood in front of me and what now coursed through me was ancient Korea. I wondered if I hadn't unwittingly taken part in a Korean black-magic ceremony. So be it—let me in. I was glad of it.

Master Han's house was split into two; the right side was for living and the left was for cooking and eating. We entered the left-hand side and she hung up her coat in a corner and asked us to sit down. The dining room was separated from a kitchen by a sliding door. There was a low table on the floor, surrounded by flat cushions; the table creaked under the weight of food. We sat on the cushions on the *ondol,* the heated floor.

There were two cabinets at one end of the room that contained bowls and plates. A small portable TV sat on a tray next to me in one corner of the room. Behind it, there was a coat stand and an ironing board, and there were a calendar and a clock on the wall. Everywhere in Korea, in every room in Korea, there were a calendar and a clock. Time watched the Koreans as they watched time, and there was never enough of it.

Master Han and two helpers had spent the entire day preparing dinner. We had wanted to take her out for dinner, but she had refused. We were in for a treat. This would be a taste of ancient Korea.

There was kelp soup with tiny shrimp inside, abalone, sesame seeds, salty and woody flowers, three kinds of kimchi: one fresh, another that was a year old, and another of the water variety.

"I only use spring water from the nearby mountains to make my water kimchi," said Master Han as she pointed at the bowl of *mul kimchi* with the thin slices of radish inside it.

Master Han was from Gwangju originally, and her relatives were scholars. As with Vivian, and all the other Hans in Korea, she claimed lineage to royalty. She moved to Haenam when she got married. She had two sons; both were now doctors.

Unlike me, she could sit in the cross-legged position for hours. She probably got up in the morning a good few hours before me, too, and could no doubt hike the mountains around her farm far faster and for far longer than I could. I was ashamed, but I was also hungry.

The table was gridlocked with food. There were steamed green strands of fresh garlic, fresh chile, steamed crabs, cabbage water, and lettuce, and *kalbi* was cooking on an electric grill that sat to one side of the table. There were small dishes of sesame oil and salt and steamed rice and pickled, blackened garlic. Roasted sesame seeds were sprinkled like glitter across everything; they speckled every plate and bowl on the table.

"I grew everything on the table myself," she said, "apart from the seafood. I buy that from the local fishermen."

This was a last supper to end all last suppers. I didn't know where to start. Master Han encouraged me with a crab claw. I picked at the flesh inside with metal chopsticks and drew it out. It scurried inside my mouth and fainted upon my tongue like a salty white sea phantom.

"If there's too much of a fish smell after eating the crab," she said, "you should eat the pickled garlic."

Master Han occasionally broke into song during our meal. She did this, she said, to better explain a point she was trying to make about food. She had a strange voice. It sounded much younger than her years. I made a *kalbi* wrap and nibbled at the blackened garlic.

She was explaining why it was symbolic to have sesame seeds strewn over the table like glitter across Marc Bolan's record collection.

"Traditionally, only rich families could get sesame," she said. "So today, it's largely a symbolic reminder of those times to have sesame on the table."

After dinner, we entered the other side of the house, where the living quarters were. She showed me a framed newspaper cutting in her living room. It hung next to a large photo of an appearance she had made on Korean television.

"I sold twelve thousand dollars of soy sauce after that article," she said, tapping at the glass frame. "At that time, that constituted thirty days' revenue in just three days."

I retired to a comfy chair while Master Han continued to sit crosslegged, this time on the living room floor. She folded her right foot over her left thigh and sat Buddha-like. She remained like that for an hour as she told stories and we shared persimmon quarters and whole strawberries, which were served on two round wooden tables in front of a huge TV.

In 1974, the family planning pressure from the government was tough. Women were encouraged to have no more than two children. Posters displayed around Korea stated messages like "Sons or daughters, let's have two children and raise them well."

Like many other women at that time, Master Han had her third pregnancy terminated. She noted with some irony that forty years later, the government was extolling the opposite message and was in the process of formulating a communist-sounding "five-year plan" to tackle Korea's chronic lack of babies.

Perhaps a similar plan was needed for food producers like Master Han, to push and promote what they do so that the Korean people might know.

ONLY K-POP SOUNDS HAPPY

It was six A.M. Mist drifted across Seoladawon tea plantation in the Haenam countryside. The small green leaves rippled like a verdant blanket across the tightly packed bushes. They shone and bristled in the breeze. This small plantation lay in a mountainous bowl, protected by a fence of pine and maple trees.

I walked through the tea plantation. It was here, at this place in Haenam-gun and only this place, that I found real calm in Korea. With only the sound of the breeze, the trees, and the birds for company. No highways hummed, there were no buzzing transmission towers, no tour groups with a loudspeaker, and no opera-playing garbage trucks.

Halfway along the plantation, and to one side, I came to a small stone hut with a wide, slightly arched roof. Two stone steps led up to a flimsy wood-and-plastic-sheeting-covered door. A pine tree grew through the roof. The hut had clearly been built in such a way as to allow the pine to prosper. Mr. Oh Geunsun sat in the hut; a mat lay on the floor and there was a radio, a newspaper, and a bottle of soju on the small shelf. He stood up, came to the door, and put his slippers on.

Mr. Oh and his wife had moved to this location after they got married.

They had been farming green tea from this twelve-acre site since 1997 and produced two hundred pounds of tea per year. It was mostly green tea, but they also made magnolia and camellia teas from the trees scattered throughout the plantation.

"It's quite famous for camellia around here," he said. His hair was thinning; he wore crimson trousers and an old quilted jacket.

"For me, it's the best tea," he said of the camellia. "It's good for your health and it doesn't keep you awake, as there's no caffeine in it."

Mr. Oh had visited China, Japan, and other parts of Korea to learn about tea growing before starting work on his plantation. He explained that it normally took sixty days from planting a tea bush to reaping the first harvest.

"With fertilizer, you can harvest in much less than that," he said. "But we choose not to, as we prefer to make it organically. It's longer and more expensive, but it tastes better and it's more natural."

When the tea is picked, it is dried outside in the shade for one to two hours. After the drying is complete, just 20 percent of the tea remains.

"If you dry them in the sun," he said, "the leaves oxidize, so you have to dry them in the shade."

As we walked through his plantation, I noticed the many varieties of trees that grew at seemingly random points. We stopped at one and he plucked a leaf, gave it to me, and told me to smell. I was instantly transported back inside my grandmother's wardrobe.

"Mothballs," I said.

"Camphor," he said. "We make tea from this tree, too, and massage oil."

Far from being random, the trees were planted in such a way as to provide shade and to attract birds that eat the bugs that attack the tea leaves. Twenty species of birds populate the hundred or more trees on the plantation.

Mr. Oh kneeled down and sunk his hand into the earth. He stood, held the soil to his nose, and drew in a deep sniff. He smiled, held his hand out to me, and beckoned me to bend my nose toward it. The soil was loose and had a distinctive smell.

"Tea," he said.

I was surprised, but of course it made sense. It had taken years for this soil to adapt to tea, but over time it had become of the tea as much as the tea was of it. I was reminded of the *meju* again, that soul of Korea. Here was a different kind of soul. And I smelled it right down there in the earth.

"It needs to breathe," he said. "Everything in the universe needs to breathe, and just like us humans, in the way that we all have our own smell, all soil has its own smell, too. And here that smell is tea."

At the farthest end of the plantation, at the base of the low mountain range that loomed above us, was a line of bamboo. The combination of trees and bamboo helped protect the tea against the wind and frost.

An osprey hunted over a lake behind the trees. Small white frothy crests of water spluttered and quickly disappeared as if the lake were flashing thousands of cotton teeth at us. I noticed a second osprey. I didn't know if they were playing or hunting.

"The male gives the female a fish tail," said Mr. Oh. "The head part is for his meal, because there are fewer scales on the head part. It's like a mating ritual at this time of year."

Mr. Oh's life seemed idyllic to me. However, I knew how harsh Korean winters could be. The wind that screamed down the peninsula from northernmost Mongolia brought with it a fearsome chill. Snow could be very deep and the cold could approach minus 9 degrees Fahrenheit.

"Is your life difficult?" I asked.

"No, it's not so difficult," he said. "We're used to the climate, and I even look forward to the cold. I really like my life—farming, it's a good life."

He dropped the earth he'd let me smell earlier. He'd been fondling it for as long as we'd been speaking. He turned his slipper over the loose dirt, scratching at it.

"Only selling is difficult," he said. "We only sell locally and we do ev-

erything on our own. The big department stores charge too much commission. This is the only problem, the fact that we can't sell through them."

Mr. Oh was not a grand master and his operation was the opposite of
Master Han's. Where she produced at scale across a variety of products,
Mr. Oh and his wife were highly specialized. We walked back to his *hanok*.
He stored mulberry juice in plastic mineral water bottles at the back of
the house, in among the cluster of more than forty earthenware jars filled
with various pickles, pastes, and sauces.

The previous night he had served us magnolia tea at a long, low,
wooden table that looked like it had been roughly hewn from a tall, wide
trunk. He and his wife performed *pansori* for us. *Pansori* are stories told in
songs where a singer is accompanied by a drummer. Mr. Oh accompanied
his wife on a traditional Korean drum, a *buk,* which he played with a thin
stick, a *bukchae.*

"What makes me sad," said his wife, Mrs. Ma Seungmi (Korean spouses
do not take the surname of the husband after marriage), "is that most
Koreans don't care about our traditional songs anymore. Many foreigners
care more, so thank you for coming to Korea and for coming to hear our
songs."

It wasn't just Mrs. Ma who was dismayed at the lack of respect given
to traditional Korean music. A Seoul-based experimental rock group called
Jambinai that use a mix of guitars and traditional Korean instruments felt
the same way. Band member Lee explained,

> "Nowadays, many Korean people don't listen to traditional
> Korean music and they don't respect Korean traditional cul-
> ture . . . We wanted to communicate with ordinary people as
> musicians through our music, but it's impossible to do that
> with only traditional music, so we created Jambinai. We found
> our own way to create new music with Korean traditional in-
> struments . . . Korean traditional instruments are really unique.
> The instruments convey certain very special Korean emotions."

Mrs. Ma sang in guttural tones, wrenched from deep within her throat. Her voice was loud and dramatic. She expressed the emotion of the song with taut, often painful-looking facial movements and with the flick of a fan in her right hand. Behind Mrs. Ma in the high-ceiling, wooden-beamed room were three long racks of CDs, a piano, more traditional drums, and a zitherlike instrument with twelve strings called a *kayagum*. She moved her arms and hands slowly while her feet stayed perfectly still. For one song, she kneeled down, always positioned at a right angle to her seated husband, whose drum was on a floor mat in front of him. The songs were about the seasons, and about love.

After they'd finished, Mr. Oh went to the small kitchen behind us to prepare some more tea. Mugwort this time.

"I have no idea what you're singing about," I said, "but all your songs sound very sad to me."

Truth was, they sounded suicidal.

"Korean songs are sad," Mrs. Ma said. "Like the soap operas of today. It's misery."

She explained that in the operatic tradition of *pansori,* a performance can last as long as six hours.

"Only K-pop sounds happy," said Kay. "But it's not real, it's not like this. This touches your heart."

Peel back the layers of the facade—the saccharine pop tunes, the twee teen singers, the bling-bling restaurants—and tradition breathes. This husband-and-wife team had chosen to dedicate their life and work to both old traditions and the newer organic way of life. The "new old." They glowed with that rare health of people who live and work outside and who eat and drink well. At this tea plantation I sensed something I hadn't really seen in Korea before: a search for well-being, for calm, for a change of pace, for a new take on ancient ways.

I DON'T KNOW

I was not hungover. How could I be? I'd just spent a night at a tea plantation that edged into health-retreat territory, a place that was officially now my calmest place in Korea. But I felt like I was hungover.

In between eating, drinking, and sleeping with Team Vivian these past twenty-four hours, we had visited two museums, two temple complexes, and a national park, walked the length of an ancient city wall, and traversed a mountaintop. I was exhausted.

We had two stops left before Team Vivian zapped back to Seoul for the night shift and I continued my journey farther south. We left the tea plantation early and soon arrived in Naju. We'd come to this town to do one thing: eat a beef soup breakfast at the White House restaurant (하얀집).

It was eight A.M., and the White House was chock-full. I counted the hangovers around me and gave up at fifty. They floated around the White House like phantoms. Red-eyed drunks supped and slurped at soups, chewing away at the bitter lumps and worn chunks of pain inside their heads.

If the couple that ran the tea plantation in Haenam were a step forward into a calmer, more holistic future, this restaurant was very much a stagger and a stumble back into an alcoholic past. The place was littered with hurting heads. Pain pulsed from diners like the popping, glowing explosions of dying characters in a computer game.

The White House is one of the disappearing, yet gloriously alive, breed of restaurant. It was a stubborn old boot that had rejected change. Beef steam hissed from the entrance to the violent kitchen, where seven women in blue aprons worked the soup vats, rice steamers, cutting boards, kitchen sink, and serving trays. An *ajumma* with rubber gloves, a perm, an uninviting glare, and a shower cap ladled soup from one of two humungous, three-foot-wide vats.

We sat down at the only free table and I crossed my legs. This particular one-dish store served *gomtang* (곰탕), and the price was fixed at 8,000 won.

There were framed laminated portraits on the wall. One of the pictures was a hundred years old. In it were the relatives who had run the restaurant in the past.

The beef was cooked very simply and slowly, resulting in a clean beef broth. Inside the hot stone bowl were the soup, strips of beef brisket, rice, spring onion, and thin, noodlelike egg strips.

"You can have it in the morning or at lunch," said Vivian. "But most people have it when they're hungover, as you can see."

There were only Koreans in here. Hundreds of Koreans. We looked out of place. We hadn't touched a drop of the falling-down juice the night before. We'd been on a veritable health kick of mugwort, magnolia, and camphor. We were like the devil incarnate, and perhaps the sick were secretly envious of our healthy glow.

"Society is moving too fast," said Kay.

She had noticed me staring at a family opposite; hungover dad, heavily made-up mom, surgically enhanced daughter, powder-puffed son. The teenagers stared at their phones; their parents seemed to be staring into the afterlife.

"Before, we used to say the generation gap was ten or twenty years," said Kay. "Now we say it's one year."

This soup was a bully. He came inside with one job to do: beat the crap out of you. When he discovered there was no hangover lurking within me, his natural bullying nature changed. He became a she, and she caressed me with beef. It was a classic soothing soup. If there had been a chaise longue in sight, I would have quite happily lounged on it for half an hour after breakfast. But, this being Korea, and this being a Korean trip, I had no such luxury. As soon as the bowls were empty and the bill paid, we were back on board the K-bus, careering toward stop two: Gochang, a city of eels.

In 1996, I had cooked for my Korean colleagues. They were shocked and told me that Koreans believed a man's penis would fall off if he so much as walked into the kitchen, let alone picked up a pickled radish, a bucket of kimchi, or a squeeze bottle of red pepper.

"These days," said Vivian, "girls look for boyfriends who can cook. It's an attractive quality to them these days."

Within a minute of our arriving, the table is covered. There was *doenjang-guk*, sesame leaves, lettuce, chiles and garlic, shredded ginger, radish kimchi, cabbage kimchi, bean sprouts, sesame leaves prepared in soy sauce, pickled onions, sweet vines and flowers, yellow radish, and the pickled intestines of a swordfish.

"Be careful with them," said Vivian. "They're delicious, but very, very salty."

As Kay had told me, Jeolla folk like to pile on the flavors, salt being one of them. Kimchi was the biggest culprit as a source of sodium, but there were plenty of other suspects in this lunchtime lineup. A few of them, including the swordfish intestines, were on the table in front of me.

"Gochang is known for having the best eel in Korea," said Vivian. "The tail part of the eel is the most delicious part."

"But why is the eel from Gochang better than the eel from, say, Jinju?" I asked. Cutting my trip to Jinju short had meant missing the chance to try the eels.

"I don't know," said Vivian. No one knew, not even the restaurant's waitress. Gochang had good eels, and apparently, everyone knew that. Unconvinced, I asked the owner, Mrs. Seol Ji-hyun. She was fifty-five years old, a Gochang native, and had opened the restaurant in 2002. If anyone knew, I thought, she would.

She looked puzzled at the question and did the clenching-teeth, sucking-in-air, head-to-one-side thing, looking deeply into the distance, imagining a lost love, a school playground far away, maybe a memory of eels, far, far away, a first taste—and then she exhaled.

"They're bigger and more delicious," she said. "That's why everyone comes here to eat them. We get through a lot of eels every month. I've no idea how many we sell, but it's a hell of a lot."

"Maybe it has something to do with the mineral deposits in the river," said Vivian. "But I honestly don't know. It's just known for eel down here. Everyone knows that."

As Mrs. Seol twirled our eels on the grill, I remembered the question I'd been asking a lot of people in Korea. I looked into her eyes. I got the sense that maybe it was this woman, this eel master, this food professional, who might just have the answer to the question I had not yet found a complete and satisfactory answer to. So I asked her.

"What is Korean food to you?"

She looked at me as if she could see through me. As if she understood me. As if this alien had tapped into the Korean heart and suckled at its soul. I awaited her response like an eager schoolchild waiting for his grade on a test.

"I have no idea what you mean," she said. "Korean people don't think about it like that. We just make good food for our customers, that's all. We don't give a damn about that stuff."

I looked at my test grade. It said one out of ten. Abysmal. Dunce. Loser. Back of the class. It was an honest response. The response of a real food practitioner. I'd seen it elsewhere. The best cooks never overthink food. That's a mainline to the navel and spiritual death. Sensing a certain degree of forlornness, a balloon pricked, Kay stepped in.

"Eels give you stamina, you know," she said. "And they're good for a woman after she's had a baby."

I remembered Korea's traditional dog-meat-eating week back in the day. The dog-meat-eating season was at its zenith between July and August, the hottest months. Three or four months after the week was over, like clockwork, Korea was a parade of pregnant women. The dog meat, it appeared, had worked its magic on the national libido.

In tandem with a decline in dog-meat eating in the Korea of today, the nation's birthrate had plummeted. The government was so worried about the dearth of newborns in 2014, they warned that

> South Korea's fertility rate is so low that the country's popu-
> lation could go the way of the dinosaurs by 2750, according
> to a new simulation commissioned by the National Assembly
> in Seoul.

With rapid development came some unwanted side effects. Korean people had no money and no time for family, and Korea's newly emancipated women didn't want marriage. And they didn't want marriage to the bits of Korean culture that were designed to keep them in their place. I wondered if the government's push for more babies would necessitate a resurrection of dog-meat-eating week. They needed something to get the national boner back up.

"Why do eels help with stamina?" I asked. "Or young mothers, for that matter?"

"I don't know," said Kay. "Everyone says it helps."

Korea, like much of Asia, has a yen for penis-shaped seafood, sperm-producing stuff, and mother's-milk promoters. Almost anything edible seemed to promise to make something harder, something last longer, something more explosive.

In 2008, one government study claimed that eating Korean food increases sperm count and makes you manlier. A team of researchers . . . studied subjects eating pork cutlets and burgers and compared them to people feasting on hearty servings of bibimbap and kimchi. They concluded that those eating the Korean food were blessed with increased sperm activity and a rise in male hormones.

The first Korean woman I ever met, Jin, the student in England, told me that Korean women were seen as nothing but "baby-making machines." If the current birth statistics were anything to go by, the baby-making machines had not only gone on strike, they were revolting. Chastity may now be out, but birth control was most definitely in.

With thoughts of sperm counts dangling before me, the *doenjang-guk* arrived. *Doenjang-guk* is delicious and I could eat it every day. If I were a bean paste girl—and by this stage in my trip, I kind of wished I was—I think I'd be quite rich. I don't have any interest in purchasing luxury goods. Think of all the money I could have saved.

"Where are you going next?" said Vivian.

"To Mokpo," I said. It was a port city in the far southwest of Korea. "There's a seafood dish I want to try. It's called *hongeo* [홍어]—do you know it?"

Vivian's eyes lit up, Kay's did, too, and Mr. Lee, the chef, seemed to suddenly understand exactly what I was talking about despite his limited English. The threesome looked like a dreamy pop group, and I thought they might break into a Ronettes song.

"Mmm . . . ," said Vivian.

"Mmm . . . ," said Kay.

"Mmm . . . ," said Mr. Lee.

"I love *hongeo*," said Vivian. "You have to have it at a wedding. If you don't, it's really bad. It's just so disrespectful for the couple."

"Korean food," said Kay. "It doesn't get any more Korean than *hongeo*."

"Mmm . . . ," the three of them repeated in unison.

They still looked dreamy as they dropped me off at Jeongeup train station. I couldn't wait to board the train south, as I was about to go eat something I'd never eaten before. Something that was deeply, deeply Korean.

WITH YOU FOR LIFE

The KTX train from Jeongeup to Mokpo stopped for 1 minute 45 seconds at Gwangju station.

Upon my arrival in Mokpo, an innocuous sign greeted me: WELCOME TO MARINE PRODUCT TOWN.

At the station, a cluster of *ajoshi*s huddled together stroking bottles of soju. Hiker couples milled about in matching clothes, with backpacks and black plastic bags full of fruit, instant noodles, and Bacchus-D energy drinks. Mokpo station was pedestrianized with flat, gray paving slabs, like every train station in every Korean city. Flowery neon lights arched over the main downtown shopping streets. There was a crowd of hotels and banks opposite. If only I had known, I mean *really* known, what Marine Product Town had in store for me, I would have gotten off that train at Gwangju. And I wouldn't have the memory. But I didn't. And now I do.

Vivian, Kay, and Mr. Lee had enthused about *hongeo,* the must-have at a Korean wedding, and I'd believed them. But if there were ever grounds for an immediate divorce, annulment, or the groom or bride to sprint like a gazelle away from the altar, *hongeo* was it.

But when I walked into Mokpo, I didn't know.

A small Kia Bongo pickup truck reversed at full speed through a pedestrian zone. It slalomed through shoppers; coat hanger rails filled with clothes and inflatable advertising columns swayed as the truck sped past, honking on a shrill horn. The driver was in a real rush to make it the ninety yards to his destination. What could possibly be so important at six P.M. on a Saturday that he would need to reverse at speed, dangerously swerve through a busy street, and honk his horn? It turned out, for this Mokpo driver, it was of paramount importance that he offload sacks of radishes at a restaurant on the corner.

I wanted to shout at Korea, all of Korea, to slow down. Take a chill pill, take the day off and stop the *bali bali* (빨리 빨리), the quickly-quickly culture that has had this nation by the throat ever since the end of the Korean War. This "can do, must do" culture took root when the country needed to rapidly develop after colonization and war. And it worked: as one industrialist who grew up in the post-war era noted,

> "When my parents were young, they didn't hurry in the same way . . . It was the children of the wartime who were the first to really experience the bali bali . . . It is the same 'can do' attitude that was repressed by the Japanese for 35 years—no rights, no culture. Now we know the real value of Koreans. Korean people now know how to win—it is bali bali. This is very useful for industry, but it is bad for the soul."

And today, it felt like Korea needed to calm down a little and take some care of that soul, lounge over lunch, rest at the table, have a chat, read a book, go for a stroll, not a march, because, really, you've earned it.

I can remember paging a friend I knew in Jeonju in the midnineties (an era when pagers were new and everyone in Korea had one). I was in a café, and I sent her a message:

"I'm in the Orchid café. Fancy a coffee after work?"

From the fourth-floor café I could see her bus arrive on her way home from work. It was about 220 yards away. I saw her run from the bus to a phone booth to check the message I had just sent, which she'd just received on her pager. As she left the phone booth and ran down the street, I sent her another message:

"I can see you. Stop running."

I watched as she stopped, looked at her pager again, and ran back to the phone booth. She checked her second message, came out of the phone booth, looked up at the café, spotted me, waved, and started running again.

But after Mokpo, after *hongeo,* I didn't care anymore. I was done. Korea could keep on with its *bali bali.* Korea was best left to the Koreans. After *hongeo,* try as I might, I knew I would never, ever fit in, and now I really didn't want to.

At this point, I suppose I should explain *hongeo* (홍어). It has been months since I experienced it, and it is still difficult to contemplate as I write about it now. But first, a short history lesson.

During the mid-fourteenth century, there were a lot of Japanese pirates off the southwest coast of Korea. This forced Koreans living on Heuksan Island to head to the Korean mainland and travel up the Yeongsan River toward Damyang. The journey was slow and fish rotted, but in the boats containing one particular kind of fish, skate, something interesting was happening. Skate excrete urine through their skin, and due to the long journey, the skate boats slowly filled with skate pee. Over time, the skate effectively fermented in one another's piss.

At this point, in any other country, the goods would have been trashed, but not in Korea. Now, I don't know who started it—I suspect it might have been a bet made during some sordid drinking game—but at some point, someone thought it would be fun to give piss-fermented skate a whirl. And, as unbelievable as it may sound, that person started to eat it. What's more, they liked it. Word spread, and a Jeolla delicacy was born: *hongeo.*

Remnants of Japanese colonial architecture are dotted around Mokpo like hard-to-remove, albeit attractive, stains. Many of the buildings look unloved, dilapidated; others are still in use, some as museums. Mokpo has been a trading port since 1897 and it was the Japanese who developed the port. As a result, Mokpo has a completely different feel to it than almost any other Korean city.

The Japanese get blamed for a lot of bad things in Korea. However, as far as I can tell, *hongeo* has not suffered that fate. *Hongeo* happened as a direct result of Japanese pirates operating on the Yellow Sea. *Hongeo*, like the *meju* that arrived with the Mongols and the Spam with the U.S. army, might never have happened without the Japanese. Regardless of foreign influence, *hongeo* is a proud Korean original.

I entered Indongju Maeul restaurant. The air was sticky with the ammonia-like odor of urine.

I was with Chris and Tom, two Canadians, both from Nova Scotia, both of whom had made Mokpo their home. Back in Canada, they were used to fresh seafood, straight from the sea, scallops eaten live, and Mokpo's take on seafood had been a revelation for them. Chris was an English professor married to a woman from Mokpo. Tom was the 2015 version of 1996 me. He worked on a South Korean government English-language teaching program. It was the same program I had worked on when it was just a pilot program and had consisted of fifty teachers throughout the country. Now there were thousands. Tom ran things for Jeollanam-do province and had lived in Mokpo for the last four years.

"My wife tells me this is the oldest, best, and most loved *hongeo* restaurant in the whole of Mokpo," said Chris. "She said we need to drink, though. It'll help the stuff go down."

"Well, I'm sure not eating it without drinking," said Tom.

I'd wanted to meet them to learn about *hongeo*, but also to get their take on Korea. What was it like living here as a foreigner in 2015? Not in Seoul or in Busan, but more "out there." In the "bloody boring" parts of Korea, as my friend Jin had called them.

The stench of Indongju Maeul was overpowering, but I immediately warmed to the cozy, rather rough surroundings. Where there wasn't a peeling advertising poster or a menu, the faded Chinese calligraphy wallpaper revealed itself. Running tabs of diners lay nestled inside small clipboards upon the tatty tatami mats that covered the floor under the low tables.

It was both Chris's and Tom's first time at this restaurant, but it was not their first experience with *hongeo*.

"It's not something I eat out of choice," said Chris.

I felt a pang of guilt, as it was I who had contacted them and I who had insisted we eat *hongeo*. A waitress showed us to a floor table and we sat down cross-legged upon the tatami.

We ordered a medium-size *hongeo* sharing plate. And alcohol.

"About weddings in Korea," I said. "I've been told *hongeo* is a must at a wedding. I haven't tried it yet, but given the smell of this place, it's hard to imagine anyone would want *hongeo* ruining their big day."

"Oh, it's essential, all right," said Tom. "There was a wedding I went to out in the countryside one time and there was some sort of *hongeo* problem. The *hongeo* wasn't good enough or something. So they delayed the wedding and organized a shipment of extra, better *hongeo* from this one particular restaurant over one hour away. Someone shot off from the wedding to go pick it up. It had to be the best *hongeo*."

"Even though," I said, "presumably, they could have picked up something nearer?"

"Yeah," he said. "*Hongeo* is everywhere in this province, but it had to be this one particular *hongeo*. The best *hongeo*. Imagine that . . . the best *hongeo*."

"I've never heard of anyone in Mokpo who doesn't like it," said Chris.

The food started to arrive. We had raw crab doused in sesame oil and soy sauce, two kinds of kimchi, dried anchovies, *doenjang*, *gochujang*, the tiny shrimp called *saeu* that I'd had with the blood-and-guts *gukbap* in Slow City of Samjicheon. Then there was rock salt, boiled kelp, and mustard greens.

"You add rice to the crab and mix it up," said Tom, who was planning to leave education and train to be a chef. "You eat it with a spoon."

The *makgeolli* arrived in a brass-colored kettle and Tom poured for us. It looked like a thin pumpkin gruel.

"Let me fill that up," he said, gesturing for me to hold up my battered tin bowl. "You'll be needing it."

In the distance I thought I could hear Darth Vader's theme. The waitress placed a plate of boiled pork on the table first and then the *hongeo*. It looked harmless, like slices of grainy tuna sashimi. It was even beautiful.

"Okay," I said. "Who's going first?"

They both looked at me. Incredulous.

"You're the one who wanted to come here," Tom said.

I couldn't deny it. I've eaten many odd things in my life—rat, cobra, sparrow, squirrel, and pig's uterus—but I found the very thought of *hongeo* repellent, and the smell of the restaurant wasn't helping. It was like a hand in the ether guiding me toward an electric chair.

"Oh, this is a small plate of *hongeo*," Chris said. "It normally arrives on a vast platter that fills the table, and it all goes. There's never any *hongeo* left."

I picked up my chopsticks and stared at our innocent-looking dinner as Tom gave me some advice.

"You have to chew it," he said. "You really, really have to chew it. That way, the strong ammonia goes up your nose. You can't get rid of it, but to help cope with it, what I do is I make a kind of pork, *hongeo,* and kimchi sandwich. But for the first time, you should try it straight, if you really want to experience it."

I took a slightly different route. I used my chopsticks to extract a few strands of *hongeo*. They flaked off easily. And with a degree of trepidation—no, with much dread—I took a bite.

It wasn't tender, but it wasn't as chewy as I had been expecting, and after a little mastication I swallowed.

"Hmm . . . ," I said.

"Well," said Chris, "how is it?"

I waited and I waited. I was expecting a car crash, a big messy one with no survivors. But nothing.

"You know what," I said, "that's okay. It's not too strong—that's not that strong at all. In fact, that's kind of good."

I felt almost let down. Chris chose the same route as me: took a few strands from a slice of *hongeo*, took a bite, chewed, chewed some more, and then swallowed.

"No, you're right," he said, a look of surprise crossing his face. He even seemed to be enjoying it. "That isn't that strong at all. You know what, that's not bad *hongeo*. Not that bad at all."

We smiled at each other and reached forward with our chopsticks for more. I felt relieved. Like I'd passed a particularly heavy test and come out the other side wondering why I had ever been worried about it. Tom shook his head; he was not impressed.

"You're both doing it wrong," he said. "You need to take a whole slice in your mouth and chew through the tendon. You see, look."

He picked up a piece of *hongeo* with his metal chopsticks and held it up as though he were a doctor talking us through an X-ray.

"You've got to gnaw through that tendon," he said, pointing at the fine white line that ran down the center of each portion of *hongeo*. "Then you'll see. The real power of *hongeo* is contained in that tendon."

Having absorbed Tom's advice, I took a slice and granted it access to my mouth. This time around, the *hongeo* was chewy. Very chewy. The texture was unlike fish; it was more like a land-based animal. Just as I was contemplating this curious sensation, I cracked through the tough tendon. This was more by mistake than design, but exactly as Tom had said it would happen, it happened. It was like I'd severed a critical pipe in a chemical factory. I imagined a bunch of mad scientists running around my head attempting to contain the toxic leak as I felt the ammonia of the fermented piss surge.

"It's attacking the roof of my mouth," I said.

"That's it," said Tom. "You've got it now. Welcome to the taste of *hongeo*."

He grinned at me, but it wasn't a kindly grin. It was the grin of someone inducting me into a lifelong club, and membership only meant pain.

The detergent-driven, soapy urine proceeded into my nose. It was spreading rapidly.

"That'll take a couple of days to get rid of," said Tom, "although the taste will never leave you. *Hongeo* is with you for life."

It was as if a urinal cake were now lodged inside me. And it was dissolving, seeding evil within. I swallowed. The image fixed in my mind, we started to exchange adjectives across the table.

"Detergent," said Tom. "Really takes your breath away, doesn't it?"

"Cleaning product," said Chris.

"Ammonia," said Tom.

"It's like soap made of pee," I said. "This whole restaurant smells of soapy piss."

I looked down at the innocent-looking platter. It seemed to shrug, as if it were apologizing to me. If it were a kid at school, it'd be the shy, quiet one who no one thought would ever amount to anything, but privately he read *The Anarchist's Cookbook* in a cupboard under the stairs after school.

The owner of the restaurant, Mr. Woo Jung-Dan, was sixty-seven years old. He originally came from an island off the coast of Mokpo, and he had opened the restaurant in the midnineties. I had to force back my disgust at his food to talk to him.

"Why do Koreans like this?" I said. "How can they like it?"

"It has a sharp, piercing taste," he said. "It affects all the senses at the same time. Many people can't handle it and absolutely hate it, but there is a small group of people who can't get enough of it. It has a distinctive taste, for sure. The older generation thinks of it as an aphrodisiac, helping them to strengthen their virility."

"We're finding it a little tough going," I said. "Do you have any advice on how to enjoy it?"

"We don't get so many Western visitors here," he said. "But it is popular with Japanese and Chinese tourists. Surprisingly, we get a lot of them each week. You should eat it the same way as our regular customers, which is with salt or *chojang* [*gochujang* and vinegar]. It's good with alcohol, so keep on drinking."

Mr. Woo got called away by another table of customers. I didn't need any encouragement on that last bit of advice—I'd already ordered more *makgeolli*. I turned to Tom and Chris.

"And Koreans really say they like this?" I asked.

"They say they like it," said Chris.

It was his turn to have a theory about Korea.

"I don't know," he said. "They say, 'My parents like it, it's Korean, so I like it.' I think that's the mentality, but I don't know if they all actually really like it. I mean . . . gawd . . . It's hard to believe anyone can like it."

He looked like he might be a little bit sick. I felt a pang of regret, since I was the one who had inflicted this upon him.

"They follow, you mean?" I said. "Because they've kind of been 'told' to like it?"

"Yeah, it's like everything Korean," he said, "from music to fashion to plastic surgery. Especially plastic surgery."

Perhaps as a way of diverting our attention away from the *hongeo*, which none of us were keen on exploring any further than we already had, we talked about Korea's most striking and obvious curio, one that no visitor to the country can fail to notice.

"High school kids sometimes get surgery done as a present," said Tom. "It's like a sweet sixteen gift from the parents."

Korea is the world leader in plastic surgery per capita. Six out of every ten people in South Korea have had plastic surgery done and the industry brings in $5 billion annually to the Korean economy.

"I was in an elevator the other day," said Chris, "and this guy, the head of the company, was talking about the Botox he'd had done at the weekend. It's very openly talked about. There's no taboo and it's not hidden. It's even envied."

There was another side to the plastic surgery industry in Korea, and it wasn't just about following your friends or trying to look pretty. It was about getting on in life, about getting a job: many job applications in Korea require a photograph.

"If you've got the money, you get work done," said Tom. "A girl in the office had work done. She came up to me and said, 'Do you think I look pretty today?' Well, yeah, she is pretty. So I said, 'Yeah, you look pretty.' 'No,' she said. 'Do I look prettier than normal?' So I looked at her more closely and said, 'Yeah, you look pretty. You always look pretty.' She had to tell me. She'd had dimples done. I mean, she's a beautiful girl, and yet she still felt she needed work done. 'All my friends have had it done,' she said. She wanted her forehead done next."

It sounded to me like she definitely did need her head seen to.

"You can get six packs implanted," said Chris, "so long as you're not too skinny."

I remembered a conversation I'd had with Min-Hee in Busan about the prevalence of plastic surgery. She was not impressed.

"I'm embarrassed by plastic surgery in my country," she said. "It's shameful: bigger eyes, larger noses, lighter skin, and bigger tits, those are what people want in Korea. They all just want to look the same. Look at the TV—Korean newsreaders look like Japanese porn dolls. It's really just so embarrassing."

Some Koreans even get plastic surgery for their pets, too: tail shortening, double eyelids, wrinkles straightened, even Botox. Yes, really—dog Botox is a thing in Korea. I'm not sure if it was dog Botox that broke the Korean government's back, but the authorities finally realized they had a bit of a monster on their hands and that perhaps something needed to be done about it. As a result, the government plans to ban some forms of public advertising, especially the "before and after" billboards common in subways and movie theaters. In addition, famous entertainers will be banned from featuring in plastic surgery advertisements. Not that this will change the public perception when every time they turn on the television, they mostly see people who have spent significant amounts of time on the operating table.

In Korea, there was a kind of game show focused on plastic surgery where you see the contestants' before and after looks. As the contestant came out to reveal the after look, the song that played was "Just the Way You Are" by Bruno Mars, a song that includes the lyrics,

There's not a thing that I would change
'Cause you're amazing just the way you are

Perhaps the game show producers should have added the word *now* to the end of the lyrics.

I had a theory (another one). Korea is a rabidly nationalistic country, a country where an argument over fermented cabbage, a clump of rocks in the sea, or the name of that sea can very quickly become a diplomatic incident. A country that, to this day, prints posters boasting of the "miraculous DNA" of Koreans.

My theory is that one day Koreans will be proud of how they look. That there will, in the not-too-distant future, be a kind of "shame," as Min-Hee put it, connected to plastic surgery. The potential second wave to hit the surgeon's blade might be, so my theory goes, to reverse the damage done. Lose the double eyelids, decrease the breasts a notch or two, shave a bit off the protruding snout. Even though I have no idea if such surgical reversals are possible, I envisage a campaign to make Korea Korean again, to save Korean Koreans from becoming extinct. And that those with cartoon eyeballs popping out of their heads would walk around with sunglasses on forever more. A yearning for the real, not the artificial, would mark Korea's final step up to confident, assured, developed-country status.

Again, I thought of Philip K. Dick and how Rick Deckard reacted upon seeing an owl for the first time in *Do Androids Dream of Electric Sheep?* Owls were a species that was supposed to be extinct, and Deckard couldn't believe what he was looking at was a real owl:

> "It's artificial," he said, with sudden realization; his disappointment welled up keen and intense . . . it made absolute bitterness blend throughout his prior reaction of awe and yearning.

Would the Koreans of the future be awed or repelled by the artificial?

When I woke up the next day, my tongue felt like someone had been scrubbing it with a soapy Brillo pad while I was asleep. An ammonia fug hung around me for days, like a Jehovah's Witness who just wouldn't go away. My clothes stank of it, my hair, too; my pores seeped it. I radiated *hongeo* and I'd barely eaten more than three slices of the stuff.

Hongeo was my rock bottom. It was as low as I could go. If tracing Korean food back to its regional roots meant this, I was beat. It was inedible. *Hongeo* is the only thing I have ever eaten that I know I will never ever eat again.

The boat to Jeju Island that morning could not arrive soon enough.

WE'RE THE LAST GENERATION

The staff on the 09:00 Mokpo to Jeju Island ferry were nervous.

After I purchased my ticket, a man shepherded me to a ticket-checking woman and she pointed me down a tunnel. Halfway down it, another woman checked my ticket. At the gate to the harbor, a man checked my ticket again. A woman then guided me onto the dock. There were three ticket checkers in front of the stairs to the ferry. As I climbed the stairs and entered the boat, a man in a starched white shirt and epaulets bowed at me. I went up the escalator; another man bowed at me as I reached the top. Then, three more men in official-looking uniforms bowed at me. Finally, another man showed me to my cabin and checked my ticket again. In total, from buying my ticket to putting my bag in my cabin, thirteen people "helped" me.

Today marked the one-year anniversary of the Sewol ferry disaster in which more than three hundred people, mostly schoolchildren, were killed. Several Korean TV crews were on board filming reports to mark the anniversary.

Just like the many trains and buses I'd traveled on in Korea, this huge ferry departed on time at precisely nine A.M. Apartment blocks, ship-building depots, fishing boats, and the small, pointed mountains of Mokpo receded. In front of us, a tugboat pulled a barge transporting large, heavy, metal bits of a ship. A group of Chinese tourists took photos of rocks in the sea as the ferry steamed under a large blue suspension bridge. And as we sailed out to sea, we passed countless small islands like witches' hats and buoys and ferries at the maritime edge of Mokpo.

I sat in the dining room amid an exhibition of hiking clothes. Grilled fish and *tonkatsu* were served alongside three-liter jugs of Cass beer and tight rectangles of rice wrapped in dried seaweed. Men drank soju from paper cups while a middle-aged couple in matching blue hiking gear drank fungus health drinks and sweetened iced coffee, and the scent of grilled dried squid twinkled in the air.

I didn't bother with the on-board lunch offerings, as I had a rendez-vous on Jeju. I'd been told Jeju food was very different from almost all other Korean food; I wanted to know how different, and I wanted to be hungry for it. I arrived in Jeju City at one thirty and headed directly to Dongmun market. I could feel the salt from the jazz of fish jabbing at my lips as I walked through the sprawling street-level shopping area that first opened in 1945. The place was crammed with seafood.

There were tables covered with hairtail fish, glinting like silver rain-bows under the roof-mounted fluorescent tubes. Buckets of crabs crawled and heaved like in a mad B-movie horror flick; preprepared, plastic-wrapped platters of sashimi looked like packs of silvery flints inside a greenhouse. Customers inspected the stalls. Their eyes were blinded by the light beamed back off the silver fish as they perused the catch.

Like the other parts of Korea I had visited, Jeju Island had dishes found nowhere else in the country, and somewhere in among the outer reaches of Dongmun market's scribble of alleyways was a restaurant serving one of those dishes. The place was known as Golmok Sikdang (골목 식당), meaning, appropriately enough, "alleyway restaurant."

It was like walking into a remote English village pub. I half expected the clock to stop ticking, the locals to turn and stare, and a dog by a fire to growl at me. It was clear that Golmok Sikdang was well lived in and well loved. It looked like something from the seventies, and for good reason: it *was* from the seventies. It originally opened in about 1975, although the current owner, chef, and sole worker had been running it only since the late nineties.

Mrs. Ahn Il-Su was originally from Seogwipo, the second biggest city on the island. She was sixty years old and had painted her face in a white shock of makeup. She arrived early every day to prepare long before she opened up for customers. Her specialty was pheasant, specifically Korean ring-necked pheasants, which are common on Jeju.

"Pheasant noodle soup," she told me from her jumble of a kitchen, which looked like more of a cupboard than a working pantry. "It used to be an autumn and winter thing, but the regulars want it all year round, so I serve it all year now."

There were a paltry six tables inside her small restaurant. Faded newspaper clips from 1982 about her and her food were framed and hung upon the wall. There were two menus: one was in Korean and the other was in Japanese.

"You have to have good ingredients for this traditional Jeju dish," she said. "There's nothing special other than that, but I think making the dough by hand to form the noodles is an important step. Most people don't use their hands anymore."

The pheasant came in a bowl with seaweed, spring onions, and those thick-cut *guksu* noodles, which she had made by hand that very morning in the kitchen. There was no buying preprepared *guksu*. Three side dishes accompanied the noodles: cabbage kimchi, radish kimchi, and bean sprouts; unlike on the mainland, none of these were spicy.

Delving into her soup was like rifling through an old cupboard and discovering the curio of a long-forgotten relative. It was something unexpected. Not just the noodle soup—Mrs. Ahn's restaurant itself was a curio. At one end of the room there was a heater, a TV, and two fridges. Bottles stuffed with ginseng sat on a shelf above the tiny entrance to the kitchen in one corner, and to one side there was a plastic shelf of plastic bottles, kettles, and water bottles. Another shelf, near the kitchen, was filled with soju and gas canisters for the tabletop cookers some dishes in her restaurant required. This place resided inside a time warp; it occupied a galaxy far, far away from smartphones, flat-screens, and K-pop.

"What kind of customers do you get?" I asked.

"No youngsters," she said. "Just regulars, and they're all from the older generation."

I wondered if she thought, as I did, that Korean tastes were changing.

"I don't know about that," she said. "You should ask food experts, not me. I just know my customers like my food, and that's all I care about."

There's a certain brash honesty from people of Mrs. Ahn's generation. Much like the eel restaurant owner in Gochang, they just cannot be bothered to think about such things. They're so much more comfortable just doing.

I was struck by how Mrs. Ahn's restaurant catered almost exclusively to the elderly. This reasonably priced shed served good, healthy Jeju staples, but the young weren't eating there, and I wanted to understand why. Mrs. Ahn had suggested I go talk to the food experts, and that's what I did. I went to meet someone I hoped could explain what was going on.

Professor Yang Yong-Jin wore a long-sleeved collarless shirt, black-rimmed glasses, and a tweed cap with a yellow ribbon badge. It was a symbol of hope that many began to wear soon after the Sewol ferry disaster.

The professor was the go-to man on the island to talk to about Jeju food culture. He was a Jeju native and had been working in food for over twenty years. His mother had been cooking traditional Jeju food for over fifty years, and the professor had long since realized how important and unique Jeju food culture was. To preserve and promote this heritage, he compiled his mother's knowledge into a series of books on Jeju food. It was a self-funded project.

I had been expecting a quiet chat and a coffee with the professor at the offices of the *Jeju Weekly*, the only English-language newspaper on the island. However, the editor shepherded me into a seminar room with a projector, screen, U-shaped table, and chairs. The publisher of the *Jeju Weekly* joined me, my translator, and the editor of the newspaper, and then the professor arrived. It felt like a formal interview, because it was a formal interview. I was granted one hour.

"There just wasn't the interest in it," the professor said of his self-publishing efforts. "No one bought it, and now it's out of print. With modernization in the seventies and eighties, traditional cooking was lost. It remains so."

It was as if Mrs. Ahn's restaurant was a time capsule; a perfectly preserved example of what Jeju food once was. The professor went on to explain why Korean food on Jeju was so very different from Korean food on the mainland or in North Korea.

"On the mainland, there is this division between food," he said. "That of the noble, or *yangban* class, and that of the peasants. On Jeju there is only ordinary food for everyone, there is no class division in food at all. "Royal" or *yangban* food like on the mainland has never existed here. You see, Jeju was like Alcatraz many years ago. The island was where the rebels, prisoners, and revolutionaries were banished. That spirit lived on in the food, and we've stuck with that to this day."

The professor opened up a battered-looking laptop to show me some pictures of Jeju food.

"The ingredients are basically the same as on the mainland," he said, scrolling through endless files of food photos. "But people over there want Korean food to be hot and spicy, but that's not the Jeju way. Also, the difference lies in the fact that we use a lot more fresh vegetables and we don't pickle and ferment so much."

I was reminded of something Joe McPherson had said to me in Seoul.

"I never thought I would miss a simple, fresh salad as much as I do in Korea," he said. "Everything is fermented, so little of it is fresh."

There was a good reason the island boasted such an abundance of fresh vegetables.

"The ocean front on Jeju never reaches freezing point," said the professor, "so the farmers and home growers can grow vegetables all year round, and we have fresh vegetables at every meal. In the fifteenth and sixteenth centuries, eating fresh vegetables wasn't easy, even in Europe, but on Jeju we could eat them all year round."

He kept scrolling through images, looking for a set of images that illustrated his point.

"Jeju's daily diet is ideal," he said. "Now we live in an era of over-nutrition, and it is the nutritionists who recommend this kind of diet, the one similar to Jeju; the eighty percent vegetable to twenty percent meat diet."

At last, he found the series of traditional table sets that he wanted to show me from the island. They were quite different from anything I had seen yet on this journey and unlike anything I would see on the rest. He tapped at the trackpad. He explained that there were not that many restaurants on Jeju that served Korean food this way anymore. He suggested a few places for me to try, including a place called Dosani.

"That's the kind of presentation you'll find in those restaurants," he said. "The table set changes with the seasons, but the basic balance of meat and vegetables, and the look, is the same."

Dosani was located down a nondescript road, next to a car showroom. It was well out of the center of Jeju City, near the KBS television station headquarters. There was a hardware shop on the opposite side of the road and, in front of the restaurant, a dried-up riverbed where, in season, a river flowed alongside an orange grove. A vicious white dog barked at me as I strolled around the front of the restaurant; a neighbor was drying bracken on a concrete walkway in front of her house.

Dosani was fake rustic, but beautifully done. It looked quite different from any Korean restaurant I'd ever seen before. It was entirely made out of all-natural wood and had more of a monastic feel about it than the more common hangover-infirmary brand of Korean restaurant. There were five tables for four people apiece and one long table for a large group, and it was all floor seating. On one side of the restaurant, there was a pile of old books sitting on top of a treasure chest. The wall was lined with framed calligraphy and fans, and an old film camera hung from a coat stand.

The perimeter of the restaurant was made up of huge sliding glass windows, which had the effect of bringing the outside into the restaurant. In the garden of the restaurant there were seven or eight trees, and in the distance, beyond the orange grove, there was an ugly white concrete church.

The menu was seasonal and consisted of only Jeju ingredients. When the food arrived, it looked just like one of the professor's photographs.

A salad plate sat at the center of the table. Orbiting around it were seven ceramic-bowl planets. I stirred at the small, reassuring *doenjang-guk;* it whirled like a murky swamp. Next to it, there was an acorn jelly salad with seaweed, cabbage kimchi, cabbage salad, picked radish, *pajeon,* and then the main event. I unwrapped the lotus leaf and a wispy umbilical chord of steam rose up to plug me into the fluttering beat of Jeju's cuisine. Inside this steamed parcel was a mix of rice, beans, grains, and nuts. I'm not sure I could ever be comfortable being a vegetarian, but Dosani gave me pause for thought. This was good, simple, light, and local, and quite the most beautiful spread of food—and the least spiced—I had ever experienced in Korea.

I met the owner, Mrs. Yang Hee-Soon, a Jeju native who had opened Dosani in 2007.

"There are a few reasons I started the restaurant," she said. "First, I really liked the old tree that now stands on the side of the restaurant. It has been around since my childhood, and the thought of trees has always appealed to me. I was kind of inspired by the tree and Jeju's traditional homes, and I wanted to reflect that idea through the interior and the food. To create a kind of rustic, homey, and comforting place."

A CD player hummed in the background, playing Korea's soundtrack: the mournful strains of a cello. The chatter of cooks mixed with the tapping of super-light wooden chopsticks in the bowls and on the wooden tables. The combination of bright sunlight and the huge windows made me feel as if I were sitting outside. The overall effect was a bit post-yoga, incense, and prayer wheels. I felt like I could have dozed the afternoon away quite happily inside Mrs. Yang's establishment.

"Jeju food is nostalgia for me," she said. "It's a memory from my past and the way food used to be cooked by my mother. We stay away from modern sauces and prepare things like in the past, using traditional methods. But the food on the island is changing because of modernization, and the eating habits of Koreans are changing."

After lunch, I went for a coffee in Cloud Nine coffee shop in central Jeju, "New City," at the crossroads of a *PC bang* (a room in which to play computer games), a clothes shop, a jewelery shop, and numerous restaurants. I watched the students on phones outside. They stared into shop windows and checked their hair, lips, and surgeons' work as they talked. One of them carefully moved the position of the cardigan on her shoulder, one had an eye patch on, her boyfriend had the same. They must have been halfway through surgery; they'd get their other eyes done soon enough.

I had made a point of asking the professor what his favorite dish was out of the hundreds available on the island, out of all those he had documented.

"*Mom-guk* [몸국]," he said without hesitation. "It's a simple pork and seaweed soup. We had a Michelin-starred chef come over from France, and when we took him out to try it, he liked it so much, he ordered a second bowl."

However, even with this Jeju original, it was difficult to find a genuine *mom-guk* cooked the way Professor Yang knew it should be cooked.

"Years ago, everyone cooked it with the intestines and served it the way it was originally served," he said. "Nowadays, most places make it with pork bones. It's really hard to taste an original *mom-guk* on Jeju now. There are simply no restaurants making it anymore, so you have to do it yourself at home and start with the intestines and the guts. You need to do this to rediscover the original taste, and you have to use Jeju buckwheat to thicken it, only Jeju buckwheat."

I wanted to eat *mom-guk,* so the professor told me of a place not far from the offices of the *Jeju Weekly.*

Opposite a Chinese language school in downtown Jeju City was a small alleyway filled with simple restaurants. Outside one, bracken was drying on a rack; it was the season for bracken. Jeju Ttosok (제주또속) was Mrs. Kang's restaurant (another Mrs. Kang). She and her husband had been working this place since 2007. She made three dishes only, and all of them were Jeju staples. I started with *bingtteok* (빙떡).

Bingtteok is a very thin crepe. She made it on an electric griddle at the front of her restaurant. The crepe was filled with seasoned, julienned Jeju radish.

"*Bing* is the sound we used to make when rolling the *bingtteok,*" said Mrs. Kang. "That's how this dish got its name. Sometimes we do a very large order, maybe thirty or fifty, and put them in boxes and send them to offices. We even send them to the mainland."

Mrs. Kang made her *bingtteok* with 100 percent Jeju buckwheat flour. Sixty percent of Korea's buckwheat is produced on Jeju, she told me proudly. I was reminded of the conversation I'd had with the two disgruntled sisters stuck in Gangneung in Gangwon province, another buckwheat-growing area.

"Many people think that Korean buckwheat comes from Gangwon-do," said Mrs. Kang. "A lot is made in Gangneung, it's true, but we grow far more on Jeju."

Mrs. Kang and her husband were in their late sixties. They kept the restaurant open every day until eight P.M., and it looked like it doubled as their front room. There were newspapers, magazines, remote controls, and phones strewn over one set of tables. I could imagine them inviting friends over for a game of cards. While *bingtteok* was a popular snack with office workers and schoolchildren, Mrs. Kang was also known for her *okdom gui* (옥돔구이, a grilled tilefish dish), and, of course, her *mom-guk*, the seaweed and pork broth so beloved by the professor.

I looked down at my *bingtteok* and reached for the chopsticks. Mrs. Kang stopped me.

"Use your hands," she said. "It's more delicious if you use your hands."

The *bingtteok* were cold. It was a surprise, as they'd just come off the griddle, but it was the radish filling, straight out of the fridge, that had cooled them down.

"In the old days," she said, pointing to the griddle, "we didn't have equipment like that. We used to use the hot iron lid of the rice cooker to make *bingtteok*. We'd ladle the buckwheat and water mixture onto the rice cooker lid. It was very hot work and hard to make, not like today. It was annoying to make *bingtteok* in the old days."

Her place was "a real local restaurant," she told me, with a good price, a fair price. She pointed at the wall; there was a sign nestled between a framed certificate and the menu board.

"It means a 'kind price,'" she said. "We don't like the word *cheap* in Korea. That means something of low quality in people's minds, so we offer our food at a 'kind price.'"

As Professor Yang had explained to me, Mrs. Kang, unlike many others on the island, used pig's intestines when she made her *mom-guk*.

"You have to use the guts to get the real taste of *mom-guk*," she said.

She went back into the kitchen to prepare the *mom-guk* and the *okdom gui*. It was almost seven in the evening. There was a soap opera on the TV in the restaurant, and to one side there was floor seating on a raised platform with just two tables on it. I had a table with a chair. I heard what sounded like a wood fire crackling, and I stood up and walked into the small kitchen open at the back of the restaurant.

Mrs. Kang placed a piece of newspaper over the *okdom* as it cooked in a frying pan upon a fierce flame on the stove. It sizzled over the soap opera and she took the paper off to flip the fish. The reason why she used the paper soon become obvious: the *okdom* flared flames as she flipped it and *okdom gui* fumes filled the restaurant. On the burner next to the fish, the murky, light-green *mom-guk* toiled on a rolling boil. Mrs. Kang added buckwheat flour to thicken it, and as she did so she showed the packet to me, pointing to the Hangul PRODUCED IN JEJU sign.

Besides the fresh vegetables, Jeju food was different from mainland Korean food in what it left out, not what it added. There was no spice, no red pepper, no *gochujang,* no fire at all—there was just the food. Even the kimchi was vastly different: it was sour, but not at all spicy. I thought about the students checking their appearance in shop windows, their caked-on makeup, their knifed-open skin. It was the opposite of the stark realism of Mrs. Kang's kindly priced restaurant, or of the other Mrs. Kang's shed of regular customers in Busan, the grand masters in Damyang and Haenam, even of the *hongeo* in Mokpo.

The sweet, tender flesh of the *okdom* flaked off the bone like a salty cotton fish cloudburst. Mrs. Kang brought the *mom-guk* at the same time.

"It's very hot," she warned me.

The *mom-guk* seemed to writhe like a trapped serpent inside the bowl as it bubbled, squirmed, and hissed at me. It was an unimaginable soup. Steamy green vapors rose like seaborne butterflies from the cauldron on my table. This *mom-guk* was emerald, complex, and divine. It was the single biggest revelation on my journey so far. Korea could learn a lot from Jeju, I thought; ratchet down the spice and let the food talk, don't punch its face in, in every bowl. I wondered how much of the excellence of this soup was down to the seaweed, not just the intestines. Seaweed is believed to contain an elusive and delectable chemical known as the "fifth flavor," or umami, and this dish was stuffed full with it. I never knew Korean food could be like this. I only knew that it wasn't like this anywhere else in Korea.

Outside, a young woman stood looking into the restaurant window. She flicked her hair into place, opened her eyes wide and looked deeply into them, and straightened her jacket. Behind her, the street was busy—people were out for food, they were out to eat, they weren't cooking tonight.

"It's the same as on the mainland," the professor had told me. "The rise of the double-income family has made a big difference. Fewer and fewer people cook at home. There's just no time."

However, this change in the pace of life, the evolving roles of men and women and the slow appearance of dissatisfaction with modern life, is ever so gradually beginning to change the priorities of younger Koreans, as I had seen on the mainland. Many young Koreans have seen more of the world than their parents have, and they don't want to copy-paste their parents' life expectations.

"A lot of mainlanders come here to enjoy the slower lifestyle," said the professor. "Jeju is the only region in Korea that shows an increasing number of settlers, and with the arrival of mainlanders, the food scene has changed."

However, there was a dilemma here. More and more people wanted to eat Jeju food, but there was less and less of it available.

"We had a survey last year about local food," he said. "People want to eat local food. That's one of the main reasons they come here, but they can't find it. So the demand is increasing, but there's no supply."

Not only that, but traditional recipes were disappearing, too. Professor Yang is involved with an international project called the Ark of Taste. The project aims to protect those dishes and region-specific ingredients that are at risk of extinction. In Jeju's case, over the last two years, eight ingredients and recipes have been added to the Ark, and another six have been applied for.

The professor is putting all his efforts into adding to this list to save these dishes. His mother has all the records of disappearing foods, and she runs a cooking academy on the island. Foreigners like to visit, as do multicultural families and people from the mainland, but, the professor said sadly, few locals go.

"Cooking at home is too difficult," he said. "Everybody buys pre-prepared food. The prices have increased ten times for some fish, like hairtail, for example. There is one hundred times less catch than there was fifteen years ago."

Not only had eating habits changed on Jeju Island, but the visitors had changed, too. A plane departs from Jeju City airport every four minutes, and the island was filled with Chinese. The influx was notice-able everywhere: in the bank, at the beach, in the restaurants—the Chinese were Jeju's single biggest foreign investors. Between 2010 and 2014, $6.1 billion was invested in Jeju alone, and 70 percent of that was in property and land. The Chinese were buying up everything, and not everyone was happy about it.

Korean vacation habits were changing, too. Twenty years ago, every Korean honeymoon photo album was identical, because every Korean couple went to Jeju Island for their two-, three-, or four-day honeymoon. The happy couples even used to wait in long lines at popular sites so that they could get their stock Korean honeymoon shots.

Imagine that: an entire country in which almost everyone with the means had an identical wedding photo album. And not only that, but they all *desired* to have the same wedding photo album. Not anymore. Those with a little money were going abroad. The only ones who came to Jeju island for a honeymoon these days either didn't have much money or were serving in the military. Along with food diversity, honeymoon-album diversity had finally arrived on the peninsula, and with it, a seemingly fixed Korean matrimonial tradition had died.

My translator, Jason Kim, suggested we meet the following day to see something else that was in very definite decline. I met him on the north side of the island, to the west of Jeju City. Jason's family had emigrated from Seoul to Iowa when he was a one-year-old. He returned to the capital after majoring in English literature at the University of Iowa in the United States, and had lived in Korea on and off since 2002.

We were sitting on a wooden podium at the beach waiting for some women to arrive. The beach was made of rough, jaggedy volcanic rock; it scarred the patches of sand like the grazed stubble of a graying, grizzled rock star. The women we were waiting for were a group of traditional Korean divers known as *haenyeo* (해녀). These women free dive into the depths, down as deep as sixty-five feet with no oxygen tanks, in almost all weather, to haul in sea cucumber, seaweed, octopus, clams, fish, and other edible crustaceans from the seabed. I wanted to talk to them, to find out what made them tick, but it wasn't necessarily going to be easy.

"*Haenyeo* can see bullshit a mile off," said Jason. "They might not want to talk to you. They have to like you."

In the 1960s, there were over twenty-five thousand *haenyeo*, whereas today there were only about four thousand left, and almost all of them were over sixty years of age. Jason had known this group for almost a year. I was hoping his familiarity with them would ease my entry into their world. As we sat on the podium waiting to see if they would arrive, we nibbled at some *kimbap* a neighbor had made for Jason.

"I mean, look at this," he said.

I looked at the plastic plate. The *kimbap* were made of rice, cucumber, and pickles rolled in dried seaweed. But there was something else inside too, something not normally found inside *kimbap*.

"They even put cheese in it," he said. "Processed cheese at that. You don't put cheese in *kimbap*, for crying out loud."

Jason was passionate about Korean food. He wrote about it in the *Jeju Weekly* and on his blog, and he discussed it on a weekly radio show, Arirang's "Wonders of Jeju," broadcast on the island. He had a dream to one day open a restaurant serving either traditional food or Korean-style fried chicken, the latter being his favorite Korean dish. Behind us was the *haenyeo*'s sorting and storage area. It was a small, white concrete structure situated between a condominium and sauna on one side and a seafood restaurant on the other.

"Here they come," said Jason, getting up to go greet them. I was apprehensive—would they talk? These women were from another era. In a sense, they were the living embodiment of everything that had disappeared over the last twenty years. They had unique insights into a unique way of life, and they had lived long enough to know what life had been like in Korea when the country had nothing. An unimaginable time, when Korea stood at the bottom of just about every global index, when it was incapable of feeding itself, a time when even Ethiopia sent help to Korea.

Jason did the talking as they eyed me up and down. They didn't look too impressed. I said I just wanted to ask a few questions about their work and their life.

"We're not interesting," one of them said. "Go to the museum. All the information you need is there."

The *haenyeo* museum on the island had opened in 2006. The memories of Andong's torpor-inducing soju museum flashed before me. I wasn't interested in another museum, especially not when I was standing face-to-face with the living, breathing subjects of that museum.

The two women in front of me were seventy-five and seventy-seven years old, respectively. Their colleague, who was running a little late, was eighty-four years old. They were getting ready to go fishing in the same way they had done, almost every day, for over sixty years.

I could see there was an inquisitive frown on the eldest woman's face. I sensed a degree of curiosity about this odd foreigner—me—someone who had appeared from nowhere and was asking strange questions. I saw the door open slightly, and I suggested Jason attempt a question.

"Your life must be so tough," I said. "People are fascinated by it. Why do you do it? You should be retired and relaxing at home by now, surely?"

"We can't relax if we stay at home," the eldest one said. I took her for the leader. "I'll keep doing this until I can't move anymore."

"There's no way we'll retire," said the younger one. "What will we do? Stay at home? We have to be active."

Fishing, for these *haenyeo*, involved a three- to four-hour unaided swim. When they dived, they held their breath for up to two minutes. They pointed out toward the green horizon, where wind chop tousled the sea.

"It's a little rough today," said Mrs. Goh, the eldest diver, after being prompted for her name and finally warming to being questioned. "But we can still go out."

The name Goh is the most common name on Jeju, and the Goh clan is one of three on the island whose mythical ancestry can be traced back to the tenth century. The "divine" presence of the Goh clan was "part of my being," said Mrs. Goh.

"The hardest part is going into the water," she said. "But it's all hard, everything is difficult. Sometimes when you're swimming, you don't know when someone else is in difficulty. Some of our fellow divers have died over the years. And these days, the ocean is more and more depleted and we have to go farther and farther out. It's more and more dangerous."

In November 2016, more than a year after I first met these women, UNESCO declared the *haenyo* an "Intangible Cultural Heritage of Humanity." The designation should form the basis of some sort of protection for them. However, international recognition is the least of these women's concerns.

"The water is pretty clear, but our eyes are not," said Mrs. Kang (yet another Mrs. Kang), the younger *haenyeo*. "With old age, it gets more difficult to see."

She sat down. She had a blue and green rocket motif on her sweater. It was windy and sunny, but it was not warm, a typical Korean spring day.

"I've heard that there are *haenyeo* in the United States. Is that true?" Mrs. Kang said. I didn't know the answer. "Maybe they can make a living from it." She looked hopeful at the thought of it.

Mrs. Goh sat on a rock wall in the shade. She wore a neckerchief with a horse and cart pattern on it. Her eyes were bright and alive. I wondered what *haenyeo* did to relax.

"We like singing and dancing," said Mrs. Goh. She launched into song and started doing a sort of jogging dance to demonstrate how she relaxed. "We have time these days, as our grandchildren are all in high school."

It was clear that diving for seafood was past being a necessity for these stateswomen of the sea. I suspected this was more about saving some money for their grandchildren's education.

All around us were condominiums and restaurants, and a leisure trail made of wooden walkways stretched around the headland out of our sight. However, it hadn't always been like this.

"A long time ago, this area was all *choga*," said Mrs. Goh, referring to the old thatched houses that were common in Korea when she was young. "We changed to the house we have now about thirty years ago."

Mrs. Goh pointed to a modern-looking bungalow about twenty yards away. It had a corrugated iron roof and a white wall around it. It looked immaculate.

"Everything has changed on Jeju," she said, "the lifestyle, the food, and electricity. We never had electricity or water back then, or even gas. We had to make our own fires to cook and stay warm."

Sentimentality and nostalgia were strong in old people in the West. I was curious to know whether it was the same in the older generation in Korea.

A look that approached horror rattled across each of their brows. Mrs. Goh shuddered; Mrs. Kang was aghast. They both shook their heads violently.

"Nothing, not a thing," said Mrs. Goh. "There's nothing to miss from those days. It was so hard, I don't even want to think about it. Just mentioning it makes me tremble. Even the simplest of things were hard back then."

She went on to explain that she couldn't go to school when she was young because it cost too much. She had to learn to read and write at a free school provided by the state after normal school hours were over. As a result, at thirteen years old, she had to start life as a *haenyeo*. Mrs. Kang started working as a *haenyeo* at twenty-one years old.

"Of course," Mrs. Goh said, "in other ways, it was easier back then. We used to collect abalone easily. Now there's practically no abalone out there anymore, as the seeds are all gone."

Just along the way from where we were talking, farther down the wooden walkway, was an abalone farm. The sea water–filled bins were divided into years. It takes up to four years to farm abalone until it is ready for sale. The farm was set up as a direct result of the lack of wild abalone on this stretch of Jeju shoreline.

"The only place where you can find abalone these days is on the south coast of the island," said Mrs. Goh. "There are far more *haenyeo* down there."

A stream flowed from Halla mountain, in the center of Jeju Island, down into the sea, near where these *haenyeo* went fishing every day. The fresh water had a negative impact on the abundance and quality of seafood in this part of Jeju. There was less of it. These *haenyeo* took time off between June and August to rest during the hottest months and to allow the clams to repopulate.

Just then, the third member of this *haenyeo* team arrived, the eighty-four-year-old. Mrs. Park was her name. The three of them suited up in heavy, thick wet suits. Before wet suits became available in the 1970s, the *haenyeo* wore flimsy cotton suits. They each carried an orange flotation device called a *taewak,* and attached to it was a net called a *mangasari* where they stored their catch. They each took a hook, too, which they used to yank octopus out of their hiding places. Lastly, they took a *bitchang,* a long knife to remove abalone.

"We know we're the last generation to do this," said Mrs. Goh as the three of them waddled toward their insertion point. She wore an orange wet suit and her mask was tied up around her head above her eyebrows. "The younger generation won't do it."

They each held a pair of flippers, but none of them had a snorkel or other breathing equipment. Their faces looked as though they had faced into the wind for centuries. The lines ran deep and rigid, but their eyes were alive, and despite those lines, they looked incredibly young and were clearly fit.

"It's a little rough today, so we'll go in over there," said Mrs. Goh, pointing to a rocky pier a kilometer or more away. I checked my watch: it was two fifteen P.M.

They looked like blubbery seals in their thick wet suits as they lurched into the ocean. We watched them swim far out to sea, so far that we couldn't see them anymore. We could only just see the orange speck of the *taewak*. Jason suggested we go eat at Jeju Haemul Bab (제주해물밥) while we waited for the *haenyeo* to return.

"The restaurant is just along the beach there," he said. "The woman who runs the place has a real interesting take on Korean seafood, and she buys the catch she serves from these three *haenyeo*."

Mrs. Lee had started her restaurant in Kapa-do in the south of Jeju. At that time, she served "royal"-type seafood; her place became very popular and she was on TV, but the local competition were unhappy about her success. Following an accident and coupled with the stress from the locals, she decided to move to the city and start all over again. She opened a soju bar, called a *soju bang* (소주방), but she ended up drinking too much and got tired of all the drunks, so she moved to this location on the seafront in search of the quiet life.

"I had a vision," she said. "I wanted to come up with a way to represent Jeju and its beautiful seafood on a plate."

She was a massage therapy major and had come to food through passion. I sensed a closet hippie, mornings of meditation, a righteous diet, and a thoroughly cleansed, soju-free body. She suggested that we try her *haemul bap* (해물밥, seafood rice), from which the restaurant took its name.

It was a mix of rice, sea cucumber, abalone, mussels, gulfweed, and vegetables. It arrived in a hot stone bowl inside a wooden box, and there were sides of fried eggs, some kimchi, and a small fish soup. In the center of the table she placed a rock upon which were slices of flounder sashimi. Like Mr. Bang in Busan, she had brought the rock to her own office, her restaurant. But this rock was from the beach, not a mountain. It throbbed with the sea that surrounded Jeju. With the sashimi spread across it, this rock was more centerfold than Mr. Bang's Zen poet's muse.

"We boil the fish bones overnight," she said as she put the fish soup on the table. "The rock symbolizes our home, as we're surrounded by ocean, but we live on rock. Rock made by the lava from Mount Halla."

The *haemul bap* was a like a happy seal bobbing in the harbor. It was full of "look at me, and me, and me, over here" ingredients. Beneath the steam and the sizzle, the bowl seemed to grow the curious whiskers of this seal. They reached out, prodding me to eat. I took a piece of sashimi as I waited for the bowl to cool down a touch.

From the restaurant window, we could see two of the *haenyeo*. They were mere dots of flotsam on the horizon, lost molecules only visible because of the orange flotation device. One *haenyeo* was closer to the shore, but to my eyes at least she too was also very far out.

"It's weird to see one of them alone in these conditions. She's too old to go too far out," said Jason of Mrs. Park. "She gets tired and can't see so well. She needs to stay closer to shore. The others keep telling her that it's too dangerous and that she should stop, but she won't listen."

I prodded at my bowl of *haemul bap*; it had finally stopped hissing at me. Now that it was calm enough, and cool enough, I took a bite. The bowl was a splendid mix of textures. The clams were like buttery beans, the rice like fluffy clouds, and the gulfweed sparkled with an ocean-deep crunch. This *haemul bap* was a health kick in a bowl, but in a good way. This was no beet juice blend and vitamin pill penury—this was stupendous. It almost felt too good and so, to balance out the health effects and give some yin to our yang, we ordered soju.

I looked around the restaurant. It was all teak, modern, chic, and clean. The regulation blue aquarium tank hidden to one side was almost the only nod to anything old-school Korean. I looked back at the plate: it was beautiful, a work of art. I could see the effort the chef had put into just thinking about how to display her food, but I wasn't happy.

"I think what I came back to Korea for is no longer here," I said. "What there is that's left of it is dying, like the *haenyeo*. All the old restaurants, they're gone and no one gives a shit. It's only old people who cook the old food. Maybe it was a mistake for me to come back."

A news report had been preying on my mind for much of the trip. It spoke of something I found unthinkable: that much of the Korean food I knew and loved, and what had brought me back to the country in the first place, had really only ever been a stopgap. The Korean food I had known was born out of poverty and postwar solutions. Prewar, and precolonization, the food had been quite different, more sophisticated, and it was this cuisine that people like Vivian in Seoul were helping resuscitate. The news report stated:

> Having known destitution and poverty, Koreans took a nononsense attitude toward food during the heydays of industrialization and rapid growth. There was not sufficient time to look back and enjoy the rich traditions that had continued on over hundreds of years.

Twenty years ago, the Korean food I knew was effectively transition food. Arguably, it wasn't really Korean food. It was more replicant than real; its incept date was war and poverty and its life span was reaching its expiration date. There was a case to argue that today, Congdu in Seoul was, historically, more Korean than the Korean food I had known and loved in 1996. Today, Korean food was going back to its roots, and its roots were hundreds of years in the past, and foreign to me. At the same time, the fruit cake pizza of Bar Sanchez was young Korea's tentative step in an entirely new direction. Korea was moving on, and maybe too far for me. I was finding it harder than I had anticipated to seek out what I'd come to eat.

"You're right," said Jason. "From your time in the nineties, it truly does seem that the food has changed a lot during that relatively short time span, but there are still some places. Some real stubborn backwaters, even in the ritziest parts of Seoul."

Our bowls of *haemul bap* were now empty; we'd slurped the fish soup down and shared the last slices of sashimi.

"I can show you," he said. "I'll be in Seoul next week."

I was here to document what wouldn't be here in another twenty years. I accepted Jason's offer, and we walked back along the beach to wait for the *haenyeo* to return with their catch.

When the *haenyeo* came back to shore, Jason told me, there were usually one or two curious buyers, tourists, and locals. These were people who knew what time and where the *haenyeo* would come out of the sea. The main buyers were the restaurant owners, who also came to see the catch.

"If the restaurant owners don't come," said Jason, "the *haenyeo* go to the restaurants and politely ask if they would care to buy the day's catch. They do not want to beg, but this puts the restaurant owners in a difficult position. They might not need the produce that day, but they look at the *haenyeo*'s age and the difficulty and danger they faced in catching the produce . . . it's hard for them to say no and not buy anything."

Good fortune to you," said Mrs. Goh, as Jason helped her haul her net onto some rocks at the shore. It was five P.M. They had been in the water for almost three hours. They trotted along a stone pathway back to their workstation to sort the catch. As they emptied the nets onto the road, sea water seeped across the asphalt like the scene of an accident. Sea cucumber squirmed alongside shellfish, kelp, and a single flounder.

"That's for my sashimi tonight," said Mrs. Goh, pointing at the flounder.

Eighty-four-year-old Mrs. Park brought up the rear. It wasn't long before the lumbering, aging, deaf, partially blind *haenyeo* got a scolding from Mrs. Goh and Mrs. Kang.

"Why did you pick that?" Mrs. Goh shouted as she looked at the contents of the eldest diver's net. "We can't sell it. It's inedible."

The creature looked almost identical to the sea cucumbers that were already in a dish and were being weighed upon a set of scales outside the workstation. A buyer eyed the weight and reached into his wallet.

"I can't see so well," said the eighty-four-year-old, dripping from her hair and wet suit.

"You should pay more attention," said Mrs. Goh.

The two younger *haenyeo* thought Mrs. Park should stop fishing, and they told her as much. A lifetime of diving and the pressure of water had severely affected her hearing, but they respected her decision to keep on going out. And despite what they said, they'd probably do the same, if they were still able, when they got to her age. The hapless and inedible specimen wriggling on the asphalt was a rock sea cucumber.

"It's too tough to eat," said Mrs. Kang. "In the old days we used to use it as a medicine for sore throats, but not anymore."

She scanned the catch; she didn't look too happy.

"There was nothing today," she said.

Jason told me that normally they would each come back with a sack containing forty-five to sixty-five pounds of seafood. In contrast, on this day, they hauled in a paltry five pounds of sea cucumber, seven pounds of hongsam, thirteen pounds of turban shells, some clumps of kelp, and the single flounder.

I was reminded of the rebel outcast reputation of the Jeju islanders as I watched Mrs. Park pack up her equipment. There was a rebel streak here. And, in 2015, perhaps it manifested itself in the stubborn bones of this eighty-four-year-old, deaf, half-blind woman who, rather than put her feet up, chose to risk her life every day of the week. The *haenyeo* were the toughest, most hard-core people I have ever encountered anywhere. While I was full of admiration for them, I was cautious about feeling too sorry for the hardship they put themselves through. They were out there every day, and they could haul in as much as sixty-five pounds of seafood per day. In monetary terms, that was up to $400 per day. That was, say, around $2,000 per week. If you were to average that out, with days off, over a month, that's an income of at least $4,000 to $5,000 per month. Tax-free.

I thought again about the students outside the coffee shop, preening their manes, dabbing their scalpel cuts, and flicking their hair. I wondered if the grandchildren of these *haenyeo* were like that. If they knew the danger their grandmothers put themselves through to give them a better life, and maybe pay for a few choice incisions along the way, too. The government had recently announced the opening of a *haenyo* academy on Geoje Island, near Busan, the same island Mr. Bang came from. There were less than two hundred divers left on the island. The aim was to train a new generation, but Mrs. Kang wasn't convinced.

"We have five years left at most," she said. "There are some younger *haenyeo* up the road. They're in their sixties, they'll keep going a little longer, but this way of life . . . it's over."

THE AFTERLIFE

I chose to fly back to the mainland. From high above Korea, the seaweed farms that surrounded the rocks, islands, and islets of the southwestern-most archipelago looked like rows of burnt-out matchsticks. The dark spindles seemed to shimmer in the green jasper. Over the mainland, the long lengths of tight black plastic sheeting used to protect vegetables resembled long rolls of *kimbap,* and when the sun caught the plastic, the plastic turned a transparent silver. I boarded a bus at Gunsan airport. I was going to the past, to Iksan, to the place I had called home in 1996.

A young woman sat in front of me on the bus. She adjusted her window curtain and held a white-and-gold phone at an angle in front of her. She clicked the shutter as the bus departed, then checked the photo. Unsatisfied, she held the phone up and clicked again. She must have been very unsatisfied with either herself or her photographic skills, as she continued to point the lens at herself and click the shutter for the entire duration of the forty-minute journey to Iksan. It has been impossible to turn off camera shutter clicks on phones in Korea since 2004. This is to prevent the taking of so-called upskirt photos and other clandestine images without the knowledge of the person being photo-graphed. However, by the twentieth minute, I was wondering whether a few upskirts weren't a small sacrifice to make to stop the incessant water torture of clicks on this bus journey. Then I remembered the vom-iting soldier, and I knew it could have been, and once was, so, so much worse. I winced at each click, looked out the window, and lost myself in the ripples of Korea that hummed by outside. I thought about the food that was about to reenter my life. The food of Jeollabuk-do, of Jeonju, the source of the best food this country had to offer.

A glut of memories arrived to counsel me. I'd been away for a very long time. There was the back street bibimbap, the beef soup shed near where I used to work, the bulgogi place that served oysters with garlic and chile as a side dish, the steaming *manduu* stalls, silkworm sellers, tofu soups, and the coffee shops. I was itching to get back. I would feast.

The bus hissed to a stop at Iksan bus station located at the southern edge of the city. I checked into the first hotel I came to and walked north through the narrow lanes toward the main downtown area. I knew the way, and looking around me, I could see that nothing had changed. I felt twenty-six again. What had Josh in Seoul been going on about? Over *galchi jorim* in Namdaemun market, he'd told me I wouldn't recognize anything.

The streets were laid out like graph paper. Above me was an idle criss-cross doodle of intersecting telephone and electricity wires; they hung there like a comforting veil. Every thirty yards, concrete telegraph poles craned over the road like hypnotized giraffes. Upon one pole, at an inter-section, were two large fish-eye mirrors. They reflected and warped the street; one mirrored south, where I'd come from, the other north, where I was going. Silver, white, and black cars lined the sides of the streets. I could already imagine the fever-pitch market; the frantic tremolo of cars, motorbikes, and buses; and the trilogy of smells just a few hundred yards away at the end of this road. I was back in the past.

I stopped at a rusting *tabang* (다방). These basic teahouses were everywhere in rural Korea, and they were used almost exclusively by the older generation. However, this *tabang* was closed, so I continued along the street. At my feet, a drainage cover had the words AMAZING IKSAN etched into it in English.

This city slogan had replaced the more cumbersome "Amazing Iksan. The City of Friendly to Women [sic]." Iksan came up with the old slogan after it was made South Korea's first-ever "women-friendly city" by the Ministry of Gender Equality and Family in 2009. In an outward display of its friendliness to women, the city created seven hundred women-only parking places in public areas. To help the gentler sex, these were painted pink and made a little bit wider and a little bit longer than regular parking spots, and they had a pink flower painted where the car should go. How considerate.

A gust of wind tousled my hair. I could smell dust. It was a particular kind of dust, a potent, dry, fusty dust. The kind of scent that arrives unexpectedly and sparks a very distant, often very minor, but very clear memory. It reminded me of a man on this street.

There was no moving traffic and there were no people and every other shop was closed. The comfort I had felt moments earlier, of being back in the familiar, dissipated with that gust of wind and the memory of that man. The air now seemed coated in a treacle of nostalgia. It was like I was walking among the dead.

It was along this street, twenty years ago, that a man hobbled out of a shop, came up to me, shook my hand, and asked me where I was from, what I was doing in his town, and please, would I like to visit his shop?

"Anytime," he said. "Please, you are welcome in my shop."

I replied that I was busy, but that one day I would indeed visit his shop. He thanked me and repeated, "Anytime. You are welcome."

And he limped off. The oddness of his approach had surprised me. Maybe that's why the dusty memory had surfaced. He'd had a soft face and none of the aggression I had grown accustomed to with some Korean men, especially a few bottles of soju deep into the night. But I never did go to the man's shop.

It was then, as the memory receded and I passed Iksan's small museum, that a man with graying, thinning hair doddered out of a shop. He came up to me, shook my hand, and asked me where I was from, what I was doing in his town, and please, would I like to visit his shop?

The same questions in the same manner and the same kindly face. It was the same man. He seemed more like a ghost to me. Perhaps it was my own fault for walking back into the past only to see it play out in front of me in the same way, albeit a little grayer and dustier all these years later.

I followed the man to his shop. He had chalky skin, blotchy with liver spots. He slid open the door and urged me to sit on a stool with my back to the entrance. He fumbled at a kettle, reached for two plastic cups and two tubes of sweet, instant coffee. He turned the kettle on to boil, sat down, and looked at me.

"I was dead," he said.

I frowned at him.

"But now," he said, "this is my afterlife."

We were in the same room, talking in the same air, but it was as if we were both elsewhere.

"This is my life after death," he said.

He seemed uncertain that I had understood his English, but I understood it perfectly well. I was still stunned that this fleeting memory from my past, caught like a smell, had materialized as a faded photocopy on a street in a quiet corner of southwest Korea.

"I'm sorry?" I said.

"I was dead," he said. "This is my life after death."

He had a beatific smile. He looked as if he were living in his own private paradise. I looked around his shop. If this was heaven, the cleaner should've been fired. It was a confusion of cloth, pins, ironing boards, coat hangers, jackets, trousers, receipts, scraps of paper, discarded junk, books, and dirty coffee cups. The front of the shop was lined with mannequins in smart suits, and there was a sign in English that read FOREIGNERS ARE WELCOME HERE. He was a tailor.

"My face is not good now," he said.

He stood up and faltered into a small anteroom hidden behind a hanging curtain. He mumbled to himself in Korean as he pottered among the wreckage, and when he came back, he had a laminated card in his hand. He showed it to me.

"This is me," he said, "when I was younger."

It was an ID card. The picture had faded, the focus softened by time. His hair was thick and black back then and he wore a beige suit. He turned away from me, picked up a glass, and swiveled back to face me.

"My face is not good now," he repeated, laughing at me. His grin had suddenly become toothless. He'd taken his teeth out and put them in a glass. A trick he found hilarious. I smiled.

His name was Mr. Kim. He was born near Seoul in 1951 and had lived in Iksan for forty-five years. In 1981, he had been in a car accident: an eight-ton gas truck hit him while he was driving. He had been badly injured and was in a coma for four months. He lifted his trouser leg to show me the damage.

"Coma," he said. "That is why I say this is my afterlife. I was dead for four months."

I wanted to tell him that I had lived in Iksan in 1996. I wanted to tell him that I even remembered meeting him then, but it didn't seem right. I'd promised to come back to his shop all those years ago, and here I was. At that moment, it didn't seem important to discuss the length of time I had taken to do it. I got the feeling that Mr. Kim approached every foreigner that improbably passed by his back-alley shop, just south of Iksan's busy downtown shopping area.

"Big change in Iksan," he said. "Many people lived and worked here before. Now everything's moved and very few people live here now."

Perhaps that explained the quietness of the streets, the ghostlike quality of the shops.

"They moved to Yeongdeong-dong," he said, referring to a district to the north of the city that did not exist during my time. "Now they move to Mohyon-dong. Korean people, they follow the apartment builders and everything else follows with them, and there are no apartments here."

The tailor had four daughters. Two still lived in Iksan and two lived in Seoul.

"I like Iksan," he said of the city of a little over three hundred thousand souls, small by Korean standards. "But it's very quiet here now."

He showed me a ledger where he recorded the details of all his customers. He had a foreign customer section and in it he had pasted and taped foreign business cards to the pages. All the foreigners in his ledger were from the Church of Latter Day Saints, the Mormon church.

There were almost ninety thousand Mormons in South Korea. I'd seen them. White males wandering around in pairs in their dark suits. I'd always thought it was they who looked ghostlike. Now I thought I must look a little like them myself. Only I was alone.

I saw phrases written in English in the foreign section of Mr. Kim's ledger. Mormons called Haizley and Zachary had been giving him English lessons as they got measured for their matching suits. The kettle had long since boiled, and he offered me a coffee. He apologized that he didn't have any sugar and he clicked the kettle to boil again. There was a black keyboard and a computer screen on a cluttered desk next to me. His wife dozed on the floor behind an open sliding door at the back of the shop. She lifted her head up, frowned at me, then put her head back down again. The coffee never quite arrived.

I thanked him and said I would come back if I was passing through Iksan again. Maybe I'd order a suit next time, I told him. He shook my hand.

"The people in Iksan," he repeated, "they just follow the apartments."

It was a muttered refrain full of melancholy. He had an image of the Virgin Mary at the front of his shop. The Koreans, he seemed to say, were just as much disciples of the apartment builders as they were of religion.

By now, it was early evening and I was hungry, but I wanted to walk the streets before eating. Along one street I saw an old, yellow sofa on the pavement; mold crawled over it. I remembered how late at night all those years ago, on the same stretch of street, I had been walking with a friend and had remarked upon a similar sofa—perhaps, like Mr. Kim, it was even the same one. A sofa wasn't something I expected to see on a street late at night, especially not one with an old woman sitting on it.

"What is she doing?" I had asked.

"She's selling her body," my friend had replied.

I looked at the old woman. She had a tight black perm, padded jacket, bow legs, bright red lipstick, thick slippers, and a body like a barrel. She looked like a puffy, rubbery, wrinkled ball. She must have been well into her seventies and was a lot less healthy-looking than the *haenyeo* of Jeju Island.

"She's selling?" I said. "Who the hell's buying?"

I passed by the clinic where I had been treated for an ear infection. The doctor had given me copious amounts of medicine and told me not to eat pork or chicken or drink alcohol or smoke until the course of treatment was over. For one month, I abstained as directed. I visited his clinic once per week for cleansing and one of his nurses injected me in the arse with something once per week.

"We've never had a foreigner in here before," she said as she slid the lengthy needle into my right cheek. "Do you have a girlfriend?"

He never did heal my ear infection. In the end, I self-medicated for a week with eardrops, which I bought from the pharmacy underneath his clinic. The infection went away the following week.

By now I was in the center of downtown Iksan. The billiard hall I used to frequent was still there, the paint on the outside peeling. I peered through a dirty window. The pool tables were gone, the room was empty, replaced by rubble—the whole building looked condemned. The photography shop was gone and the department store, Iksan's pride and joy in

1996, was now surrounded by a flimsy metal fence. It was unsafe and would soon be knocked down.

The central, covered market through which I used to walk every day, had been completely redeveloped, but there was no one there. Near the market, there was a series of narrow, alleylike streets that were home to stacks of restaurants, but none of the restaurants I used to eat in were there anymore. Whole swathes of street were given over to rubble and were surrounded by red-and-white plastic tape. It was Friday night, and in this part of Iksan, there were more rotting buildings than open restaurants.

I found one of the few open restaurants. It was called Hwi Ne Bunsik (회내분식). *Bunsik* generally means "snack food" or "cheap fast food." It was opposite a knocked-down building and next to another. I felt sure that this restaurant was not long for this world.

It was small, brightly lit, white walled, wooden floored, neat, and clean. An elderly man sat on the floor and a woman pottered in the kitchen at the back. They both greeted me and I sat down. The man wore a baseball cap, navy trousers, and a polo shirt. He told me he was seventy-seven years old and had learned a modicum of English when he served with the U.S. military during the Korean War.

"It all started about ten years ago," he said, "when Iksan started to move from here."

There used to be an excellent bibimbap restaurant on this block. It was so good, people came from Seoul to eat there, and there was a superb *dak galbi*, too, a great *samgyeopsal*, and fabulous sashimi.

"There's nothing now," he said. "There are no good bibimbap in Iksan anymore. It's all gone."

What surprised me was that he wasn't at all sad about the change of fate for the area. This couple seemed to be biding their time until the inevitable bulldozer arrived outside their front door.

"So," I said, "where can I get a decent bibimbap in Iksan now?"

He pointed at the table in front of him and smiled. The restaurant was completely empty, apart from him, his wife, and me. There were eight floor tables and one table with chairs, and a TV showing a baseball game.

"The only good bibimbap is in Jeonju now," he said.

His wife served me a *kongnamul bibimbap* (콩나물 비빔밥). It is a minimal rendition of bibimbap, made with only bean sprouts and rice. As such, it is more of an abstinent monk compared to the nipple-tassle-wearing, cigarette-holder-flicking glamour puss I knew I would soon meet again in Jeonju. However, there was a spicy soy, sesame seeds, spring onion, and chile powder sauce in a side dish to rouse it, although it came with a warning.

"Don't add too much," the wife told me through her husband, but I understood the Korean. In addition, there were two kinds of kimchi.

I was reminded of what Vivian had told me in Seoul and what Professor Yang had said on Jeju. Jeolla province was all about the heat. However, it was only now, all these years later and all these miles spent circumnavigating the country, that I felt I understood that Korean food in Jeollabuk-do was different, that it was special, that it was spicy, that it was the hottest food in all Korea.

I took the chef's advice, as I wasn't sure I could handle the spice. I'd had so many warnings, I felt almost brainwashed. It was like I'd never lived here and never survived it day after day, month after month. I put a small spoonful into the bibimbap and asked for a beer.

"No beer," she said.

"*Makgeolli?*"

"No *makgeolli*," she said.

"Chung Ha [청하]?" I asked, referring to the light alcohol that's a little easier on the palate than soju.

She shook her head.

"Soju?" I asked, somewhat resigned, but feeling the occasion of my return to Iksan deserved at least a little alcohol.

Her husband looked at her and then looked at me.

"I can go out and get some for us," he said to me in English.

But his wife, who seemed to suddenly understand English perfectly, replied for him.

"No."

And so it was that my first dinner back in Iksan was accompanied by a warm tumbler of barley water. So very un-Korean, it was almost neo-Korean and simple to the core: a crunch of bean sprouts, a filling of rice, and a spicy needle to the tongue.

If there was one place on this entire trip that I felt anything approaching melancholy, it was in Iksan. Not for Korea, nor for Iksan, but for me, for my youth. Iksan made me feel old, and everything I had once known here had aged badly.

By day, my hotel opposite the Iksan bus station was a black, faceless block. By night, it was lit in yellow, white, and blue neon bulbs. The reception had a sign in English that said FEEL SO GOOD. I had thought it strange that the reception was so small and that I couldn't see the receptionist without bending down and staring through an improbably small letterbox-size hatch.

It was only after I looked more closely at my room that I saw the words LOVE MOTEL etched onto the wall above the television.

There was a whirlpool bath and condoms in my gift package. There were drawings of damsels washing themselves on the bathroom walls. Next to the bed was a mind-boggling assortment of oils, creams, and lotions. The lighting system was so complex, it came with its own manual. It took me half an hour just to figure out how to get rid of the soft, low, throbbing red effect, and it took much of the following day to work out how to turn off the bloody bathroom light. Meanwhile, the TV remote looked like something you'd use to land a space shuttle, and I didn't risk pressing any of its buttons.

I looked out the window. Neon crucifixes lit the sky; it was like a Korean Golgotha. I decided to get up early and walk through the city to Yeongdeong-dong, where the apartments were located that Mr. Kim told me all people followed, like concrete disciples.

In the center of Iksan there was an orange church spire. Near it, a band of noisy birds perched in a tree on the main road. They seemed to taunt the birds in cages outside a pet shop opposite. A line of phone booths stood like dead ears. I doubt they even worked. Wood pigeons cooed in the treetops around a park at the base of Mount Baesan. On a path, a face-reading fortune teller related a fortune to a woman in glasses with short hair. These soothsayers were having a hard time in the Korea of the twenty-first century. The epidemic of plastic surgery meant that they could no longer read their clients' true faces.

Yeongdeong-dong did not exist in 1996. Back then, it was little more than a couple of streets, whereas today it was a vast modern district, filled with enormous shops, rack after rack of twenty-one-story apartment blocks, movie theaters, restaurants, banks, and fashion stores. In a few short years, the Koreans had simply moved the entire downtown, and everyone, just as Mr. Kim had told me, had followed. Yeongdeong-dong was teeming and I now knew that what Josh had said in Seoul was right. I didn't recognize downtown, because I'd never known it.

The blimp-size Lotte Mart shopping mall was next to the equally vast Homeplus shopping mall that was opposite the almost as big CGV movie theater, which was next to the large Starbucks and the two-story McDonald's. Cars and buses rumbled along a six-lane highway, and pedestrians clambered across overhead walkways and through underpasses. The area was ultra-modern, packed with people and buzzing with cars. This wasn't mere change—this was a wholesale transplant.

I had arranged to meet Mark. He was from Canada, worked at a nearby university, had lived in Iksan on and off since 2007, and was married to a woman from the city. I wanted to meet him to see what it was like to live here in 2015.

"This part of town is getting ready to shut down," said Mark. "The new up-and-coming area is Mohyon-dong."

I think I gasped—I couldn't believe it. Not only had the old downtown I'd known died since my departure, but the downtown that had replaced it in the interim, the one in which we were sitting, at a little over a decade old, was about to repeat the dying trick.

"Back home," said Mark, "There's always a 'bar street.' You know, an area where all the bars are. It never changes during your lifetime, but here, entire downtown areas just upshift and move wholesale, as if overnight."

The new up-and-coming area, Mohyon-dong, was the area I used to live in. I'd walked past it that morning and seen my apartment block; it had been brand-new in 1996, but looked old and tatty now. Where once there were rice fields glinting green and gold far into the distance next to my home, there was now a gigantic new apartment complex. It rose from the paddies like the bastard brood of a crazed cubist student. And there were bigger plans: Iksan would soon be home to a mammoth $500 million Asian food hub called Foodpolis, designed to attract domestic and international food companies, produce an output of $15 billion annually, and generate twenty-two thousand new jobs. Iksan wasn't just a new city—it was a new solar system. In the words of a longtime Korea resident and current affairs blogger, Matt Van Volkenburg, "It's much easier to talk about the things that have changed than to try and conceive of the things that haven't."

Mark and I sat in an outdoor area at the back of a coffee shop. The Tulip, Lily, and Rose apartment blocks that made up a colossal complex called Golden Castle towered above us. They were so high that they blocked out the sky. Mark tugged on a cigarette as we chatted. Change had come in other ways, too.

"Most Koreans don't even smoke in their own apartments anymore," he said. "Maybe it's not a written rule where you can't—the smoking ban only came in recently—but now you have kids who didn't care about smoking before, and now, within one month, they're telling their folks to stop smoking in the house. In Korea, men could smoke anywhere they wanted, when they wanted. It's as if the country changed an entire ideology within the space of one month."

This part of town seemed to embody everything about modern Korea. Everything new I had seen on my journey was mirrored in every shiny glass building. However, some of the old Korean guard didn't like the twenty-first-century version of their country.

"The old *ajoshi*s who can't cope with all the changes, they move," Mark said. "You hear about them in Vietnam, up to the same old tricks. They move that lifestyle overseas, because it's not welcome here anymore."

Week in, week out, Southeast Asian newspapers report on Koreans arrested for dodgy dealings. A couple in their fifties, wanted by Interpol in a $9.1 million fraud case, were found holed up in Hanoi. One South Korean company executive fled Vietnam without paying a thousand garment workers at his company. South Korean men are reportedly the biggest clients of prostitutes in Southeast Asia. Even more alarmingly, they are the "No. 1 source of demand for child sex trafficking" in the region, too, according to a report by the state-run Korean Institute of Criminology.

However, there was also a positive side to more Koreans traveling overseas.

"Koreans have traveled and most appetites have gotten wider," Mark said. "For example, I teach a bunch of kids and we have a class on roasting, baking, sautéing, and all that. Three years ago, none of the kids had an oven at home. Now three or four kids tell me that they have one in the home, even if they don't know how to use it. But the parents have been abroad and they want to try and replicate whatever it was they tried when they were away."

As I talked to Mark and saw the new part of town, my melancholy lifted. I was glad I had come back, and I didn't feel like a ghost anymore. This part of Korea, like everywhere else I had visited, had moved on far faster than my brain was capable of computing. I was full only of admiration for what Korea had achieved.

I went to the Iksan bus station. Unlike other bus and train stations on this trip, there were no burger bars or pizza outlets inside. There was a *manduu* restaurant in one corner. I entered it and sat down. I'd been here many times before and I didn't even look at the menu to order when the waitress came over to my table. I just said, "*Gun manduu* [군만두, fried dumplings]." The waitress hollered my order to the open kitchen. I could see that the place had been redecorated, but it looked much the same. The bus station itself had not changed since the seventies. The clocks on the fleet of Iksan bulldozers outside were surely clicking very loudly.

The *manduu* restaurant was a typical bus station joint. Bus and train station food are a major part of Korean life. The country always seems to be on the move and everyone ate in these places.

A soup warmer on the serving top contained a pork stock and there was a rice cooker the size of a washing machine next to it. Two nattering woman worked the joint; one was fat, the other thin. In another life, they could have been a comedy duo. They both wore designer eyewear. The thin one grated cabbage in the kitchen, while the fat one constructed *kimbap*.

My simple lunch arrived, the *manduu* glossy with the sizzling remnants of hot oil. The dumplings were gathered around a squiggle of ketchup and mayonnaise. They came with two small side dishes: pickled yellow radish and cabbage kimchi. There was also some chile-infused soy sauce, a bowl of the pork stock soup, and a stainless-steel tumbler of water. This was my farewell to Iksan.

As I ate, I looked at the menu, which was illustrated in pictures above the kitchen. There was udon noodle soup, soba, *naengmyeon,* and various kinds of dumpling, but there was no *gun manduu*. I took a mouthful of fried wonton and picked up the menu on the table. No *gun manduu* there either, but I was eating *gun manduu*.

Without realizing it, I had ordered off-menu. I had simply ordered what I had always ordered in that place, without thinking, as if it were yesterday that I had last sat down there and eaten the same dish. And for a moment, I almost felt like a ghost again.

People I knew once upon a time could be in the same market, in the next car, at the next table, in the bus passing by the window. Students I once taught might have served me in shops, pushed their children past me in a stroller, or cooked for me in a restaurant. I'd lived here before the Internet was widespread, so I'd lost touch with most people I knew from Iksan, but not everyone.

I caught the next bus to Jeonju, the home of Korean food. I was going to meet an old friend.

IT'S ALL IN THE WATER

S he met me with a quizzical air, as if to say, *Where the hell have you been for these last twenty years?*, while in the same instant she seemed to also say, *But it's great to see you*. We had worked in the same state school together. Mrs. Lee was the head of English, and I was the school's first-ever foreign teacher. She had recently retired, but she seemed to be busier than ever. She volunteered at a drop-in center to help migrant wives adjust to Korean society, translated here and there, and taught part-time at a university. She possessed not only a sharp intellect and a dry wit, but she also had that most prized yet elusive of items, something desired by many Asian women: a perm that worked.

"Do you remember the secretary and the filing cabinet?" asked Mrs. Lee.

"Yes," I said. "It's a little difficult to forget her."

The secretary had been in her office and embroiled in what sounded like a rather heated argument. We were in the staffroom next door. After five minutes or so, along with the voluminous shouting, screaming, and wailing, a repetitive banging sound began. Two solid objects were hitting each other, and judging by the sound of crashing echoes, I deduced that one of those objects was metal and the other was flesh and bone.

More voices joined the cacophony, sounding concerned, even hysterical. I stood up, as I, too, was concerned. Suddenly, the door to the secretary's office burst open and the secretary ran out. Blood spewed from a gash in her forehead. She raised a hand to stop the flow, but the blood seeped between her fingers and down her arm. Some teachers screamed at the dervish flailing through the otherwise peaceful workspace. She ran toward me. I stood transfixed; she saw me and quickly bowed. A teaspoon of blood splashed at my feet. I moved out of her way and she continued running and dripping the length of the staffroom. It was a horrific sight.

"That was her *han* [한]," said Mrs. Lee, referring to the near mythical Korean term that seemed to encapsulate irresolvable pain, unrealizable dreams, and desperate yearning for impossible revenge.

"Her *han* was like a volcano," said Mrs. Lee. "It was too much for her. And she exploded."

"And so," I said, just rechecking the facts, "she head-butted the filing cabinet in her office."

"Correct," said Mrs. Lee.

"Repeatedly," I said.

"Yes," said Mrs. Lee. "Many times."

"Until she needed hospital treatment," I said.

"Unfortunately," she said, "that is also correct."

Apparently, this thing called *han* was responsible for this. *Han* was something I had been told that I would just never understand.

"You're not Korean," my cultural interpreters would tell me. "How can you ever know? It's something that is shared by all Koreans and only Koreans."

Han had a big KEEP OUT sign attached to it. Koreans wanted it all to themselves. They'd invite you for food, get shitfaced with you, sing and swap languages with you, but mention *han* and the response was a very clear but petulent teenage groan of "You just wouldn't understand." It was as if the Koreans guarded their own private, unique pain in much the same way as they guarded the demilitarized zone. Another interpretation was that *han* was the national chip on Korea's shoulder.

And it seemed to flood all aspects of Korean life. I always thought that Korean coffee shops were a mirror of *han* in that they seemed to feed this feeling of melancholy. Mournful, plastic songs always played in the background in Korean coffee shops. Lonely women stroked tall mugs of hazelnut coffee and stared blankly, but meaningfully, into space. The same image was reflected on TV every night in the wildly popular rash of soap operas. There was always a scene with a woman staring into the void, out to sea, over a river, or off a cliff, the implication being that at any moment she might jump. I often wished she would. I didn't know if the soaps were reflecting life or if Korean life was reflecting the soaps. Regardless, *han* was a curious misery dappled with a dreamlike hope, a misery Koreans yearned for and clung to.

But I could not believe that Koreans, and only Koreans, shared a human emotion that no other brand of human could ever know or experience. Mrs. Lee had sowed a seed in me, and I needed a plan to test what *han* meant to Koreans in 2015.

But I had to eat first.

I'd spent twenty years longing for a Jeonju bibimbap (전주비빔밥). There is no substitute, not in Seoul, not in Busan, not in New York City, and not in Los Angeles. You have to go to Jeonju. I know this to be true, because I'd only ever eaten bibimbap like it in Jeonju and I've tried it in plenty of other places, both in Korea and abroad.

Bibimbap is one of the most quintessential Korean dishes. While the variations in Andong and Jinju were interesting and quite delicious,

Jeonju is the Daddy. It arrives packed with rice, vegetables, seasonal roots, nuts, a raw egg, grains, and a little meat. Deep inside are a variety of textures, from soft acorn jelly to the healthy snap of bean sprouts and the sugary heat of *gochujang*. Bibimbap stuffed a broad spectrum of Korea's edible excellence into one fabulous bowl.

The Korean government used bibimbap in one of its misguided, multimillion-dollar cultural awareness campaigns overseas. They'd produced a ridiculous K-pop video with an even more ridiculous song about bibimbap. It included the unforgettable refrain,

Wanna be healthy?
Then you know we got the best.
We got strawberry, ginseng, love that kimchi.
Keep the skin so beautiful and full of energy.

The problem with bibimbap is the look of it. As in Jinju, it looks beautiful when it is served, with the ingredients laid out inside the bowl like a sunflower. But once you've mixed up the ingredients, as you must do to eat it, it looks a little different, less like the stunner you picked up in that Seoul bar that night and more like the one you woke up to the morning after. There's an empty crate of soju at the end of the bed, a man with a drill inside your head, and the stunner has her face plugged into the toilet. It's not a good look, and neither is mixed-up bibimbap a good look. It's a multicolored mush the consistency of baby food.

I'd arranged to meet Mrs. Lee at a crossroads on the old main street in Jeonju. She'd told me, "I'm retired. I'm all yours for a week. What do you want to eat?"

I arrived early at Gajeok Hwaegwan (가족회관). The street was quiet. It was a single-lane road, filled with jewelry, wedding dress, and *hanbok* shops. The old city hall used to be down this street, but the city outgrew the building and so the hall had moved. At the crossroads, there was a stamp-making shop, a bank, a branch of Korea's national post office, and the bibimbap restaurant. Although it didn't look that old, this was the oldest street in Jeonju.

A man in a yellow vest and white face mask collected trash with a broom and put it into a cart. On a corner, another man sat under an umbrella in front of a sewing machine; he looked like he'd gotten off the bus in the wrong decade. A woman in black PVC trousers and a black-and-white sweater talked into a phone while half walking, half jogging. Another woman pushed a stroller past me; she had a box of fruit in it. Her eyes bulged unnaturally and she had a huge bandage across her nose. The scent of jujube berries mixed with smells from a bakery farther down, and at the far end of the street, just before the small Chinatown area, was a garish, psychedelic, rotating sign indicating a beauty salon.

To think this narrow street was once the epicenter of the city, Jeonju's most crowded, most commercial area. Now it was just a quiet side street, a relic only visited by the dwindling number of Koreans who still chose to get married and needed to visit the wedding shops, and by those who wanted to eat bibimbap.

Mrs. Lee arrived. She'd texted me moments earlier to tell me that she would be one minute late. This was an ongoing theme in Korea, this hyperconscientiousness when it came to time.

"There are knighthoods for cooks in Korea," she said. The brains behind this bibimbap restaurant was the first to get one in Jeonju. "She's the thirty-ninth to get one in Korea. They're not quite knighthoods, but honorary masters of food, approved by the government."

She was referring, of course, to the grand masters. Mrs. Yang had opened this restaurant in 1979 and was part of this small elite along with Master Ky of Damyang and Master Han of Haenam.

As we entered, I noticed a poster. It explained how this restaurant was the first place in Jeonju to grow and use "upside-down bean sprouts." The idea is that the bean sprouts somehow retain more nutritional value by growing upside down. I was bamboozled by the logic, but could it be true . . . ? How could growing anything upside down improve it?

"In my opinion, this is the best bibimbap in Jeonju," Mrs. Lee said, and she should know. She'd grown up in Iksan, studied in Jeonju, and worked and lived between the two cities all her adult life.

Inside, the brickwork was old and white, and the restaurant rattled with the sound of metal chopsticks on brass bibimbap bowls, the clank of side dishes, the scrape of chairs, and the squeak of trays moving across the glass-topped tables.

The kitchen was spread along one entire side of the restaurant. A man took a photo of his family eating bibimbap; they were Korean tourists. There were over twenty tables and no floor seating. Each table was prepared with aluminum kettles, cups, tissues, and chopstick boxes. Age etched itself into the wooden chairs.

"You can get everything in Jeonju," said Mrs. Lee as we sat down at a table, "all manner of ingredients, and that's why Jeolla is famous for food, because we grow everything here."

There were two bibimbap options: with meat for 15,000 won and without meat for 12,000 won. We ordered with meat.

"The mountains are less than one hour away," said Mrs. Lee. "And the sea is two hours away for everything else. That's why I think Jeolla people are good at cooking. We have easy access to great ingredients."

The side dishes arrived first. The selection dazzled: small sweet potato chunks with sesame, shredded pickled radish with grilled sesame seeds, salted persimmon and *gochujang*, fermented salted fish, fermented plums, mushrooms, cabbage kimchi, glass noodles with sesame, mung bean jelly, an earthenware pot of the scrambled eggs called *gyeram jim* (which I had eaten earlier in my trip at Namdaemun market with the hairtail fish dish). And there were sweet chiles covered in sesame seeds, salty radish with slivers of nuts, a bowl of bean sprout water, some wild greens, and, finally, the bibimbap itself. The table looked like a soccer game: the action was happening all over the field and our bibimbap bowls blocked the opposing goals.

"You have to eat this with *moju* [모주]," said Mrs. Lee. *Moju* is a mildly alcoholic drink packed with ginseng, cinnamon, and jujube. She poured for me and I took a sip: it tasted a bit like a cold mulled wine. Mrs. Lee told me that it was served hot in the winter. To my right was an enormous pyramid of brass bowls on an aluminum table, and next to it were trays filled with side dishes, ready for the next customers to arrive.

"*Jeon* means 'perfect' in Korean," said Mrs. Lee as she explained the city's name. "Therefore, we think Jeonju is the perfect place to live. There are no floods, no drought, it's not too hot and it's not too cold and there isn't much snow."

Steam issued from one end of the kitchen where the rice cooked. Vapors enveloped the rice chef whenever she opened the lid. Like the Lady of the Lake, she would appear and disappear from view between blasts of rice mist. The air inside Gajeok Hwaegwan was dense with a nuttiness from years of roasting sesame seeds. An old woman with a red net hat trundled past pushing a cart laden with jostling trays of side dishes.

"There were many places selling bibimbap back in the seventies," said Mrs. Yang, the daughter of the other Mrs. Yang, the seventy-eight-year-old owner. The younger Mrs. Yang sat down with us for a chat. "But this was the first place that sold only Jeonju-style bibimbap and nothing else."

The younger Mrs. Yang was fifty years old. She'd had her eyes done, and wore a white blouse and a gray jacket, with a diamond necklace dangling over her blouse. Her leather-and-gold purse sat between us on the glass-topped table.

"The secret to a good bibimbap is the preparation," she said. "It's very easy to eat, but very hard to prepare and to keep those colors and the character and to preserve the personality, the look, and the size. We need one size for all the ingredients. It's very important that it looks right when it's served."

Despite her age, Mrs. Yang's mother still cooked in the kitchen, preparing five hundred bibimbap per day and double that over the weekend. Twenty women and one young man also worked in the restaurant. Five of those women had worked there for more than twenty years.

"It's those five who do the cooking and the serving," said Mrs. Yang. "They're the experts and they're the ones who keep the quality this high. Along with my mother, of course."

The younger Mrs. Yang had followed her mother into the restaurant trade, but not to the letter. She had recently opened her own bibimbap restaurant in Jeonju's *hanok* village. The tourist village was an area of mock *hanok*s, filled with knickknack shops, small museums, and places to stay and to eat. She had taken the concept of bibimbap and stripped it down.

"I serve buffet-style bibimbap," she said as she scrolled through photos on her smartphone to show me her concept. There was a vat of rice and a long line of trays with all the ingredients laid out. It looked like a by-the-pound candy store.

"The idea is that you make your own bibimbap," she said. "Lots of people want to arrange their own style of bibimbap. This way, they can choose what they want. Make it their own way."

"How does your mother feel about this break with tradition?" I asked.

"She doesn't like it," Mrs. Yang said. "She thinks I shouldn't dabble and change how things are done, but there's a market for this. I serve five hundred people per day, too, and people tell me they like it."

At this point, Mrs. Yang's mother arrived. Unlike her daughter, she had a sweaty brow and tousled hair and wore a stained apron, and there were no diamonds or gold on her. She frowned at her daughter.

"No, it's not the way to do it," the septuagenarian said.

There had clearly been a reasonably good-natured family dispute about the newfangled restaurant, or "the future," as the daughter saw it. I'll admit, I sided with the elder Yang; the industrial cafeteria-style line of ingredients was no match for the artful creation served in Gajeok Hwaegwan.

I wanted to know what made Jeonju bibimbap so special, why it was so different. Mrs. Lee had already explained to me that Jeonju's location was important for the supply of ingredients, but I felt there was something more, perhaps in the cooking style. The mother, however, had a different answer.

"The most important thing with bibimbap is the water," she said. "It has to be Jeonju water, and then, the ingredients, they have to come from the Jeonju area. Without those two things, it's not Jeonju bibimbap and it won't taste right."

She sneered when I told her about the restaurant signs I had seen advertising "Jeonju Bibimbap" in Seoul, Busan, and elsewhere. I felt sure the same signs could be found in London, New York, Los Angeles, and Tokyo.

"No such thing," she said. "There's nothing Jeonju about that, and not much bibimbap, either. It has to come from this area."

The line of Yang family chefs would not end with Mrs. Yang's daughter, it seemed. The twenty-two-year-old granddaughter was also keen to enter the trade, and she was at college learning about it.

At the restaurant's exit, there were cabbages and trays of eggs piled on the stairs all the way up to the next landing. In one corner, there was a row of large water bottles, and next to the cash register were bottles of moju. By the time we left the restaurant, it was full of customers. I asked Mrs. Lee if she'd visited her daughter's restaurant.

"I have," she said, "but I didn't like it. I don't like the concept, and anyway, I can make it better myself at home."

We reached the air of the street. Unlike Gajeok Hwaegwan, the wedding shops were all empty. It was as if Koreans were more married to Jeonju bibimbap than they were to marriage.

"However," Mrs. Lee said, dragging my thoughts back to food and looking up at the restaurant sign at the crossroads, "I can't make bibimbap better than this place. No one can."

Mountains loomed beyond Jeonju, white apartment buildings peeked at me in blocks, and cars juddered past on a six-lane highway. Rainwater leaked from under the highway bridge. I was standing next to the small Hanbyeokdang pavilion at the city limits. It was originally built in 1404; cranes and dragons were etched into the edges of the roof tiles. It was, quite probably, completely rebuilt—it didn't look ten years old, let alone six hundred. Opposite me, by a bend in the river, were rows of wooden decking under the trees.

"This used to be the best view in Jeonju," said Mrs. Lee. "But not anymore."

The concrete expressway bridge thundered with whizzing Hyundais, Kias, and Daewoos. The cars were so close I could read the license plates, so close that the heavier trucks shook the pagoda.

To our left, above the bend in the river, were some small mountains; at their base was a village with *hanok*s, some with blue roofs. In front of me, on the other side of the bridge, was a hill covered in trees. Mist dabbed the mountains, but I could just make out a tall, white Buddha near the top of one.

"It used to be just a small railway bridge here," said Mrs. Lee, "but the government wanted a big bypass road."

A heron flew over and a magpie mobbed it, while another crowed from a nearby tree. Centuries ago, poets would congregate here to recite poetry and travelers would come to take a rest. It had once been a meditative stop, but no more. The only glimpse of calm came whenever the red stoplights on the road on one side of the bridge conspired to create a couple of seconds of motionless traffic.

We walked back down under the expressway, alongside the river. A group of men exercised on the river path near three catfish restaurants. We were going to eat another Jeolla dish; this one was called *o-mo-ga-ri* (오모가리), a hot, red, fish soup.

"In other parts of Korea, *o-mo-ga-ri* doesn't come with vegetables," said Mrs. Lee. "But that's the way we serve it in Jeolla province."

At the entrance, just outside the front door, catfish skulked inside a blue aquarium.

"We're going to eat the small fish," said Mrs. Lee, pointing to a second aquarium. "It has hard, stiff bones, not like the catfish. People tend to come to this restaurant because it's the oldest one."

Mr. Kim, the restaurant owner, was an old friend of Mrs. Lee—they had gone to university together. His parents had opened the restaurant in 1945, the restaurant next door opened around about the same time, and the third restaurant came sometime later. They all served the same dish, but only Mr. Kim's establishment had remained within the same family since the beginning.

Mr. Kim was a slim man, with a smile brimming with teeth. He invited us inside. And inside meant the kitchen, as all customers, friends or otherwise, had to walk through the kitchen to get to the restaurant. I liked the up-front honesty of the concept, although, I suspected, it was not a concept at all. It had just been the most convenient place to put the kitchen all those years ago and no one had ever thought to change it.

An industrial stove with a gas supply direct from the volcanic core of hell blazed to my left; small fish flipped inside furious black earthenware pots as feathery red flames licked up the sides. Staring into that mire was like bearing witness to a bloody massacre at a lava spring. The red chile delirium sneered, spat, and hissed at me. I imagined a Raymond Chandler short story.

"The pot is very specific to this dish in this area," said Mr. Kim, pointing to the row of seething pots. "They're called *dolsot bajang*. You won't find *o-mo-ga-ri* served in this kind of pot anywhere else in Korea. It's a Jeolla thing."

As he talked to us, he brought a small Korean table in and placed it upon two others at one end of the kitchen, resulting in a three-table-high structure. He laid a sheet of paper across the table, put a gas burner on one side, and then filled the side dishes, spooning the food from stainless-steel containers, and laid them out on the table one by one. When the table was complete, he carried it through to the waiting customers. The soup, still inside the *dolsot bajang* and angry as hell, followed. The chef carried it with a large metal pincer device. I dreaded to think of the carnage that would ensue if she ever dropped one.

A row of thirty-kilogram sacks of salt lined one side of the restaurant. Mr. Kim told us that he went through two hundred sacks like that every single year. I thought about Korea's worrying salt intake once again.

"I put radish leaves and pak choi into the big brown plastic bins outside the restaurant," he said, as he began to lay out a second table. "One layer of vegetables, one layer of sea salt, all the way to the top, and I leave it like that for at least one year."

There were ten vats outside the restaurant, huddled together like slumbering tramps. There was another cluster of them up the stairs at the back, under an awning on a rooftop patio.

"The secret to this dish is in the radish leaves," he said. "I gather them every autumn as the first leaves come out at that time, and they're the ones we need, the young leaves. The second and third leaves are too tough and not tasty. It's these fermented radish leaves that are the key to my restaurant's popularity."

Mrs. Ok, the restaurant's head cook, boiled cuts of fish in water before adding the fermented radish and pak choi leaves. Then in went some small shrimp and the prepared soup, which was filled with garlic, roasted wild sesame seeds, chile powder, and some *doenjang* to add saltiness and tang. No oil is used in the making of the soup, and the taste comes from the fermented radish leaves. After a year spent bathing in salt, the leaves are taken out and washed three or four times to get rid of the salty taste. Once they are drained, they are ready to use.

"If you don't do it this way, the soup won't be good," said Mr. Kim. "The important thing is to keep the texture of the vegetables."

We entered the restaurant and went into a back room. It was unusual for a restaurant in that it was completely barren. We sat on cushions on the floor around an empty space. I felt like I was at a meeting of Quakers, and then Mr. Kim walked in and I remembered where I was. He brought our table, put it down on the floor between us. The space filled, the room immediately looked as it should, the Korean restaurant jigsaw puzzle was complete.

Side dishes crammed the small table set for five people; here was sweet, hot, young spring onion doused in fire and sesame seeds, there was kimchi and a dish of salty fermented chile leaves—the long, green chiles themselves lay on a white dish next to them—and the smallest dish held salted fermented razor clams.

"One of the other differences with this dish here is that it is made with ground wild sesame seeds," said Mrs. Lee. "In other provinces they don't have that, or they just use ordinary sesame. In Jeolla, people like the wild sesame taste, both ground and as sesame oil. If you toast wild sesame, the taste is different, it's stronger, much stronger, and we like strong tastes in Jeolla."

Again, I was reminded of what I had been told throughout my journey: that Jeollabuk-do, and Jeonju in particular, was the Korean hobnail boot kicking down the door to your taste buds. Get booted in the face long enough, and you begin to yearn for the particular kind of sweet pain only Jeolla can give you.

"If you don't toast them . . . ," Mrs. Lee made a scrunched-up face. "Well, it just tastes like ordinary sesame." A look approaching pity passed over her face.

Mr. Kim's *o-mo-ga-ri* had its boots on; they were laced up and they meant business. Supping in the heat, crunching through the leaves, swiping at the side dishes, I took on the challenge of this broth that was more street fight than soup. That fearsome Jeolla chile heat was irresistible. I came through it bloodied and cut, but content. This was the real taste of old Korea, I thought, this was the one the kids were turning their noses up at.

After the soup, Mrs. Ok brought us a shell of burnt rice. It looked like the singed dome of a soccer stadium.

"It's another Jeolla thing," said Mrs. Lee. "It's known as *durungji*, but we call it *gambak* here. It's burdensome to make this in a busy restaurant and it's unique to the restaurants in this area."

It takes thirty minutes to make *gambak*. The rice takes twenty minutes to cook along with a handful of black beans. Then the rice is burned for ten minutes inside the stone cooking pot over high heat, after which it's scraped and peeled and dragged out of the pot in one piece and placed onto a serving plate as this domed structure.

"Old people like it and kids, too," said Mrs. Ok as she served it to us. "They like that mixture of sensations, the crack combined with the soft."

There is no taste to *gambak*; it possesses only the faintest memory of burning. As such, it's purely a texture food, tobacco brown in color, cracked on one side and soft and fluffy on the other.

Mr. Kim told me that his family had been buying fish from the same place ever since the restaurant opened.

"There are a lot of clean streams and rivers in Jeolla province," he said. "Therefore, the quality is great. However, more and more we are seeing Chinese fish on the market, but they're not good. They use some kind of anaesthesia to put the fish to sleep and then they tie the fish up. When they untie them, the fish wake up, but it's not a healthy way to keep and eat fish".

"It's true," said Mrs. Lee. "Fish and prawns from China are not clean."

She seemed very annoyed at these cheap, shoddy foreign invaders, much like Areum had reacted at Namdaemun market in Seoul to the news that replicant Chinese kimchi was spreading like an invasive plant throughout Korea's restaurants.

"Those small vendors you see on the street," said Mrs. Lee, "you know, the old women. I went up to one and she opened a sack of prawns. She told me they were from such and such a place, but they were so cheap, too cheap, and they were still jumping about. That's not normal. I didn't believe her and I walked away."

I remembered that Jason had mentioned a Jeolla dish to me when I was on Jeju Island. It was called *chueotang* (추어탕), a mudfish soup. He wasn't keen on it, but I'd never eaten mudfish before and I wanted to try it. Namwon is about 30 miles south of Jeonju, and it is the home of *chueotang*. Mrs. Lee introduced me to a contact there, the appropriately named Mr. Chu, and I went to Namwon to meet him.

Mr. Chu was an English teacher. He had worked at schools in Namwon for sixteen years and had trained with Mrs. Lee when they were at university.

"There used to be a season for *chueotang*," said Mr. Chu. "But now there's no season. We can eat it anytime we want."

Namwon had a history of poor city slogans. The current one, "Jump Namwon," had replaced "The City of Love Namwon." I eagerly awaited future incarnations.

"Back in the ancient times," said Mr. Chu, referring to a period of time some thirty years ago, "after the rice harvest, mudfish were always very easy to find. They live in the rice paddies and we have a lot of paddies around here, as you can see."

South Korea plants rice in June and July and usually harvests in October. In April and May, the paddies surrounding Namwon looked like open wounds waiting for the balm of the planting season to begin. We arrived at the restaurant, a bland, gray-and-brown-brick building. I took this as a good sign. The less pretentious a place is, the more heart you find inside.

"There are not too many traditional restaurants left in Namwon these days," said Mr. Chu. "But this place does *chueotang* the traditional way. You won't find a better one than this in all Korea."

Namwon is an agricultural area, like much of Jeolla province, and there are no factories in Namwon. Apart from rice, the area was known for strawberries, vegetables, and grapes, and, Mr. Chu told me, peach growing was becoming more and more common.

Although he still worked as an English teacher, these days it was

Mr. Chu's daughter who taught her father English. She'd studied overseas and her English was better than his, and now it was he who needed to pass an English exam. Years ago this would have caused acute shame, but not now. With the movement of people, there was a realization that that's the way things had evolved in Korea. It was almost funny, and Mr. Chu could see the humor in it, too.

"*Chueotang* is not the same outside Namwon," he said. "It's difficult to find, anyhow, but very few places do the real mudfish soup. But I promise you that this is the real one. I don't come here very often, but I like it when I do, so I'm glad you came. Although my wife's friend has a *chueotang* restaurant in Jeonju. You could have gone there—it is very good, too."

The taste is the usual Korean ironmonger's branding upon the tongue: scorching chile, scorching heat, a propulsive jet of garlic, and the cooling crunchy radish leaves, but there's more. The mudfish thickens the soup into almost a stewlike consistency. I had a notion that what it really wanted to be when it grew up was a porridge. As a result, I figured, the mudfish almost felt hard done by; *chueotang* wasn't a soup, it wasn't a stew, it wasn't a porridge—it was simply a *chueotang*. It wanted for more, and so did I. I wanted to have it again, but I was only in Namwon for an afternoon, so I asked Mr. Chu about the restaurant in Jeonju.

"This mudfish restaurant in Jeonju," I said, "what's it called?"

Then, I had a thought.

"No, hang on," I said. "Let me have a guess. It serves the same dish as this place, right?"

"Yes, yes," he said. "Exactly the same, the way it should be made."

"And Namwon," I said, "is the place everyone comes to eat *chueotang*, right?"

"Yes," he said. "That's right."

I thought about it: mudfish paradise, the home of mudfish, mudfish king, and then I remembered I was in Korea, and it dawned on me.

"Would it, by any chance, be called . . . Namwon Chueotang?"

"Yes," he said, his eyes widening. "How did you know that?"

I bent forward, looked at him intently, and pointed at my eyes with two fingers.

"Mr. Chu," I said as I pointed my two fingers at his eyes, "I can read your mind."

For a second, I think he believed me. There is something both dully predictable and reassuringly pragmatic about Korean restaurant names. There is zero pretension in any good Korean restaurant, it is what it says it is, and there is no need for any fancy imagination to dress it up in a feather boa, heels, and a cocktail dress.

You could almost wade through a bowl of *chuoetang;* eating it, I could almost imagine I was devouring an entire swath of rice paddy. Whole. Mr. Chu told me that the very peculiar sensation was because of the way the fish are prepared, and we went to the kitchen to learn more. The scullery was a narrow galley scattered with the engine parts for *chueotang.* Mr. Chu asked the husband-and-wife team, Mr. Oh and Mrs. Suk, to talk me through the method of cooking.

"First, you have to clean the mudfish," Mr. Oh said.

To demonstrate, he opened a door at the back of the kitchen and returned with a red bucket. It pulsed with live mudfish.

"You boil them while they are still alive," he said. There was no pity in his voice as the mudfish flipped and flopped between his hands. They looked about as annoyed as mudfish can look. Looking at them, I felt no emotion, either—why would I? I'd been eating their sisters and cousins. I was stuffed, and I had decided mudfish were delicious.

"Second," he said, "you have to divide the flesh from the bones. After that you grind the meat in a machine."

The gruesome end for the mudfish had a touch of the mafia about it: the machine looked like a mini cement mixer.

"The soup," he said, "is made from the water boiled with the mudfish bones."

The boiling was done in a large pot, big enough to shelter two chubby babies.

"Then you filter the soup through a bamboo basket," he said. "This gets rid of all the small bits. If it's not filtered with bamboo, then the small bones can get through. After that, we need to add the radish leaves."

"We gather them in the spring and the fall," he said, echoing Mr. Kim at the *o-mo-ga-ri* restaurant in Jeonju. "There's more texture to them at those times. We gather them twice per year. The fall leaves are better, and we store them in boxes and freeze them."

Mr. Oh had his own gripes about imported Chinese radish leaves. They weren't up to the job. Radish leaves had to be Korean.

"A lot of dried radish leaves are imported from China," said Mr. Oh, "but they're very sticky. That's the difference. You really have to have young Korean radish leaves."

Korean bean sprouts to make *meju*, intestines to make *mom-guk*, Korean radish leaves to make soups the "right way" . . . I was beginning to feel that I had garnered a few kernels of knowledge on this Jules Verne–like quest into the Korean stomach. However, one thing I hadn't done to excess yet was drink, but I knew it was coming. I knew Koreans loved to drink, that their guard dropped once alcohol was imbibed, and Mrs. Lee had promised to let me in on a semi-secret place to learn of Jeolla's ways. She phoned to tell me.

"Tomorrow," she said, "we will go drinking."

"Drunkenness is an outstanding feature in Korea. And it is not disreputable. If a man drinks rice wine till he loses his reason, no one regards him as a beast."

"You can't get in on a Saturday night," said Mrs. Lee. "It's packed."

Makgeolli Sul Jjib did little to advertise its presence. The tatty restaurant was on a cobbled street, next to a flower shop on the edge of Jeonju's *hanok* village. The small frontage was a mix of dirty white tiles and steamed-up aluminum-framed windows. It was difficult to see inside, and maybe that was the point. However, it was not difficult to hear the revelry already underway. It was eight P.M.

Down the street, mobile phone antennae crawled across the rooftops and loudspeakers clung to the lampposts. A single bicycle outside Makgeolli Sul Jjib belied the packed interior. Before I even entered, I felt tomorrow's hangover tap me on the shoulder.

I imagined the "too drunk to drive home" taxi service were regulars at this place. For a fee, *dae-ri un-jeon* (대리운전), or "replacement drivers," will come and drive a drunk home in the drunk's own car. A staggering seven hundred thousand people in South Korea use the service each day.

"This is one of the famous places in Jeonju," said Mrs. Lee.

As is so often the case in Korea with restaurants, bars, shops, and markets, Makgeolli Sul Jjib is run by women. Three were throwing food together in a small kitchen inside a cubbyhole next to the entrance and one was serving, along with a student who worked as a waiter.

"There are many, many dishes to eat in here," said Mrs. Lee as we entered. "But you must drink, because if you drink more, you eat more. That's how it works in here."

Inside, Makgeolli Sul Jjib looked like the playroom of an anarchist child. Someone had gone psycho with a Sharpie. The walls were entirely covered in graffiti written in black ink. There were drawings of faces, hearts, drunken scrawls, and the more concentrated and intricate, but wobbly, patterns of the severely alcohol impaired. There was not a spare patch of wall space that was not written upon. I looked up at the ceiling and it was the same story. Koreans clearly came here to play and to leave their mark.

There were seven of us at a long table. I sat opposite Mrs. Lee and her husband, Mr. Jang, and next to a man called Mr. Park, who was the most enthusiastic drinker of the group.

The first time I ever got drunk on *makgeolli* was with Mrs. Lee and others somewhere in Jeolla province. I'd boarded the bus on the school teachers' trip at six A.M. one Saturday. The men started on whisky at 6:05, karaoke kicked off by 6:15, soju entered the fray by 6:30. The men on the bus were all blind drunk and on to brandy by 7:00 and sleeping by 7:30. I had found it a somewhat trying trip. The *makgeolli* started at around ten A.M. on top of a mountain in a forest near a Buddhist temple. The school principal dared me to drink a bowl. He was a man with a reputation, but limited stamina. He had once invited me into his office and unlocked a padlock on a vast metal cabinet. Inside, it was filled, top to bottom, with alcohol. We ended up sharing a bottle of soju from North Korea. I eyed him in the mountain air, brought the *makgeolli* to my lips, and sank the pinky murk. Then it was his turn. However, as he leaned his head back to sup, the hooch dribbled down his chin and slowly, ever so slowly, he began to fall. Cartoonlike he went, flat on his back, and the bowl clanged upon the concrete floor. The four-foot-tall bespectacled ball laughed away offers of help and proceeded to crawl under a table of female teachers. It was then that he started to grope the geography teacher. She screamed, he was immediately hauled away, placed back in the ski lift, put in a taxi, and driven the four hours back to Jeonju alone.

"So you remember that, too," said Mrs. Lee after I had recounted the story to her. I think she was surprised at how many of these stories I could remember from all those years ago.

"I asked the geography teacher if she wanted to make a formal complaint," she said. "But she declined, she just wanted to forget it. The behavior of men back then was just too much. It's a lot better now, but we still have a long way to go."

I was handed a battered bowl, like the one I'd drunk from on that mountaintop. Mr. Park poured for me. His English was poor, but he repeated what Mrs. Lee had told me.

"Drink more," he said. "Eat more."

The *makgeolli* bowl was made of cheap, light, brass-looking aluminum. Mr. Park told me that it had been invented in the seventies, and mine looked like it dated from that time. Either that, or it had fallen down a very long, very hard set of stairs. It looked like my head would feel the morning after—maybe that was part of the concept behind Makgeolli Sul Jjib.

Mr. Park held the brass-colored kettle up and poured—he poured big and he poured long. The abundance of kettles that hung from the wall at the entrance looked like a Mad Hatter's Christmas tree. I downed the brew, picked up my chopsticks, and took a couple of dried silkworms from the petri dish in front of me as I perused the spread, feeling a fizzy warm glow from the *makgeolli*. Mr. Park poured for me again.

Upon the table there was pork *samgyeopsal*; snails; broccoli; small, thin fish; octopus; kimchi; sweet mussels; doenjang paste; edamame; carrots; sweetcorn; raw Chinese cabbage; squid; tofu draped in chile; kumquats; spiral-shell clams; a cabbage salad covered in mayonnaise; a green salad with a sesame oil dressing; a couple of slabs of tofu drizzled in soy sauce and speckled with sesame seeds; and there, on its own, nodding sagely like the king at his court, at one end of the long table was a lone plastic plate lined with three thick slices of fish. The tell-tale line of white tendon broke the flesh down the middle. The memory of Mokpo returned, and I could almost taste the reeking urinal breathing from the distant plate. For the rest of the evening I would do my best from my end of the table to maintain that distance.

"At first I hated it," said Mrs. Lee of *hongeo*. "My parents-in-law are from Jeollabuk-do and every Chuseok and summer we'd have *hongeo*. You have to prepare and eat it over and over, many times. That's what I did, and it grew on me. Now the smell is very attractive to me. Preparing it so often made me love it."

The human being is an incredible creature: it can get used to anything, it just needs to endure. I admired Mrs. Lee for her sacrifice, but I refused to follow in her footsteps. She took a slice of the *hongeo*. I hit up the octopus instead.

Some South Korean restaurants have a button on the table. You push it, a bell rings in the kitchen, and a waiter arrives, but not here. Mr. Park tapped our brass kettle with his metal chopsticks. It was empty again and it made a hollow rattle. The waitress scooted over with a refill of the pinky *makgeolli*. The student waiter followed with a tray filled with more food, and we reconvened. Among the new spread was the greasiest, fattest *pajeon* I'd ever seen.

"It's good with alcohol," said Mr. Park, sawing into the pancake with his chopsticks. Grease splurged at the edges of the plate. "It's like a sponge."

Mr. Park was a former student revolutionary. In the 1980s, he was the "union man" at university, and he ended up spending 270 days behind bars for his revolutionary activities under the Chun Doo-hwan government. These days, he was a manager at Hyundai. He was dressed in a dark suit with a tie, the salaryman outfit. In a statement that was both factually accurate and somewhat profound, Mr. Park said, "I like drinking."

And he poured for me again.

Mrs. Lee had an explanation for the likes of Mr. Park, for the revolutionaries of Jeolla.

"The river runs from south to north in Jeonju," she said. "It's the only river that does that in Korea. It kind of proves to us that we have a revolutionary, or at least contradictory, spirit in this area."

I found the link a little difficult to follow, but Mr. Park's refills made sure I accepted her wisdom unquestioningly.

"One of the kings from long ago," she said, "didn't want any ministers in his government from Jeollabuk-do because of the river. It seems to represent this rebellious, revolutionary mind of the people. Maybe that comes out in the food, too. You know, all that fire, heat, and spice that we love. To this day, there are fewer people in the government from Jeolla than from any other province."

Tap. Tap. Mr. Park summoned another kettle of *makgeolli,* along with a seaweed-rice dish and crab.

"I never came here before I got married," said Mrs. Lee.

It almost sounded like an apology, but there was no need. I adored the place. It was raucous and rough with that playful psychotic graffiti, like a spider's web of insanity enveloping the entire den. This was the Korea I'd come back to see.

"We used to go to another street that was filled with *makgeolli* bars," she said. "We'd drink and eat there because it was cheap and we got plenty of food, as you can see. But you had to get drunk to eat enough."

It was a simple concept, one that I can't help thinking should be universal.

The *makgeolli* we were drinking, like all *makgeolli,* had been made from rice. The Japanese forbade the making of *makgeolli* during colonial rule to preserve rice stocks for eating. So Koreans made it illegally—it was their moonshine, an alcoholic finger to the imperialist Japanese. It is ironic, therefore, that in more recent years, it was the Japanese who reinvigorated interest in *makgeolli* in Korea. Japanese women got a taste for it in 2011, and the trend crossed back to Korea. Restrictive laws on the production of alcohol were relaxed, small producers proliferated, and a *makgeolli* boom was born.

"Makgeolli Sul Jjib was always cheap when I was a student," she said. "There were none in Iksan where I lived. They only existed in Jeonju."

Tap. Tap. Another kettle. More *makgeolli.* A pig's trotter arrived. It added an air of the medieval to the table, not that we needed it. Mr. Park looked regally drunk, but I was assured he could keep going longer.

"Oh, this is nothing for him," said Mrs. Lee. "He can keep on going all night if he's allowed to."

She looked at Mr. Park's wife, who had been quiet all night, happily, drunkenly quiet, nodding back and forth like an ornamental puppy. Mr. Park could have been Henry VIII holding court as he went about slicing the meat from the trotter.

"There's an abattoir there by the bridge, when you come into Jeonju from Iksan," said Mrs. Lee. "There are a lot of pig's trotter places there. It's good, simple food. Many laborers work there, that's why it's easy to buy this food in that area. It's good drinking food and it's good for pregnant women."

As in other parts of Asia, Korean women are encouraged to eat pig's trotters during pregnancy and after birth to encourage the production of milk. It takes four hours to steam this Korean-style pig's trotter, and it's served with garlic and spring onions. We ate it with the tiny salty shrimp that act as a fishy salt in Korea.

Tap. Tap. Another kettle arrived. And tempura-covered prawns with ketchup, some crabs in honey, and *gochujang*.

"People drink less now," said Mrs. Lee. That seemed hard to believe, scanning the red eyes around the table, but I think she was referring to the younger generation.

"Our culture started to change maybe five or ten years ago," she said. "It was around the time when domestic violence became a 'thing.'"

I remembered the couple upstairs where I used to live in Iksan. I never saw them, but I heard the beating sessions every Sunday afternoon.

"Domestic violence was not thought of as a problem when you lived here before," said Mrs. Lee. "We never talked about it. The same was true for child sex abuse. Men had to be careful, and when they drink soju, they can lose control. All the drinking just exacerbates those kinds of problems."

Twenty years ago, things had been very different indeed. Mrs. Lee was like another woman, or maybe she treated me differently now, more like an adult, less like a son.

Now there was a court case, she explained, involving a navy sergeant and an underling; soju was a factor and sexual harassment charges followed. It was just one of an increasing number of cases on the peninsula.

A drinker at a table next to us asked his companion to look at a video on his phone. A K-pop band enthusiastically gyrated across a vast stage. I could just make out the tinny music over the rumpus of the bar. Mr. Park noticed it, too.

"Korean culture is becoming popular in Europe, isn't it?" he asked.

"I wouldn't say it's popular," I said. "It's more known that it was, but it was completely unknown before."

Unlike in the United States, where K-pop has found a modicum of Billboard chart success, where K-pop concert tickets sell out within hours and *The New Yorker* ran a lengthy feature on a K-pop girl group. K-pop stars have caused traffic jams in South America and much of Asia, but in Europe the fanbase is much smaller. While there had yet to emerge a Justin Bieber– or Rihanna-size global K-pop sensation, it seemed only a matter of time.

Mr. Park wanted to know about Korea's place in Europe because the entire table was planning a group trip to Italy in the next two years.

"From north to south," said Mr. Park as he tapped for yet another kettle. "For the food, and the drink, of course."

A trip like this would never have happened twenty years ago. Economically it would have been tough, there was no time, and, more to the point, there was no real desire. Kimchi was a rare commodity in rural Italy, and back then, the Korean who would travel without first securing a kimchi supply route beforehand simply did not exist.

As we exited the drinking den, I looked on the opposite side of the road. There was a posh new *makgeolli* inn, advertising dishes like bibimbap along with the plastic bottles of alcohol. It was silent and almost entirely empty. A roar went up inside Makgeolli Sul Jjib, and a very drunk man started to sing what sounded like Italian opera. It seemed appropriate, like a send-off for Mrs. Lee and her friends to Mediterranean shores.

"You know where to go tomorrow morning?" said Mrs. Lee. We were all a bit wobbly. My hangover had one arm over my shoulder now, grinning at me like an asylum patient. I did indeed know where to go tomorrow: there was only one place to go in Jeonju the morning after. It was a place well used to my friend from the asylum.

A chemical I could not place had pierced my brain. It would take time and a little help to shift. I'd been told bean sprouts were the answer. Hyundai-ok was once a small, rough shed in a back alley. I knew it well—I'd eaten in it many times in the midnineties—but it was no longer a shack. Today, Hyundai-ok was filled with apron-wearing women, a machinelike preparation area, a faceless kitchen, and a modern seating area. The grunge of yore, which had once been mainstream, had been eradicated. Now Hyundai-ok was a franchise and it was open 24 hours a day, 365 days a year.

It was nine A.M. Baseball was on the TV; there were eight customers, young and old. Some looked rough, and I'm sure I did. There was a box of tissues on the table and a dried seaweed holder next to a chopstick box. A young man wheeled soup to my table on a cart. He could have been in a hospital ward, and in a sense, he almost was. I had a hangover cure to acquire, and Hyundai-ok was my doctor.

Hyundai-ok's *kongnamul gukbap* (콩나물국밥) is a bean sprout soup. It came in a stone bowl and it fizzed with a curative bean sprout fog as it was placed upon my table. In a small metal bowl next to the soup were two eggs, just ever so slightly cooked. On a wooden platter, there was a small dish of those tiny shrimp again, some cabbage kimchi, and a bowl of salty fermented octopus.

The staff wore red shirts. A woman with a white-painted face separated seaweed into strips and placed them inside plastic wrappers, ready to serve. Another woman with a permed bob washed the small metal bowls for the eggs.

I spooned a little soup onto the eggs to cook them further, added a few shrimp to the soup and a little octopus, too. In other countries, hangover cures involve tomato juice, vodka, sugary soft drinks, greasy alcohol-absorbing food, and ibuprofen. I had never considered bean sprouts as my go-to ingredient to cure a night on the sauce—until I lived in Korea, that is.

"They have a quality which makes the stomach feel more comfortable," Mrs. Lee had told me. "People in Korean markets drink a lot, and so they eat a lot of *kongnamul gukbap*, too. It's been common here for a long time. We need *kongnamul gukbap* to calm the soju in our stomachs."

She had told me this as if soju were a constant in Korean stomachs, and given the consumption rate, she was probably right. Soju is the world's most popular alcohol. Koreans drink twice as much liquor as Russians and four times as much as Americans. Of the hard liquor sold in Korea, 97 percent is soju. As a result, Korea may also have the highest number of hangovers, too.

Korean corner shops are lined with hangover cures that come in small medicine-like bottles or cans, or in chewing-gum form. However, most Koreans still believe in the power of *kongnamul gukbap* to cure the morning head pounding. Most Korean food items are either hangover cures, health enhancers, or boner givers, and I am pretty sure nothing else would sell. In addition, Korea may have the perfect drink to enjoy the evening before a morning after *kongnamul gukbap*. It's a natural hangover cure and a genuine, homegrown Korean one, too, according to science, no less.

One news article reported, "Australian scientists at [the Commonwealth Scientific and Industrial Research Organisation] found that consuming [Korean] pears or pear juice before drinking can dramatically reduce the symptoms of hangovers."

As I bent in toward my *kongnamul gukbap* and supped at it, the chile forehead sweats began to bleed my hangover out. The guttural groans of my fellow sufferers resounded around Hyundai-ok. The curative foundation of *kongnamul gukbap* is cemented by the crunch of bean sprouts, the anchovy-based stock, and the chile at the bottom of this regional powder keg. A wide metal lid rattled as a cook checked on the bean sprouts in the kitchen. Mobile phones whistled the *"kakao"* sound of the ubiquitous KakaoTalk messaging app, a service which transmits a mind-bending seven billion messages a day across the country. Chopping was constant, it was an uneven rhythm, like the beat of a tribal drum, only the drumskin was a cutting board, the drumstick was sharp steel working its way through a hundredweight of scallions. I was largely oblivious. *Kongnamul gukbap* is a ridiculously good soup and I supped ever onward.

The current owners of Hyundai-ok bought the place in 2009. There are roughly 150 branches of Hyundai-ok throughout Korea. The one I was in was "almost the first one," according to the owner's son and chef, the appropriately named Mr. Kuk, a twenty-seven-year-old from Jeonju. It was, he said, the only place in Jeonju where they sell *kongnamul gukbap* for 5,000 won.

"It's unlike any other place selling the same dish," he said.

Even though it looked like it was exactly the same as every other place selling the same dish and it was a franchise? Mr. Kuk explained to me the secret to a good *kongnamul gukbap,* and it was not what I expected.

"There was a woman who learned everything about making *kongnamul gukbap* here in our restaurant," he said. "She opened her own place and followed the recipe exactly, but she couldn't get it to taste the same. It just wasn't any good."

It wasn't the ingredients she was using, it wasn't the way she was cooking, and it wasn't the place she was cooking it in—it turned out to be something far simpler.

"Heat," said Mr. Kuk. "You have to have heat, a lot of heat in your fire, and she was using electricity, but that doesn't generate enough heat. You have to use gas to get the temperature you need because it's the heat that defines the taste."

The restaurant had started to fill up since I had finished eating and the interior continued to clang with the sound of dropped chopsticks and the constant chopping. It was a sound that needled the various hangovers dotted around the Formica tables and seated upon the cushioned chairs. My own hangover was now numb, and I felt incomparably better for the soup.

"We get the hangover crowd in the mornings," said Mr. Kuk, unsurprisingly. "At night, drinkers might come here for the 'final stop' to 'wake up' their hangover. The eggs and the bean sprouts help with that. We have a lot of trouble with drunk customers, because they smoke, they're noisy. It's very typical Korean behavior after drinking too much. We try to stop them from drinking more—we don't serve them soju, for example—and we tell them to smoke outside, but these people don't care about anybody else."

Mr. Kuk wanted to leave Jeonju to live in New Zealand, where he had studied for ten months. His girlfriend, from the nearby city of Masan, was not convinced. His restaurant was located in a slightly older part of Jeonju, and by older, I mean from the 1990s.

"Companies buy all the old places," he said. "They turn them into convenience stores and coffee shops."

Gentrification was a phenomenon happening all over Korea, something that was painfully obvious to any visitor traveling around the country. Some people, like the artist Choi Soyeon, who together with two other artists founded an open space called Takeout Drawing in Seoul circa 2005, tried to make a stand. The landlord of her spot was the famous singer Psy, and he wanted them out so he could renovate the building.

"Some people call this phenomenon the evaporation of culture," said Choi. "Gentrification replaces the independent businesses with wealthier franchises and this changes the characteristics of visitors. But culture diminishes, and businesses increase."

Gentrification had left open scars from the demilitarized zone to Jeju, scars that would take a radically different approach to urban development to heal.

I left Hyundai-ok feeling restored, and I called Mrs. Lee to see how she was coping. Plus, I was curious as to why Jeonju in particular should be known for its bean sprouts. They were easy to grow all over Korea, so why here? Mrs. Lee had a theory.

"In Jeonju, the water has a lot of iron," she said. "To decrease the iron, people need to eat bean sprouts, and the bean sprouts are different here, it's a fact. Everyone says they're better. The conclusion that I've come to is that it must be the water. Do you remember what the chef said about the secret to a good bibimbap?"

I did.

"Water," said Mrs. Lee. "It's all in the water."

It was my last day in Jeonju, and we were debating lunch options.

"I think it's illegal now," said Mrs. Lee. "I haven't seen it for a long time."

She was referring to the practice of eating pig's fetus, which had apparently been a thing for a while. I wondered what else had been perfectly normal until recently but was now illegal.

"Some men catch snakes," she said. "They boil them to eat in the mountains and others make alcohol with them, but I think that is illegal, too, now."

For some reason, the method of making the snake alcohol, whether or not it is true, seemed to symbolize, in a very direct way, the female viewpoint of the nebulous Korean pain that is *han*.

"To make the alcohol," she said, "they catch a snake and put it in a bottle while it is still alive, and then they fill the bottle with alcohol. The snake drowns in the alcohol, and some months later, maybe even years later, it is ready to drink."

I imagined female *han* was the bottle, the Korean man was the snake, and the alcohol was the Korean's temporary relief from *han*.

"But," she said, referring back to the pig's-fetus restaurant. "I'm pretty sure it's illegal now, and anyway, it's too far away. Let's go and eat *sundubu* instead."

I'd eaten the fresh *sundubu* made with sea water in Gangneung in the north east of South Korea. *Sundubu* is one of the most common dishes in South Korea, but it is only ever exceptional when made and served where the beans grow within view of the restaurant, as in Gangneung and as on the road out of Jeonju toward Jinan.

"We'll be hungry by the time we get there," she said.

There are several *sundubu* restaurants on the road between Jeonju and Jinan. It is an area of tranquil beauty, surrounded by green mountains, trees, and bean fields.

"This is my favorite road in Jeolla," said Mrs. Lee. "The trees form a kind of tunnel, and at this time of year, it's at its best."

There are two seasons to visit Korea: spring and autumn. Summer is too hot and sticky, winter is too cold, but the rest of the year is perfect. The tunnel of pink trees seemed to be pushing me toward the end of my journey, squeezing me out the other side back to where I'd come from. We stopped at the smallest of four or five *sundubu* restaurants at the base of the mountains.

The area between these mountains has long been known for tofu. During the Chosŏn dynasty (which started in 1392 and ended in 1910), people used to walk toward Jeonju to sell vegetables, fruit, and livestock. They'd leave very early in the morning, and by the time they reached the place where the restaurants are today, they'd be hungry. The only crop that thrived there at that time was beans, and so the people developed tofu. The restaurant we were going to eat in and the few others along this section of road were all that remained of that past.

"Tofu's good for your health," Mrs. Lee said. "And it's cheap and easy to make. Back in the old days, when the traders had finished selling, they would get together in this place to eat. The farmers and the merchants would all eat together here."

It was hard to imagine the life of those sellers almost two hundred years ago. The road would have been little more than a track, and where they came from must have been completely inhospitable. Looking up at the mountains from the comfort of the restaurant, it looked like a tough enough trek in 2015.

"They stuck together," said Mrs. Lee. "Back then, there were a lot of big animals around this part of Korea, and there was safety in numbers. But ever since that time, this area has been famous for tofu."

We were sitting on the floor. I leaned against a cabinet at one end of the restaurant; it housed a four-screen karaoke machine. A group of senior citizen cyclists in spotless and luminous Lycra cycle-wear filled the only other small room in the restaurant.

When the *sundubu* arrived, the tofu wasn't silky like you find in most city-rendered *sundubu*—it had more the consistency of scrambled egg. It was similar to what I had tasted in Gangneung, minus the sea water. The soup was Jeolla's signature molten-fire foundry. But much as a fireplace is a place you convene around, to feel comfort from, the heat of the main dish was not the only thing that holds your interest. It what's going on around the fire that is often more interesting.

This *sundubu* came with fresh kimchi and a small wild green shoot called a *dolnamul* (돌나물). It's a sedum, or stonecrop, a kind of succulent, and it only grows at springtime. The young leaves are plucked from the rocks in April and May and drizzled with *gochujang*. They were ever so slightly crunchy.

The succulent leaves I was eating now would be replaced by something entirely different come summer. These surprise seasonal offerings you find on the table are one of the best aspects of eating in the countryside in Korea. They are almost always wild, be they roots, berries, ferns, leaves, seeds, grains, or bracken. If it's edible, it'll find its way onto the table somewhere in Korea when it's in season.

"It's full of vitamin C," said Mrs. Lee of the young, green leaves. "In the old days we never had it. We do now because it's more widely known about and more commonly available in the countryside."

Thinking of the bounty of the Korean table, I wondered how many other things that had not been eaten for a long time were yet to find a return to the table. Like Vivian's rediscovered dusty recipes.

The tofu restaurant's location was idyllic. This part of Korea was a leafy, rugged pillow, a stretch of countryside that had never heard of apartment blocks. It was an escape from the big city, but there were no shops nearby and there were no schools. It was into these kinds of neighborhoods that a lot of migrant wives were moving to from the megalopolises of the poorer reaches of Southeast Asia. I couldn't help thinking that if the change of pace didn't break the incomers, the winter would.

"A Vietnamese girl told me she thought everyone in Korea lived like they do in the soap operas," said Mrs. Lee.

Korean life depicted in soap operas is upper middle class. It's a fantasy world where everyone has money, everyone consumes, and everyone looks immaculate. There's nary a bubbling bowl of tofu-filled fire, nor even a side dish of kimchi visible on a soap opera set, and most of the characters are utterly miserable. I felt there was a connection between these two things.

"They come here," said Mrs. Lee of the influx of foreign wives to Korea, "and many of them end up having a tough life in the countryside in places like this. They say they can have that life in the countryside in Vietnam or the Philippines or wherever. They didn't expect to find it here. It's a kind of shock to them."

There was a TV program about migrant wives broadcast once a week in Korea. It was called 다문화 사랑, *Multicultural Love*. I'd seen it a few times. One episode looked at the life of a migrant wife in Korea, living on a farm, and then followed her back to her home country with her Korean mother-in-law. The tough Korean mother-in-law suddenly saw the reality of her daughter-in-law's life back home. She felt remorseful and sorry for her daughter-in-law and vowed to change her ways. It was an uplifting take on an ordinarily miserable story.

"It's a kind of propaganda," said Mrs. Lee. "That TV program only shows the good stories."

Mrs. Lee worked with migrant wives, and she'd seen plenty of bad stories. The South Korean government begged for foreign women to come marry their men and populate the country, as Korean women had largely given up on the challenge. As a result, the nation was headed toward a potentially catastrophic population crisis. So the foreign brides came, but they had few rights and life was hard, suicide rates high, divorce and separation rates higher still. It was help centers like the one Mrs. Lee worked at in Jeonju that were sometimes a lifeline for the foreign wives.

"One Filipino woman," said Mrs. Lee, "came to Korea and married a man without having ever spoken to him."

Such was the problem that in 2014 the Korean government tightened the law on mail-order marriages, requiring foreign spouses to pass a language test and show proof of income.

"Why?" I asked. "Is it just desperation fueled by poverty? Is the Korean husband an escape route?"

"They don't think before they come," she said. "And they're not educated."

I'd heard another take on the difficulties facing foreign wives from Tom in Mokpo.

"There's this attitude from the Korean husband," he said. "It's like he's almost bought her. And, you know, 'You're in Korea now, so you must become Korean, you have to speak and read Korean, you have to do this and do that, just like a Korean woman would.' It's like they have to be more Korean than a Korean woman, and of course, they want a baby, and quick."

I looked into the fiery pit of my lunch. The satiny clumps of gentle tofu looked like unlikely guests at the wrong party. They'd dressed up for the soft toy, pajama sleepover, but they'd arrived at the nuns and whores slutty swingers' night. I tucked in; red pepper flooded my taste buds. My mouth was pleasantly on fire.

"About what we talked about the other day, Mrs. Lee," I said. "This . . . *han*."

To try to begin to understand the concept, she told me, I first had to understand a little of where it was coming from, at least from the woman's point of view.

"For a woman," she said, "after marriage in Korea we say that she must spend three years without speaking. She only says 'Yes,' then three years just listening. In Korea, first, women have to follow the father, then the husband, and then the son."

The way she described it, marriage sounded like an unavoidable prison.

"Dreams can never be true for a Korean women," she said.

She asked me if I knew of the traditional Korean game, the seesaw game. I said I did. It was like any seesaw game the world over. Only in the Korean version, the seesaw players stood up.

"But," she said, "do you know how that game originated?"

I did not.

"Women used to play it," she said. "So that they could jump up and look over the wall. To see another life."

Houses in the old days were often surrounded by a protective wall, and women were not allowed beyond the wall. The repression and misery did not stop in the nighttime.

"At night women would wash clothes," she said. "The wife and the mother-in-law would do it together while the men went out drinking. The women would beat the tough cotton clothes as hard as they could to make them perfectly flat. As they worked, the mother-in-law would imagine she was beating her husband and so she would beat harder and harder. Whereas the daughter-in-law imagined that she was beating her husband or her mother-in-law, or both. This would go on all night. Meanwhile, the husband was out drinking with girls. And all night, the sound of beating."

The tofu was sliding down, coated in the molten fire. A fire that seemed to reflect the rage felt in the lives of the women Mrs. Lee was describing to me.

"Korean men don't have *han*," she said. "Korean men are *han* makers, and only if a man fails repeatedly can he ever know *han*."

And there was a sinister edge to those who felt their *han* a little stronger than the next person.

"In their heart there is only anger," she said. "Some consider murder and some suicide. *Han* is a combination of unfulfilled dreams and anger. You know, we say that a Korean woman with overwhelming *han* can make it frost in June."

In addition, the cherry on the most miserable cake in Korea was its inevitability.

"You can't change *han*," she said. "Maybe by education, but endurance is the best policy."

There were no merchants or vendors in Jinan these days, only packs of passing mountain bikes and, in the fields, those migrant wives and workers.

"One blood," she said. "All Koreans believe this, all of us, one hundred percent and it's very difficult to change that. It'll take generations."

Of that I wasn't sure. I was beyond impressed with the speed of change in Korea of the physical things—the roads, the buildings, the infrastructure—but more so I was astounded by the change in the people. The attitudes, particularly male attitudes, which had seemed so fixed, stubborn, ignorant, bigoted, and, quite frankly, psychotic to me twenty years ago had matured dramatically.

The influx of foreign brides, the increase in intermarriage and international travel only bode well for a future where Korea could finally reject the Hermit Kingdom descriptor of yore.

However, *han* still didn't make complete sense to me, at least not in the modern era. I could envisage the miserable existence of Korean women a century or more ago, or even just twenty years ago. And although life was far from perfect for many Korean women in the twenty-first century, change was afoot. There was a female president, the first immigrant member of parliament was female, there were more women in the workplace, they had more independence, they were saying no to marriage. It was clear that, more and more, it was the women who were calling the shots.

I was reminded of a young woman I knew in 1996. She had been twenty-six years old, and as such she was of marrying age. She wanted marriage, she wanted children, but she wanted her career too, she wanted to be an independent woman. And she was ridiculed at work for it: her nickname had been "THE Miss Lee." She was a revolutionary back then. She's more the norm now, like the miniskirt-wearing cigarette smokers.

We walked out of the restaurant. The owner showed us where she picked the young green succulent leaves, which grew in a rocky area behind her restaurant. I picked a clump, nibbled at them, and looked to the hills. Black nets covered small plots of ginseng among the green and in the far distance, where bears, lynx, and amur leopards once roamed, transparent black greenhouse tunnels were just visible. There was so much history in this one place, I thought. However, apart from the mountains, nothing recognizable remained from those times when traders would hunker down over tofu before they went to town to sell, or headed home to start the process all over again. There probably weren't even any photographs—only the stories persisted.

Mrs. Lee dropped me off at the Iksan railway station.

"Don't stop," she said. "It's desert between here and Seoul, nothing but apples. Just keep going."

I didn't need her advice. I had an appointment in Seoul, and a plan.

21

A WORMHOLE IN MYEONGDONG

*She dug out a long octopus tentacle from the soup, put it in her
mouth, and chewed enthusiastically.*

—*Jung Mi-Kyung, "I Love You"*

Myeongdong, the capital's trendiest district. Friday night and
Seoulites swarmed. Teeth glinted, eyes smiled, fashion racks
jostled, and phone case sellers and street food vendors elbowed
each other. Towering buildings tasered the sky a bleeping pink, yellow,
green, and blue. A bubblegum beat thudded, and the air frothed with
tteokbokki, dried squid, and sweet fried cakes, as the spinning top of
another night in Myeongdong whirled into kaleidoscopic gear.

"I told you I'd bring you somewhere old-fashioned," said Jason Kim.
He smiled at the irony. "It's just around the corner. It's about as old
school as it gets in Seoul these days."

Myeongdong was anything but old. It was the epicenter of shopping,
dancing, drinking, posing, and picking up. Jason had flown up from Jeju
Island for work, and we'd arranged to meet for dinner.

Around the corner were more crowds. Koreans coursed like black-capped corpuscles through Myeongdong's mammoth machine. A girl with glittery makeup and dyed-blond hair walked past. She held hands with a tall, slim boy in a black suit and a porkpie hat. They paused at a makeup shop. She checked herself in a mirror and reached for a lipstick while all around them screens twinkled, sellers hassled, and passersby nudged as the night gunned down an electric neon barrel. I felt disorientated and hemmed in.

Jason pointed to an anonymous, narrow alleyway leading out of the night. On the left of this oddly located crack in time loomed a colossal glass-fronted building, while on the right there was a branch of a famous American shoe shop. On the sliver of battered wall that framed the alleyway crack was a garble of stickers, scratches, and scribbled messages. At head height there was a small navy blue plaque and on it, written in white, was the number 37–3.

Lining the alley were electricity meters and wires, and the floor had brown tiles. Orange paint peeled from the walls, fluorescent lights throbbed above. Walking along the length of the alleyway, I felt like a patient on a gurney, being wheeled along a hospital corridor. Alleyway 37–3 was a restorative wormhole out of the dizzying Myeongdong din.

At the end of the twenty-yard-long corridor was a frosted-glass door and upon it were the words 명동할매낙지 (Myeongdong Halmae Nakji). *Nakji* means "octopus," a creature with no skeleton and with the ability to creep into the tiniest of crevices. It looked like this restaurant had done exactly the same thing sometime before I was born. And it had never bothered squeezing itself back out again.

Halmae Nakji first opened in 1950, and entering it was like walking onto the set of a Korean B movie. There had been an attempt to redecorate in the sixties and another in the seventies. After which it appeared that the owners had looked around the place, looked at each other, and said, "Stuff it." They'd added a TV and put some posters up to mark the turn of the century, and then left it at that. It was wonderfully ramshackle.

The only windows in the restaurant opened onto a wall. Myeongdong had built itself around, above, and under Halmae Nakji. The chairs were bendy, basic, dark brown, and covered in PVC. Hite beer posters peeled from the walls, and a yellow plastic menu hung next to the ubiquitous photographs of TV personalities and framed newspaper articles.

The cooking area was right next to the entrance and commanded a view over the restaurant. Three ladies worked in this crevice. The cook, Mrs. Park, had been behind the wok for over twenty years. She found it difficult to talk, as she had a medical problem that made her voice quiet and husky. She looked like a DJ at a frying-pan deck. Under her wheels of steel, and looking like a child's art project, her workspace was covered in grease and chile-spattered newspaper. She told us that the restaurant originally started by serving squid, *ojingo* (오징어), in the fifties and sixties, but nowadays, it was all about octopus.

"We rely upon our regular customers," she said. "A lot of places are not doing so well in this area."

She used a spoon to dip into a pot of minced garlic next to her stove. Alongside that was a bigger pot filled with *gochujang*. A spicy sheen reflected from the pot in the fluorescence, broadcasting the heat of the dish she served: *Nakji bokkeum* (낙지볶음), one of Korea's spiciest dishes.

It is a stir-fried, hot octopus dish. It is believed to have been invented in a tavern in the Mugyo-dong district of Seoul in 1965 by a woman called Park Mu-Sun. In the sixties, Mugyo-dong was the most fashionable area and was also a part of modern-day Myeongdong. *Nakji bokkeum* quickly caught on. Word spread, and a national favorite was born.

A colander of sliced onions and a basin of octopus morsels completed DJ Park's selection for the evening. On the handle of her heavy, deep, frying pan was a bandage. Once upon a time it had been white; it was a muddy gray now.

"You have to cook it on a high heat," she said, shaking the pan. "And quickly, too. That way you keep the octopus tender."

Another woman washed dishes and served. The third woman was very old. I watched as she cleared a table.

"She just comes in now and again to help," said Mrs. Park.

The woman moved slowly across the floor, her back hunched—she must have been ninety years old. She was not related to anyone in the restaurant, and she had something of the air of a helpful ghost about her.

Halmae Nakji was the guts of Seoul, a crumb of the past, a stubborn bloom, a fantastic find. Yet the cook had no interest in nostalgia for the past, even though, in this cubbyhole, it was the past that surrounded her.

"There's nothing lost from modernization in this area of Myeongdong," she said. "Everything is better than before. I can't think of any downsides at all to the changes you see around this part of Seoul."

Mrs. Park added dried anchovies, leeks, and onion, then spooned a mixture of fine and coarse sugar into the pan. In 2014, she told us, a newspaper visited and a journalist ate her stir-fried octopus.

"There were lines out the door," she said, waving a hand toward the entrance. "All the way down that alleyway and out into the shopping area, but the economy is not so good these days. That's why there are no lines now."

She tossed the octopus. A single fluorescent tube on the ceiling lit her face as she cooked. On the wall behind her was a calendar, a patchwork of pinned receipts, and a plastic bag hanging from a nail. A cushion with a flower pattern sat upon the stool where she rested when she wasn't cooking.

"We get all sorts in here," she said. "From our regulars, who then bring their children here and so on. Then there's the blog crowd."

Jason had told me about the "blog crowd." Like everything in Korea, they were ranked and divided into subsets, from very popular to not so popular to wannabes to unknowns. Some Korean bloggers boasted super-star status, but this seemed incongruous with Korea's modernity. Blogs are seen as somewhat old hat in most of the rest of the developed world, but they were highly relevant in Korea. And this digital elite had power.

With a tap of the return key, they could drive a legion of food seekers down hidden alleyways, under the neon blanket of the Korean capital.

"Naver is a big thing in Korea," said Jason, referring to the dominant Korean-language blogging platform. "One mention on there by a well-known blogger, and this place, any place, explodes in popularity."

I'd talked about the food-blogging phenomena with Charles Montgomery, the American professor of Korean literature.

"On the weekend," he said, "you'll see that some restaurants have lines of thirty people out of the door. My friend calls them 'velcro lines' 'cos it's like they're stuck to each other. And that's because a food power-blogger has mentioned them on Naver. The place immediately becomes trendy. The prices immediately go up, and the quality immediately goes down."

The *nakji bokkeum* arrived with side dishes of bean sprouts and radish. We were each given a bowl of rice and a small bowl of fish paste soup. The glossy red octopus came mixed with onions and laid tangled, redolent on a sharing plate. It was tender, as Mrs. Park had promised it would be. A single bite kicked the Korean fire back into me. It was the same fire I'd shared the previous day with Mrs. Lee and with Hyun-Ae in Chuncheon and Soo-Jin in Busan. Only this furnace was a little sweeter and a little hotter. *Nakji bokkeum* is a sensational Korean dish.

"It's amazing," said Jason, "that a place like this can survive, when you look at everything that is going on on the other sides of these walls, out there in Myeongdong."

Jason had a list. It was called the "one hundred best restaurants in Seoul." He found it in a Korean newspaper, and he had been working his way through the list and writing about each place. The list was unofficial, and afforded no protection to the restaurants mentioned on it. Many of the places, Jason said, almost seemed to have a death date stamped upon them and the date read "coming soon."

"You have to hope," said Jason, "that the restaurants on the list won't get messed with, or closed down to build yet another coffee shop, but I wouldn't count on it."

I got the feeling that, if Mrs. Park had the means and the desire, she'd rip Halmae Nakji up and relocate it to the basement food court of a twenty-story shopping mall. And this freak show in a crevice in perfectly manicured Myeongdong would be unceremoniously sealed up by the powers that be and forgotten about. And yet, surely, the vibe of the crevice was the big sell. *Nakji bokkeum* is not that tricky a dish to cook, and the customers came, I'd wager, because of what the place reminded them of, less for what it served.

That a culture can so willfully rip up the past remained anathema to me. It was an alien concept, but it was normal to Koreans. Culture shifted, it wasn't static.

"I've seen firsthand the transformation of people's eating habits during the past ten years in Seoul," said Jason, "particularly with the younger generation. There's been this massive move from Korean to more 'fusionized' dishes that incorporate Western ingredients."

By fawning praise over these more traditional places, I wondered if I wasn't imposing my own fixed view of what Korean food culture should be. Why can't good things change?

"Although I hate to admit it," he said, "traditional Korean food has taken a step back for Koreans, but undoubtedly, and ironically, it has found itself popular with international tourists and chefs."

It was true. Gochujang was a hit in New York. I was reminded of Roy Choi's Korean fusion taco truck and of David Chang's *ramyun*. Later that week in Seoul, I attended a *makgeolli*-making class at Susubori Academy. It was run by foreigners and the participants were all foreigners. Like Mrs. Ma in Haenam had told me, "most Koreans don't care about our traditional songs anymore. Many foreigners care more." It was as if foreigners had latched on to Korean food at a time when Koreans themselves were setting a course toward an entirely different culinary stratosphere.

Just because foreigners like Jason and myself didn't want them to change hardly seemed relevant. Indeed, it was of no relevance at all. Korea was Korean, and that meant it would never, it could never, ever stay the same. From the outside, Koreans had a very peculiar way of forgetting and moving on in almost anything.

"I think Korea wants to forget about their devastating past," said Jason. "They don't want to be reminded of it in some ways, and I think that food is a big part of that."

We walked out of the crevice and back onto the street. The multi-colored flashguns of the Myeongdong night jabbed at us like a thousand paparazzi photographers.

"Most of the places that I have come to love and cherish will be gone," said Jason, "only to be replaced with another damn coffee shop or Western-style eatery."

The peace of Halmae Nakji smashed and splintered back on the streets of Myeongdong as Seoul hit the boost button and stepped back onto the gas for yet another relentless nighttime ride into oblivion. Into the future.

22

WE'RE NOT ALIENS

You can get this food in Chicago," she said, "but you can't get this restaurant."

I was in a *kalbi* restaurant in the Mapo district of Seoul with Jung-wha. As I was leaving Jeollabuk-do to go back to Seoul, Mrs. Lee said to me, "You should meet my daughter in Seoul. I don't think she's really Korean. She's lived abroad too long."

Mrs. Lee's daughter, Jung-wha, had grown up in Korea, but had studied abroad for a long time. She looked around the ground-floor hangar in Mapo. Pork spat from the oil drum–size barbecue tables, shot glasses crashed, *kalbi* grills clanked. Laughter mingled with shouting and sweet soy, sesame, and ginger–infused porcine fumes permeated the air. Mapo Kalbi at nine P.M. on a Saturday was a bacchanalian BBQ bistro bar none.

"The sounds, the smells, the atmosphere . . . ," she said. "You can only get this in Korea."

I'd been introduced to the place by food wrter Joe McPherson. It was a glimpse of the Korea I loved, but it was a glimpse made almost modern. This restaurant, Mapo Jeong Daepo (마포정대포), was gloriously bizarre. It sat among a motley snot-nosed brethren of *kalbi* restaurants in one of

Seoul's many high-tech visions in the district of Mapo, a district that was the face of an advanced Korea. However, the architect behind the design of this district had somehow let the *kalbi* gang carry on. This band of BBQ misfits didn't look like they belonged.

When Marvel Studios came to Korea to scout out locations for their 2015 blockbuster film *The Avengers: Age of Ultron,* it was Mapo they went to. The Korean government paid the filmmakers "close to $2 million" to film there. The hope was that the film would show Seoul in a favorable light, as a sophisticated, high-tech, advanced city.

"Mapo is probably the single best place to try Korean barbecue in Seoul," Joe had told me. "The quality and the variety is all there, and the restaurants have an atmosphere that is lacking in other parts of the city."

Mapo was home to an original Korean barbecue style: unsurprisingly titled *Mapo kalbi* (마포갈비). It was a variation on the traditional marinated pork *kalbi* and a seemingly simple enough twist at that.

In the moat around the grill, instead of the water that was usually there to catch the pork fat, there was scrambled egg to which the waitress suggested we add kimchi. The egg, pork fat, and kimchi all mixed together as the *kalbi* grilled. It was a style of food that had spawned copies in Korea and beyond. There were restaurants in Los Angeles called Mapo Kalbi. It was so popular, it had almost become something of a Korean brand.

The restaurant was particularly well known for *galmaegisal* (갈매기살), a marinated pork skirt-meat grilled at the table. *Galmaegisal* meat is redder than *kalbi,* resembles beef in texture, and is massively popular with Koreans.

Jung-wha and I sat down. Charcoal grumbled all around us under the multitude of shiny, well-worn, heavy-duty metal kalbi grills. A woman banged past us, holding a hot grill with a metal vise in her gloved hand. Another pushed in the opposite direction, carrying a bucket full of hot coals.

"It started twenty years ago," the waitress said, referring to Mapo-style *kalbi*. "I've no idea who it was who first made it, but the style just stayed. People got a taste for it around here."

This joint was in another location for four years before it moved here in 2008. The waitress took some of the meat from a plate and started to cook for us. The flesh tensed upon hitting the hot metal. Twenty years ago, places like this would have been thick with smoke, of both the meat and tobacco variety, but not anymore. Above us, there was a warren of matte-gray pipework. It took a circuitous route around the hangar and intermittent vents whirred as they sucked the greasy exhalations from the restaurant's interior.

Jung-wha was not used to eating in places like this, but she liked it. Outside the most committed food-blogger circles, most Koreans of Jung-wha's generation preferred their restaurants to be like a neat, crisp, fresh-faced, digital selfie and not the much-thumbed, half-torn, faded Polaroid that was Mapo Kalbi.

The waitress told us that the restaurant made its own marinade and its own kimchi. This was clearly a badge of honor, and for good reason. Most restaurants, even respected restaurants in Korea, buy their spices, their marinade, and their kimchi from mass producers or, God forbid, from those electric kimchi purveyors, the Chinese.

"For this kind of *kalbi*," the waitress said, "you need to turn the meat a lot. We shave the meat really thinly and then we lay it on the grill in a way that complements the way we cut it."

She twisted the carcass on our grill with her gloved hands as she talked to us. A toilet paper roll hung from a holder attached to a pillar under two brown, sticky, stained electric sockets. Three straggling sheets of the flimsy paper fluttered under the air vents. A tubby man in a blue shirt put his soju glass down, tore the sheets from the roll, and wiped his face.

"It tastes better if you turn it a lot," said the waitress. "If you keep turning it, you keep the juice. When it's cooked well, it has a shine to it. See?"

I looked closely; Jung-wha bent in, too. The meat glistened like mercury. It seemed to throb with life. However, there was more to Mapo-style *kalbi* than shiny meat and an egg moat.

"You have to dip the meat into bean powder and soy sauce," said the waitress. She took a slice that she had deemed ready for consumption, dabbed it in bean powder, wrapped it in a sesame leaf, then inside a lettuce leaf, and handed it to Jung-wha, who popped the parcel into her mouth. I copied her. This particular combination of sesame leaf, meat, and bean powder was at once new to me and yet resolutely familiar. It was a taste I could have chomped anywhere in the world and yet been instantly transported to a smoky hut somewhere in Seoul. Eating a piece of wrapped, grilled *kalbi* in a place like this was possibly the most quintessential Korean dining experience.

"With traditional *kalbi,* there is no bean powder, only *ssamjang,*" said the waitress, referring to the sauce commonly served with grilled meat and made from *doenjang,* garlic, sesame oil, soy, *gochujang,* and spring onions. "At the weekend we get busy with friends and family gatherings. During the week, like tonight, it's all about office workers and a lot of drinking."

Jung-wha had the confident air of the overseas educated. She was part of a generation at odds with traditional Korea. She had studied abroad since her early twenties—her "gold" and "silver" age, the time the Korean society textbook says a Korean woman should traditionally be looking for a mate. However, she had returned to Korea in her "bronze" age and was still unmarried.

By now, her old friends were all married and on Korea's corporate hamster wheel. That same torpor Jin-Young had described to me in the kimchi restaurant when I was last in Seoul. For the most essential years of a young Korean woman's life, as viewed by Korean society, Jung-wha had been absent. As a result, she had enough distance from her native country to have an objective insider's outside eye. Jung-wha was phase one of my plan to get to the bottom of *han.*

"About this Korean concept," I said, "*han.*"

She looked confused. It was not something she'd heard much about. She turned the *kalbi* and slugged from her Hite beer.

"Hmm . . . ," she said.

She thought very hard, to the point of confusion. I could see her dredging through a long-forgotten file in a cobweb-covered dossier inside a dusty filing cabinet in a redundant part of her brain.

"Do you mean that thing . . . ," she said. She frowned, as if frowning helped her sweep the dust from the memory. "That thing . . . where you kinda feel sad . . . or you feel love for someone . . . or . . . you desire something . . . but . . . you can never ever have it? Do you mean that?"

"I think you're on the right track," I said. I glugged back the weak beer. "Sounds kinda *han*-ish to me."

"And then you want some kind of revenge for that?" she said. "For that . . . feeling . . . Is that what you mean?"

"Well, yeah," I said. "I think so—you tell me. Apparently, all Koreans have it, don't you?"

"Not really," she said. "People don't think about that anymore, and I don't think it's uniquely Korean. Maybe Korean people frame it in a way that they think is unique, but over time I'm sure they'll realize it's not something unique to Korea. It's kind of pathetic to think that only Koreans can think and feel this thing. That's closed-minded."

The restaurant was full now. Men prodded at meat, women served drinks. The restaurant was loud, it was a happy place, people smiled, laughed, shouted, and gossiped. There was a young couple at the next table; the woman grilled for herself and her boyfriend. She wrapped some meat in a sesame leaf and placed it in his mouth.

"I mean, we're all human," she said. "Black, white, yellow. Koreans don't experience uniquely Korean emotions. That's absurd. They're just emotions within a Korean context, they're not unique to us."

The couple looked into each other's wide eyes. They both looked surprised. Surgery had made them appear as if they were watching a twenty-ton bus come screaming toward them. Forever.

"I mean," said Jung-wha, "we're not aliens . . ."

She looked over at the couple and then back at me.

". . . are we?" she finished.

"No," I said. "Of course not. That would also be absurd."

"You know," I said, "there's a theory that *han* is actually Japanese. That it was effectively imposed during colonial times as a kind of pseudo-psychosocial control mechanism to keep the people down, and that when the Japanese left, the Koreans clung to it as their own."

Jung-wha didn't seem at all surprised. She was open-minded to the idea—I liked that.

"Most Koreans don't really know who they are or what is Korean," she said. "They just repeat what they've been told."

Andy, my food-writing friend, was also a martial arts expert. He told me that tae kwon do (태권도) had come in large part from the Japanese. It was an adaptation of the Japanese martial art karate. And that the genuine, homegrown Korean martial art was called *taekkyeon* (택견). *Taekkyeon* had almost died out during the Japanese occupation. The sole surviving master and his lone student were the only practitioners left who knew it. From these two people it had slowly begun to make a resurgence through the eighties and into the nineties. But before that, and even to this day, most Koreans see Japanese-tinged tae kwon do as the most well-known Korean marital art.

Jung-wha clearly enjoyed the food at Mapo Jeong Daepo.

"I'm going to bring my boyfriend here," she said. "He'll really like it. It's a wonderful place."

I wondered if Jung-wha knew much about food.

"Can you cook?" I asked.

"No," she said. "I'm really spoiled. My mother sends me food nearly every week. She freezes it and I eat that during the week, or I go out to eat."

Mapo Jeong Daepo heaved and there was a line forming outside. We got up to leave. I paid at reception and we each took a chewing gum from the basket at the entrance and walked out toward the Mapo station. It was surrounded by towering, modern, dark-gray office buildings. The tops blasted out the names of Korean companies in neon Hangul. The large intersection in between felt staked out, as if it were ready for some grand battle.

"Our generation is very different," said Jung-wha. "We have a different attitude to almost everything. There are a lot of young people opening up these small, intimate places to eat and drink now."

We talked about Bar Sanchez. Jung-wha knew several other places like it.

"These are the people who can afford to fail," she said. "But they don't mind failing, and this is very new in Korea. Failing, or the possibility of it, might one day become, maybe not desirable, but accepted."

I imagined the next big, most unlikely hit band in Korea: they were called The K-pop Rejects and were made up exclusively of losers, bums, and unstyled failures.

Jung-wha's was a sentiment I found heartening to hear. We said good night. Jung-wha got into a taxi and I decided to walk. Transparent garbage bags lay stacked next to the bus station entrance, a neon crucifix burned the sky high in the distance, and yellow taxis whizzed by in packs. Down silent alleyways, bicycles and motorbikes dozed among empty soju crates. Some offices were still lit up with white, yellow, and orange lights. As sleep began to suffocate the city, I recalled a similar conversation that I had had with Charles, the Korean literature professor.

"The generation that I'm teaching at the moment are international," he said. "I don't know if it'll happen or not, but they tell me that they're not gonna do what their parents did. They say, 'I'm not gonna force my daughter to take piano, send them to the private school in the evening, or force my boy to take tae kwon do.' Who knows? It's easy to say those things when you're young. But just look what happened to the hippies."

23

LIKE MOM'S FOOD

I magine a rag soaked in juice from a colossal vat of kimchi, and imagine that juice was magic. Imagine ringing out that rag on a patch of concrete down a pokey alleyway in Seoul. And then, imagine the restaurant that might grow, "Jack and the Beanstalk"–like, on that very spot. What would it look like? Gwanghwamun Jjib (광화문집), in the central Seoul district of the same name, might be your answer.

It was located off the people-filled main street in Gwanghwamun and down a narrow alley hidden in among the surrounding squash. Outside the brown front door, it was a mess: an empty crate of soju, stools, old buckets, trash bags, slabs of wood, and brown plastic vats of kimchi. The owners, you would have thought, could have made an effort to make the place look more inviting, but hadn't. And I was glad they hadn't—this looked like a stupendous find.

I stepped into the nook. There were just five tables downstairs and a cramped nest upstairs. Prepared pans of *kimchi-jjigae* waited upon old newspapers on a set of tatty, blue wooden shelves. The open kitchen was next to the shelves at one end of the small room. An *ajumma* greeted me as she wiped down her work surface.

I sat at a corner table. The air trembled with a sour syrup of vinegar, garlic, and *gochujang*. The tabletop was scratched to the bone with what looked like the panicked nail marks of someone who'd awoken to find himself alive inside a coffin. A fan whirred above the front door; flowery gold-and-beige wallpaper bubbled up the walls. Breaks in the paper were fixed with thick brown adhesive tape that looked like Band-Aids on an ancient patient. This was the most unlikely of gastronomic dens to find in central Seoul, and I immediately felt at home.

"What do you want?" asked the *ajumma*. "*Kimchi-jjigae* and omelet?" She didn't wait for an answer.

"It's what everyone has," she said with the confidence of a doctor who had just diagnosed a patient, and she walked away. She was the head chef at this plastered-together shack. Such utter confidence—some might interpret it as arrogance—is a mark of the utmost quality in a Korean restaurant, because they do know better than you what you need.

A black cast-iron burner sat upon the table, attached via a thick hose to the gas supply. The wallpaper had discolored above the burner. I noticed it was the same at all the tables, and the effect was like a tide-mark that rippled all the way around the tiny shack, under the requisite calendar, clock, and framed photos of celebrity visitors.

The *ajumma* came back with a pan from one of the blue shelves and placed it on the burner. I peeked under the lid: inside were chunks of pork, sliced onions, kimchi, and islands of tofu that looked like sponges floating in a red sea. She turned the gas on and lit the stove. Another *ajumma*, the sous *ajumma*, arrived with the appetizers: an omelet, rice, and side dishes of bean sprouts, radishes, greens, and kimchi.

"So simple, but it's so good," said the sous *ajumma* about the omelet. "Nothing but good eggs, salt, and spring onion."

Five women in total worked in this restaurant. They looked like a five-a-side soccer team in matching uniforms. The head chef toted a Burberry purse and wore a pair of blue plastic shoes. She sat down to talk as I nibbled at the omelet and waited for the *kimchi-jjigae* to cook.

"Years ago," she said, "we had ten menu items, but not anymore."

She had been working here for twenty years, although the restaurant had been open for over thirty, was in her sixties, and lived with her family forty minutes away by subway.

"We used to cook octopus and all sorts here," she said. "But it got to be too much work because we got too popular, so we reduced the number of items on the menu to what we have today."

Two young women entered the restaurant and took the table in front of me. They didn't order, either—the food just arrived, the same as mine had.

"I make all the kimchi myself," said the *ajumma*. "I don't use any salted shrimps in the preparation and I leave it to ferment for a minimum of six months."

The two young women took out their cameras and started snapping. I was surprised at how young they were, because Gwanghwamun Jjib did not strike me a young person's kind of restaurant.

"Oh, I'd say nine out of ten are the younger crowd," said the head chef *ajumma*. "Mostly students and young office workers. We get a lot of food enthusiasts. My grandson tells me there are people who write about this place on the Internet. He showed me some photos once."

I took the lid off the luminous, brilliant *kimchi-jjigae* in front of me. The broth toiled like a salaryman on a treadmill, working off a particularly tough berating from his boss. I spooned some upon my rice, and with each mouthful, comforting flames of vinegar licked at my insides.

Thomas Carlyle, the Scottish historian, said, "Music is well said to be the speech of angels; in fact, nothing among the utterances allowed to man is felt to be so divine. It brings us near to the infinite."

It was a notion with which I agreed. However, in Seoul, it was the sheds like Gwanghwamun Jjib that competed with the angels who worked the same beat. And these deities came with dyed-black perms, not harps or hymn sheets, and they were hellbent on connecting us with the infinite via their cooking. At Gwanghwamun Jjib, they had succeeded. Great *kimchi-jjigae,* as this was, is like a twinkling arrow to the taste buds. It hits you dead straight, stops you in your tracks, and instantly makes you a believer. I greedily gobbled my way through their boiling red sermon.

A trader passed the restaurant as I ate and shouted out the price of his goods. Heard through the door, his voice was almost lost to me in the crowded jelly of echoes that rattled along the passageway outside. The *ajumma* checked with one of the other chefs.

"Did he just say 5,000 won?" she asked. That was a little less than five dollars.

She got up and shouted into the alleyway, and the trader, who must have been the same age as these old women, entered the restaurant. He had a large sack of onions, packed tight against their mesh sacking.

"How much did you say?" asked the *ajumma.*

"Five thousand won for twenty kilos," he said.

"Okay," she replied. "Put them at the back of the kitchen over there. We're not strong enough to carry them."

She handed over the money, and now she had onions enough for the rest of the week.

I'd always thought of *kimchi-jjigae* as a test for non-Koreans in Korea, something of a third hurdle. The first hurdle was the difficulty of using shiny, slippy, metal chopsticks. The second hurdle was kimchi. *Kimchi-jjigae* was that bigger leap, the third hurdle. At first it seemed an impossibly high jump.

It was a Canadian who had first pushed me to try *kimchi-jjigae.* He'd lived in Seoul for two years before I arrived, and had fallen deeply for the dish. At that time, I couldn't imagine anything worse to eat than a stew made of rancid Korean cabbage. One night and less than one month after first moving to Korea, I took the plunge in a one-room shed near my apartment in Iksan. It came on a gas burner in a cheap metal pot with a bowl of rice. It looked just like what sat in front of me at Gwanghwamun Jjib. Eating *kimchi-jjigae* that first time was like gobbling down a grenade full of bees. I'd been stung, but I was hooked on the pain, and as a result, I was hooked on Korea—I was a believer.

By the time I left Gwanghwamun Jjib, the place was full of smartly dressed Koreans. And just as the head chef had told me, they were all young. For those who were not as fortunate as Jung-wha to receive packages of food from their mother in the mail, this restaurant was a good substitute.

"It's like their mom's food," said the head chef. "That's why they all come here."

24

THE PYONGYANG CONNECTION

The skinny girl sitting at the table next to me was staring into her phone. She had a mocha iced coffee and three doughnuts, which she chomped at like an enthusiastic pet. There is a theory that eating with your mouth open keeps the body cool. There was a case to be made for open-mouth eating during a *kimchi-jjigae* blowout, but not, I would argue, while hogging down three sugar-coated American-style doughnuts in an air-conditioned Dunkin' Donuts.

I was in a Dunkin' Donuts in the City Hall district of Seoul because I couldn't go to North Korea. I wasn't allowed in. For a year before this trip I had been living in Senegal, and unfortunately, the West African nation had recorded a single case of Ebola. A man from Guinea had caught it in his own country and brought it to Dakar, where I had lived. He'd been quickly quarantined and eventually recovered and returned home. That was almost six months before I arrived in Seoul and no new Ebola cases had been reported in Senegal since. However, North Korea had banned entry to anyone coming from an Ebola-infected country. That one case barred me from Pyongyang, and that's how I ended up in Dunkin' Donuts, that scion of Western capitalism, to meet a bit of North Korea in South Korea.

Mr. Choi arrived, and as we talked, a waitress wiped our table like she was swabbing the deck of a boat. Over the years, I'd been told many a time that North Korean women were the most beautiful and that South Korean men were the most handsome. Mr. Choi was neither ugly nor overly handsome. He had thick, black eyebrows, an open smile, and thinning hair. Loose strands of it fluttered under the air conditioning like tree branches against a winter's sky. He had escaped from North Korea in 1999.

"There is nothing to compare to life in North Korea," he said. "It is a hell."

We ordered coffees. I took a double espresso and Mr. Choi ordered what the girl with the open mouth was having.

"Living there," he said, "you don't know any different. There is no information about the outside world—you only get what you are told. You have no way of really knowing anything, so you believe everything."

Mr. Choi grew up in a coastal town in the province of South Hwang-hae, a part of North Korea that is very close to a number of South Korean islands.

"You know Yeonpyeong?" he said. "It's the island the North Koreans bombed. Where I come from is the frontier of that conflict." Yeonpyeong Island is part of South Korea. During a border skirmish in 2010, the North Koreans bombarded it, killing four South Koreans and injuring nineteen.

Getting information into and out of North Korea is notoriously difficult, and it was no different for Mr. Choi. "I heard that my sister had gotten married," he said, "and that my father had died, but apart from that, I've had no news of my family."

After he escaped to China, he went to the German Embassy and subsequently gained asylum in South Korea.

"You cannot imagine what life is like in North Korea," he said. "It is unimaginable to anyone who hasn't lived it."

He worked at a human rights organization in Seoul and was learning English through an organization funded by the U.S. government. He was also writing his life story and looking for a publisher.

"I visited Cambodia once," he said. "Compared to life in Cambodia, the facilities in North Korea are better. However, education and society are far, far worse in North Korea."

Vivian Han was extremely proud of her North Korean heritage and of the food. It was, she had told me, more refined, cleaner, and purer. I was keen to hear Mr. Choi's take on his food, the food he grew up with, his version of the South Korean mom's food I had recently eaten inside Gwanghwamun Jjib.

"It's hard to explain the difference between the food in North Korea and South Korea," he said. "Take my favorite food, the one I miss the most, *naengmyeon*. It's a simple cold soup with noodles, but once you've tasted it in Pyongyang, you can appreciate the difference and the quality. After you've tasted it there, it can never be the same anywhere else."

He went on to tell me that there are two different styles of *naengmyeon* and that the flavor varies depending on which city you eat it in. Hamhung, North Korea's second largest city in the east of the country, has quite a different style of *naengmyeon* from Pyongyang in the west. The noodles are chewier than those in Pyongyang, as they're made from sweet potato and not from buckwheat as they are in Pyongyang. In addition, the soup tastes stronger in Hamhung, according to Mr. Choi, although it was the Pyongyang taste he preferred.

North Korea is more mountainous than the south, has a harsher climate and less arable land, and rice is difficult to grow. As a result, the north came to rely upon buckwheat and potatoes for its starch intake. More potato and buckwheat noodles are consumed in North Korea than rice.

By now we had finished our coffees and walked outside. We stood at a crossroads waiting for the lights to change. It's easy to feel small and lost in Seoul, especially in City Hall, hemmed in by concrete, glass, and flashing lights. I figured Mr. Choi must have a bolthole, a secret spot in the south, somewhere he could go to relive the north. Regardless of where we come from, we all need that when we've been abroad for a long time. A taste of the mother's teat suckled from afar.

"You must miss the food from home," I said. "Is there anywhere in Seoul that you go when you want a taste of home?"

"I go to Pyongyang Myon Ok [평양면옥]," he said. "There is another place that people like, but I prefer the taste at Pyongyang Myon Ok. It's in Dongdaemun, near the spaceship."

He could see that I did not understand what he meant. Korea was not known for space travel, beyond Yi So-yeon, the Korean astronaut who took kimchi into space with her.

"What spaceship?" I asked.

"You'll know it when you see it," he said. "Just go to Dongdaemun, you can't miss it, and Pyongyang Myon Ok is on the same road."

An electronic bird chirped as the lights changed at the pedestrian crossing. It was the signal for us to cross. Sun washed down in sheets between the skyscrapers, violent swirls of dust glittered, women in work suits trotted, men marched, a few faces hinted at a salty madness within; eyes like fish in a desert, they urged the workday to end and the first drink to begin.

Halfway across the road, I remembered my quest to find out about *han*. If *han* was a feeling that all Koreans knew, what was the North Korean take on it? On the other side of the road, the bird stopped chirping and we came to a halt at a cheeseburger stall on the sidewalk. Wan burgers limped across the griddle.

"People are very sensitive in South Korea," he said. "Society has developed, but people don't know how to express themselves freely."

A mother and daughter approached the stall. They had their arms linked and had matching eyes. One face wore memories, the other was as white as steamed rice.

"Especially women from the older generation," he said, noticing the two women. "They've learned to do this, to hide their feelings. Until finally, one day, they explode."

The mother and daughter ordered from the burger stall. I imagined them exploding right there and then, like a pair of live shrimp out of the sea, twitching angrily at each other on a patch of sidewalk in downtown Seoul.

"If Koreans could only learn how to express themselves properly," he said, "there wouldn't be so much stress."

I found it ironic that it was someone from North Korea, a nation not exactly known for freedom of expression, who was advising South Koreans to free their minds and, for sure, their asses would follow.

"You know," he said, "I see Italian soccer players who cry very openly when they lose or when they win. We can't do that in Korea."

"So, *han* exists in North Korea?" I said. "It's a feeling people have?"

"I'm not sure," he said. "Because when I was there I never learned about that. I've never felt any kind of *han*. I only heard about it when I moved here."

Had *han* been replaced by common garden-variety stress? The statistics suggested that this might be the case. Look at the results of almost any global stress survey and Koreans come out as the most stressed people on Earth. At the same time, pretty much any happiness survey finds Korea at the bottom or close to it.

Dongdaemun Design Plaza looked foil-wrapped. It is an all-in-one art gallery, museum, conference, and exhibition center. It was the spaceship Mr. Choi had told me about. This part of Seoul was a confusion of neon and silver, like something from the opening scene of *Blade Runner*. In comparison, Myeongdong looked old-fashioned. I half expected to see Harrison Ford zooming overhead in one of Philip K. Dick's spinners.

Fluorescent lights dripped like cotton balls on a wall of neon stars at the Maxtyle fashion mall. At a crossroads, a series of elephantine TV screens beamed the plaza with a glacial brilliance that illuminated the darkness. Behind them, atop a building, was a gleaming hotel sign that read K-POP RESIDENCE. Farther along the road was a church covered in ivy, which looked like a fuzzy error in Seoul's matrix. And there, between a car dealer and a coffee shop, was Pyongyang Myon Ok.

There was a menu on the wall at the entrance to the restaurant, but my attention was distracted by the parking garage. It was black and in the shape of a tower and it rose high into the sky. I watched as a chauffeur-driven blacked-out Porsche pulled up and the garage door into the tower opened. Inside, there was a double elevator shaft. A parking attendant drove the car inside, walked out of the tower, and pressed a button on the wall. The doors closed, the tower spewed out a ticket, and the car zoomed up the tower. It was a novel solution to the lack of parking in this overpopulated, traffic-packed city.

The staff inside Pyongyang Myon Ok wore red aprons. I walked across the wooden floor, scraped white by years of chairs being moved over it. One wall was mock brick. I remembered a story I had heard of a foreign filmmaker who had visited Seoul and refused to film in any restaurants with a mock brick wall, as it was "not authentic enough." I sympathized with the filmmaker, but the truth was that mock bricks were more common, even more authentic, than real bricks in the Korean restaurants of today.

Pyongyang Myon Ok had a large kitchen. I could see the six cooks working behind the aluminum-framed windows separating the restaurant from the kitchen soups. Vats steamed like an iron foundry while ten waitresses buzzed between the serving hatch and the packed restaurant. One man stood with his arms folded, the floor manager. He had perfect skin and wore a white shirt. His hair was stroked and glued down. He looked absolutely immaculate, like a finalist in a hairdresser's exam.

Pots and jars of vinegar, *gochujang*, chile powder, and ground pepper sat upon my table. There was a framed menu upon the wall and a newspaper article featuring the owner, Kim Dae Sung, who opened the restaurant in 1984. The metal-framed Formica tables each had numbered blue badges on them. My waiter arrived, a young man with dyed-light-brown, permed hair. He looked like he could have been one of the K-pop rejects. Maybe I should have started recruiting right there and then. There always seemed to be a lone young male working in these popular, traditional Korean restaurants. The rest of the staff were always women in their fifties and sixties. The young men, like this one, invariably wore a hunted look. He took my order, and within minutes, my food arrived.

Like the other cold noodle gruels I had eaten, my *naengmyeon* inhabited a metal bowl. A moat of thin, transparent soup surrounded the noodle castle, which was topped with half a boiled egg, a slice of boiled fatty pork, and a slice of boiled beef. Below were pickled strips of radish and cucumber. My *naengmyeon* looked like a Pyongyang skyline: gray, poor, humble, and full of unspoken grievances. This bowl of noodles had taken an extraordinary journey to get here, a history conjured out of a horrific magic hat. The truth was, Pyongyang Myon Ok was staffed by North Koreans in exile: defectors, escapees, those with families sliced in two by war. Pyongyang Myon Ok was a trumpet in the twilight, a connection, like the thin thread of a string telephone back to that impossible place, Pyongyang, 120 miles to the north. I took a taste.

It was super-clean, pure, cold, deep. I felt a song coming on, a psychedelic number written by the K-pop rejects. Each spoonful caressed my mouth with incandescent star shells filled with painted pepper candles. This soup was clearly the product of a deliciously troubled vinegar mind. I added some mustard to my bowl, stirred, and tasted again. More cooling star shells—this soup was astounding, how could I have never warmed to this all those years ago?

I looked around the restaurant. Diners burbled like a choppy chattering sea, mouths sipped at metal tumblers of hot stock, some eschewed the most popular dish and went for bulgogi. After all, *naengmyeon,* like *makguksu,* is summer food. The blotchy hands of the elderly man next to me tapped inside his bowl.

As I succumbed to the fantasy lick of this alien soup, the psychedelic song came back to me. I glanced over at the kitchen, the haze of steam seemed to throb like a peacock's vibrating feathers. I thought I could see empires gleam, skies condense, a time stair, moons burning silver, a nightshade colony of plague owls, was that a sitar I could hear? *Pop.* Another star shell. They say that if you have one too many, you may turn, and at that moment I think I did. It had taken me twenty years to come around to it, but this *naengmyeon,* in this place, had turned me. Finally, I was a cold-noodle-soup convert. I gobbled down the rest of the bowl like a raging dog, and in a glorious fit, I texted Vivian Han.

"I'm at Pyongyang Myon Ok. It's amazing."

She replied at once.

"Oh, that's my favorite naengmyeon!! That's what we North Koreans call soul food."

These cold, vinegary noodles were her equivalent of my bacon and eggs. Unbelievable, when you think about it, how we humans tune in to vastly differing frequencies when hunting down our soul food. I was starting to think I was wrong about *han*. The Koreans who came up with this soup were clearly operating on an entirely different vibration than the rest of us.

Vivian had told me that hundreds of years ago, Pyongyang was the richest part of Korea. And that it was very open to food trends from China and other places. Many North Korean dumplings, noodles, and soups had been introduced at that time and they had heavily influenced native Korean cooking, whereas in South Korea, even as recently as the 1950s, many Koreans had never heard of dumplings. *Manduu*-style dumplings, of course, were now common all over South Korea, but back then, the food simply had not traveled that far south. The influences that arrived in the south a little over half a century ago were from the somewhat more culinarily challenged American soldiers with their Spam, hot dogs, and baked beans.

As I slurped my last, I sat back, satiated. The manager came over. I was the only foreigner in the restaurant.

"Did you like it?" he asked.

He could see that I did.

"What makes it so good?" I asked.

"I'm not sure," he said. "Our food is simple, which appeals to some people more than others. Some people like it so much that they come regularly."

"But there's nothing special that you do?" I said.

"We just cook it the traditional way," he said. "We use a machine to turn the *maemil* [buckwheat] into powder. Everything is just done the traditional way. So, no, nothing so special, really."

"I've been told," I said, "that North Korean food is more refined than the food in the south."

"I'm not sure if it's more refined or more flavorful," he said. "But there is this subtle aspect to it where people get addicted to it and they get addicted quickly."

It was as if he could read my frazzled mind, as he was describing me. I'd heard that a lot of restaurants in China had been shut down because they were found to be putting opium poppies into their food. I suppose it was one way to keep the customers coming back for more. However, I didn't think that was the case here. I told the manager about my journey around the country, the things I'd eaten and the changes I'd seen. I wanted to know if he thought Korean tastes were changing.

"I don't know about that," he said. "But people like our *naengmyeon*."

I got the sense that not only had he never thought about it, but he didn't really care. That he, too, was riding this Korean wave of never-ending change and that the wave would break wherever it broke. And so be it when it did. It was all rather Zen—did I hear another sitar?

I paid my bill at the entrance. Twenty or more transparent plastic sacks of whole white radishes were bundled next to the bathroom. There was a framed painting on thin paper of a tiger. Tigers were a symbol of good luck and strength in Korea. Amur Tigers, the largest cats on the planet, were thought to live in the uninhabited, undeveloped, demilitarized zone between North and South Korea. But no one could go there, so no one knew for sure if they lived there.

I walked outside as a Mercedes came out of the towering tin-can parking garage and a BMW went in. Two different makes of car, both designed and built in Germany, a country once divided, east and west, but now unified. A similar result for the two Koreas seemed a distant dream.

While the south says reunification is desirable, they admit it would be costly. South Korea's Financial Services Commission estimated that reunification would cost $500 billion. Analysts reckoned this was crazily optimistic and put the potential cost as high as $5 trillion over two decades. More than cost, I couldn't see how the two countries could ever get along together.

The physical, mental, emotional, cultural, even linguistic barriers seemed almost insurmountable. Yet there was this food, this great, great food, and I saw hope in the food. After eating my South Korean version of a North Korean *naengmyeon,* part of me wondered if reunification wouldn't be worth it. Especially if it meant South Koreans could tootle up to Pyongyang for an evening to get a taste of real *naengmyeon* in the place where it was born. That, I thought, might just be worth tearing down the DMZ and stumping up $5 trillion for.

25

AN ALLEYWAY IN SEOUL

I don't really like soju," I said.

"No one does," said Jason.

What an obvious and true statement. Drink enough of the stuff, and you grow an unnatural desire for more. This is not good and must be resisted. Any level-headed taster will tell you that your bog standard, off-the-corner-shop-shelf soju should never, ever be drunk, but we all do it. Why? It's the Korean-ness of it that I liked, not the taste. I could never imagine drinking regular soju anywhere but in Korea.

"This is the only way to drink it," said Jason.

We were sitting at an alleyway stall in the Jongno district of Seoul. It was run by two grandmothers who served simple seafood dishes from a shed they had built out of prefabricated pieces. In another life, this shack would not have looked out of place on a building site. The name of the shed, Byukdam Pocha (벽담 포차), described the wall and the brick that the shack itself was made of.

"So-maek [소맥]," said Jason. It was another one of those handy Korean portmanteau words, a marriage of soju (소주) and maekju (맥주), beer.

Jason poured a soju shot into half a glass of beer and whacked the glass with metal chopsticks. Inside the glass it looked as if an aspirin was dissolving.

"The beer dilutes the taste of soju," said Jason.

It's still there, of course. Soju won't just go away on its own. It's evil that way, but at least when you drink it in this manner, it quietly mutters to itself in a small echoey padded room and doesn't come at you in its more customary banjo-playing, chainsaw-wielding Frankenstein fashion.

A minimal menu was stuck to the wall of Byukdam Pocha with heavy-duty duct tape. One of the grannies came over. Jason knew them well, as he was a regular here whenever he visited Seoul.

"She never disappoints us," he said. "She's got this amazing mom's-cooking touch to each dish."

"What is it that you want today?" asked the sixty-year-old cook.

She wore a checked shirt, a red apron, and a ready smile, while her voice was of tobacco gravel. We ordered a spicy baby octopus dish called *jjukkumi bokkeum* (쭈꾸미 볶음).

"You'll need bean sprouts with it," she said. "After the spice, they will help you to cool down."

The two grannies had worked this place for over twenty years.

"We get office workers in their thirties, forties, and fifties," said the gravel-voiced granny, as a call came in to arrange takeout for a nearby office. After the call, she came back with a tray of tofu, radish, seaweed, kimchi, greens, and *gochujang*.

"Our space is government owned," she said. "We rent it."

The two friends had put down a $5,000 deposit to secure the spot and paid $150 per month in rent. In an area of Seoul where land prices were astronomical, this sounded like a good deal. However, they lived outside of central Seoul.

"I live over that way," she said with the wave of a hand that could have meant pretty much anywhere in Korea.

She told us that she was born in Chungnam, to the south of Seoul in South Chungcheong province. It was a region I had been told was desert. She started "pick-up" work in the construction industry when she first moved to Seoul in the eighties.

"Cooking was just something I could do," she said. "I'm not a particularly good cook. I just cook the way I was taught. We buy seasonal food from the market and do what we know best with it."

It was Gwangjang market she went to. I'd eaten *pajeon* there several weeks earlier with an American photographer, and he'd asked me if I had any worries about communicating on my trip, a fear that, mostly by chance, had turned out to be largely unfounded.

"We go there every single day," she said. "We don't buy any frozen food."

The baby octopus arrived.

"Extra eggs for you," she said. "Look, can you see how many there are?"

"Is it imported?" I asked.

A look of horror and disappointment fell over her face. I felt I had perhaps unduly shaken her *han*.

"This is a Korean octopus," she said. "If it was imported octopus, it wouldn't have so many eggs."

I made a note to myself: *Check to see whether female Korean octopus is more fertile than foreign octopus.*

The cooling bean sprouts were cooked into the dish and were soft. She added *gochujang*, red pepper powder, and young green peppers—Korea's spiciest peppers—chile, and onions, and placed a bowl of *odeng guk*, fish paste soup, on the plastic table next to the main event.

When we told the granny where we'd eaten octopus recently, the *nakji bokkeum* in Myeongdong, she nodded in approval.

"That's a good place," she said as she placed a comforting toilet paper roll on the table for us to share. "They've been on the job even longer than us."

The octopus lay hacked to pieces in a red pan. I took a bite. It was like gnawing through deep-sea butter. The tentacles swam inside a chile-driven turboprop sauce, a sauce bent on powering our taste buds into a seafood rainbow consisting only of shades of fiery red.

These two grandmothers were the living embodiment of everything that was good about the Korean dining experience: shed + pavement + good, fresh food + cheap, crappy booze = good times.

It was a simple equation, and it was what I'd come back to Korea to taste. But what connection, if any, did the grandmothers feel to what they produced?

"Korean food to me is survival," said the granny I'd been talking to. "This is how I make a living, and I'm lucky to have regular customers who enjoy my food. It took me a long time to make the dishes as good as they are today. It was by trial and error, and I know I'm lucky to have been in business for so long."

More customers arrived. They filled the remaining tables along the alley and the grandmother scuttled off to tend to them. I turned to Jason.

"I think you're right," I said. "These places don't stand a chance."

"Korea prides itself on its image," said Jason. "And I think traditional Korean food will reinvent itself with that in mind. It will evolve into something more presentable, palatable, and, more important, exportable. Much like the rapid transformation of Seoul into a modern, sophisticated, and trendy city."

Modern Jongno craned down upon us, seeming to dwarf the shed like an angry bully. Jason told me he thought these traditional dishes would soon be refined and modernized by younger chefs. Cooks who had less of a connection to Korea's past.

It was here, sitting on one of the grandmother's plastic stools, in that alleyway, surrounded by golden skyscrapers, that I felt more connected to Korea than anywhere else on this journey. I'd been plugged back into the mains. Perhaps these alleyway places felt more alive because they were closer to death.

Jason had a dream. A half-hatched plan.

"So many of these places are disappearing," he said. "It spurs me on to want to open my own restaurant in the future. To honor the foods and the establishments that have already disappeared. I really feel it's my calling."

LONG DESERTED, THE DREAMS

*I lifted my bowl to my mouth. When I had finished emptying it,
I could see him holding his bowl to his mouth and drinking with
his eyes closed. I thought to myself with some feeling of regret
that the time had come for me to get up and go.*
—Kim Sung-Ok, "Seoul: 1964, Winter"

I entered the restaurant in Jongno. There were four round tables on a bare concrete floor and only one of the tables was full. A group of salarymen in white shirts and dark ties occupied it. They smiled at one another, drank soju, and ate grilled pork belly wrapped in lettuce and sesame leaves. I took a blue plastic stool and sat down at an empty table. My dining companions were running late.

Dong Dong Sot Bul Gui (통통숯불구이) was a *samgyeopsal* restaurant. It was the sort of restaurant that was a bruise on Seoul's surgically enhanced skin. It was more garage than restaurant, a bit like an obsessive's den of engine parts, electronics, and dirty rags with a Krautrock sampler playing on repeat. However, the engine parts in this restaurant were porcine, and in place of engine oil, there was soju; in place of Kraftwerk, there was shouting, laughter, and TV.

The air hung damp with burnt pig, bean paste, and the crackle of alcohol. Fat from the thick cuts of pork belly popped and snapped. I looked over at the salarymen; they looked a little younger than me. Tomorrow, before dawn, they'd be in their suits, at the subway, hungover, reeking, commuting through the concrete vinegar to their office jobs. Their days as I imagined them were a kind of death to me; total obedience to the boss for life, married to the company first and the wife second. As I watched them eat and clash glasses, I remembered something Mark had told me in Iksan.

"If I were a Korean man," he said, "I would've killed myself by now."

It was an extreme sentiment, but one I could understand, if not entirely agree with. I both admired and felt sorry for these salarymen. It seemed to me that at every juncture in their lives, the system had them by the balls.

Andy arrived. I'd told him I wanted my last night to be like the old days. Hence, we agreed to meet at this tiny, anonymous den.

"Look at these old dears," said Andy. "I doubt they'll be around the next time you're in these parts."

One of the two *ajumma*s waddled over. She looked like she could handle herself with a crowbar, a set of wrenches, and a problem with a gas burner. She fired up the tabletop grill and it whooshed to life. The other *ajumma* rustled among a car crash of pots, pans, bowls, dishes, crates, and bottles and somehow put together a tray of pork, sesame leaves, lettuce, dips, garlic, chile, kimchi, bean paste, *doenjang,* and rice.

Andy was still pondering the age of our cooks.

"There's an extraordinary victim mentality here," he said. "For anyone under the age of forty, like those guys over there, there's nothing to complain about. Unlike these two women, most Koreans did not grow up in poverty. There should be a difference between the generations by now."

Andy was, of course, referring to the monsoon-size grievances many Koreans clung to.

"There's still this sense that 'we are the most unfortunate generation,'" he said. "This feeling that Korea is one of the most grossly victimized nations in history and that everything bad is everything from 'the other.'"

I looked over at the salarymen. As hard as their lives must be, it was a struggle to believe they had it tougher than their parents had. But then there they were, ensconced in a little pocket of Korean heaven, inhaling pork and snorting alcohol. I couldn't think of anything to complain about at that moment, and I'm sure they couldn't, either.

A serving of *samgyeopsal* is like a board game of repetitive moves. Grab leaf, insert meat and bean paste, wrap, dip, eat, drink. Now it's your move. And like any board game, the competitor's eyes are mostly fixed on the moves made by others. Who is turning what meat, which pieces are ready, which look most delicious, do we need to ask for more lettuce, sesame leaves, garlic, soju?

One of the *ajumma*s, Mrs. Kim Young-boon, came over to refill our lettuce and sesame leaves. She told us she was originally from Kyunggi-do in Deokso, a place a little to the east of Seoul. She had opened this grill shed in the midnineties. She was wonderfully dismissive when I suggested that Korean tastes were changing.

"I don't really think about that," she said. "I just keep doing my job and work hard. I feel good when people eat my food, that's all. I don't think Korean tastes are changing. So far as I can tell from my customers, they're not changing, anyway. Nothing has changed, but you foreigners really like Korean food these days, and I'm happy to see that."

She took a pair of chopsticks and turned our meat. She didn't have to, but I think she just had to feel like she was doing something as she stood and talked to us.

"There's nothing particularly special you need to do to make a good *samgyeopsal*," she said. "But I do have a lot of experience in picking the right meat. I usually check around at different meat suppliers and choose quality meat. Touching it and looking at its color are the best ways to see its quality."

"I've long been told that *samgyeopsal* and soju is a marriage," I said. "Why is that?"

She smiled and a look of pity came over her face, as if she thought I was utterly clueless.

"Of course it's a marriage," she said. "We don't even have to think about it. It's just a natural thing for most Koreans. I guess that, since it's kind of a greasy, oily food, the soju washes down that oil perfectly. For me, though, when I see people enjoying my food, and drinking, it makes everything worthwhile."

A Dutch journalist named Anouk joined us. She'd been adopted from Korea at birth in the 1970s and had grown up in Holland. She was writing a book about locating her birth parents in Korea and had contacted Andy to help her. Unfortunately, she was vegetarian and she picked forlornly at a *doenjang-guk* and some rice. She'd picked up on our conversation. I'd been telling Andy about the differing opinions I'd heard about *han*.

"What's *han*?" she asked.

I was curious that she didn't know what it was. However, she didn't speak Korean, nor could she read Hangul, and she knew very little about Korean culture and history. Andy explained the concept of *han* as briefly as he could.

"No," she said. "I've never heard of that."

"But," I said, "do you feel it?"

"Not at all," she said. She seemed confused. That an entire race, her race, should feel this thing that she could not feel. I could see her searching for a connection to her Korean-ness. I wondered if I hadn't implanted in her an additional sense of loss to accompany the one from her childhood.

"Although," she said, "I have noticed how Korean people are always bumping into each other like they somehow lack coordination. I'm like that, too, I do it all the time. Maybe there's a connection there?"

Andy looked unimpressed, and I think I did, too, but I felt something approaching relief at her lack of empathy with *han*.

"This concept that Korean culture is imprinted into your DNA," said Andy, "it's just baloney. It's romanticized. Especially by Koreans in the diaspora, many of whom can't even speak Korean. And they have this kind of handed-down romantic view of Koreans and Korean culture that has nothing to do with Korea today. There is no *han* in today's generation. Those who want to find out, they go and find out, but most don't know anything about it."

The remains of the pork whispered on the grill like autumn leaves. The *ajumma* came over and turned the gas off. We sipped at our soups, drank the remains of the soju, and got up to leave.

Anouk glided off into the night, no doubt with thoughts of *han*. Andy told me that he knew a place to seal the night, a *pojangmacha* (포장마차).

Pojangmacha, the orange tents so beloved by so many Koreans, had been completely absent during my trip. The garish tents with the glow of a dim lamp inside were uniquely Korean, but now they were illegal. According to one tally, fewer than three thousand remained. They had been dragged off the streets kicking and screaming, as they didn't quite fit the cookie-cutter design-school template for a developed country—

plus, the owners never paid their taxes. One estimate reckoned that the average orange tent earned about $5,000 per month and the more popular ones in excess of $1,000 per day. So they were banished, and as a result, outside of one dull, regulated *pojangmacha* zone, the last surviving tents spent their time scurrying around Seoul looking for quiet, dark holes to pitch up in. The quest to find one in Korea today was akin to donning Ahab's shoe to go in search of the white whale.

In between tall buildings and off the main roads, Jongno by night is a nest of alleys that creep with life. We came to a *kalbi* shed; it was closing, the round metal grill tables were gathered and stacked inside the restaurant. Two tables remained outside and a group of old men in baseball hats drank at them. The first casualty among them lay slumped, seemingly attached to the stainless-steel table. We marched on, and soon we arrived at a clearing on a narrow street. Trestle tables lined the sides, where a huddle of one-man operations toiled under plastic sheeting, but there wasn't an orange tent in sight.

"It's not quite a *pojangmacha*," said Andy as we agreed on which stall to eat at. "But this is as close as you'll get to one in Seoul nowadays."

We sat down at a table and the middle-aged man at the cutting board acknowledged our arrival with a firm welcome and a bow. The transparent tent covering the stall flapped slightly in the breeze. Seafood swam and snaked inside a small aquarium. The table next to us was filled with empty bottles and half-eaten plates. I turned to Andy.

"Vivian Han's chef told me that he missed the *pojangmacha*," I said. "He couldn't understand why they had to be shut down. He seemed genuinely sorry that they'd gone. They were a Korean fixture to him."

The cook, in a padded jacket, apron, and glasses, wandered over to us, holding a knife dripping with black ink and sea water. We ordered soju and *sannakji* (산낙지). The man bowed, plucked a baby octopus from the tank, and returned to the cutting board inside the jumble of his kitchen.

"You know these places only really started after the Second World War," said Andy, eyeing the tarpaulin row that lined the avenue.

"No," I said. "I had no idea."

I hadn't thought about it before, but *pojangmacha* were mere blips in the Korean timeline. To me, they were the most Korean of Korean places to eat Korean food, yet they were already fading from living memory. A friend had called me earlier that day to tell me he had visited the site of the only *pojangmacha* he knew of in Seoul, but it was gone. When he asked what had become of it, he was told it had to go to make way for a new coffee shop.

"You know there are 'indoor *pojangmacha*' now," Andy said. I nodded—I think I flinched, too. Mark in Iksan had shown me a row of them. They served iced beer, some served beer with whipped cream on top.

Even the meaning of the word *pojangmacha* had already begun to morph. I was told that Korean children now used the word to describe small street-corner snack stalls. *Pojangmacha* were meeting, eating, and happy drinking places, yet they were frowned upon by conservative Koreans, who saw them as a bastion of cheating husbands and drunks wheeling their way home. Korea's self-appointed moral police force said they were places no good could ever come from.

The cook hacked the squirming octopus into half-inch-size pieces, put them on a plate, and sprinkled them with sesame oil and toasted sesame seeds. He brought the *sannakji,* soju, a dipping sauce, and some freshly cut cucumbers to our table. I held my glass, Andy poured the drink.

"I hate this stuff," said Andy as I picked at the squirming snack on the table. "Can't bear it."

A tentacle twisted one way and the other between my chopsticks. It was blindly reaching for something, anything other than the finality of death.

"However," Andy said, putting his shot glass down, picking up a pair of chopsticks, and grabbing a tentacle, "this stuff, on the other hand, is really rather delicious."

I dipped the *sannakji* in the sweet *gochujang* sauce and bit into it. *Sannakji* is one of the most tender and delicious Korean food items. It felt apt to finish my journey with something so Korean, so straightforward and so pure. And as our snack squirmed in front of us, I realized that the Koreans truly were the mad scientists at the cutting board. That fruit cake pizza was really part of a long tradition of alchemical experimentation that took in live baby octopus and piss-fermented skate, and married Spam with kimchi, hot dogs, and baked beans. *Sannakji* was probably one of those very first experiments, and it remains to be seen how many of today's alchemists manage to create something that fixes itself quite so steadfastly into the Korean culinary consciousness. What was certain was that the Koreans would never stop experimenting. In fact, they were only just getting started.

"So," Andy said, "when's your book coming out?"

"Probably in about two years from now," I said.

He snorted.

"By the time it comes out," he said wagging a finger toward Jong-no's high-rise illuminations, "everything you write about will have been knocked down, closed, or moved. Korea is a rapidly moving target."

By now, it was almost two A.M., and subdued conversations crowded the lips around us. It seemed that the night was sprinkled with thoughts of the new day that had already begun. The last of the tentacles had almost stopped wriggling between us, and I looked around the tent. It was then that I noticed that this was the only place I had eaten in Korea that didn't have a calendar or a clock. Time didn't exist inside these endangered tents, and at once it seemed to me that Koreans, more than most, needed more places like this, not less.

Korea had grown a very unpredictable set of wings while I'd been away. They were wings that beat fast and were intent on flying to some very far-out places. They were places that I wasn't sure I understood. Andy was right: Korea would never be the same, no matter if I came back next month, next year, or next decade. And I knew I could only ever hope to click and catch a single frame in time on my journey around Korea's kitchen.

ACKNOWLEDGMENTS

I wish to express my gratitude to the following people. They all ate with me, pointed me in an interesting direction, introduced me to someone, explained something to me, or helped in some way during my time in South Korea: Andy Salmon, MBE; Joe McPherson; Josh White for setting up my camera, and taking the magnificent photograph on the front cover and the one of me at the back of the book; Areum; Ji-Young; He-Ryong; Fiona Bae; special thanks to Vivian Han for her time and passion and for touring Jeolla with me; Lee Hwan-Eui; Justin Talbot; Charles Montgomery for Korean literature recommendations; Breda Lund; Mr. Choi; Alex; Mrs. Kim of Andong; Mrs. Kang at Jagalchi market; Soo-Jin; Yoo-Jin; Min-Ju; Chris Tharp and Min-Hee for being such excellent dining companions; Mr. Cho; Kay; Grand Master Ky; Grand Master Han; Oh Geunsun; Ma Seungmi; Chris Devison; Chris Strugnell; Stentiar; special thanks to Lee In-Wha for being my go-to Korean food, culture, and quirks expert ever since 1996; Mr. Jang; Mr. Park; Mrs. Hong; Mrs. Chuoi; Mr. Chu; Dr. Anne Hilty; Stewart Ho; Song Jung-Hee; Darren Southcott; Professor Yang Yong-Jin; special thanks to Jason Kim of mykoreaneats.com for passion, enthusiasm, sharing many meals with me, translating, and undertaking additional research; Mrs. Park; Mrs. Oh and Mrs. Kang aka the incredible *haenyeo* of Jeju Island; Mr. and Mrs. Kang in Jeju City; Paul MacDonald; Lucy Williamson; Jung Wha-Jang; Susubori Makgeolli Brewer's Club; Sung-Chang; Daniel Tudor; Sonja from bburi kitchen; Anthony Bourdain for believing in me again; my agent Kim Witherspoon and everyone at Inkwell Management; book designer Sara Wood for listening to my ideas; and my editor Gabriella Doob for her clear eye and incisive guidance.

I listened to the following music during the writing and editing of this book: *Ambient 1: Music for Airports, Music for Films, Discreet Music,* and *Thursday Afternoon* by Brian Eno; Symphony No. 1 "Low," Symphony No. 4 "Heroes," and *La Belle et la Bête* by Philip Glass; "Islas Resonantes" by Eliane Radigue; *Vrioon* by Alva Noto and Ryuichi Sakamoto; *Blade Runner* film soundtrack by Vangelis; 1950s surbahar recordings by Annapurna Devi and Ravi Shankar; "Celestial Power" by Henry Flynt; Bach's Cello Suites 1–6 performed by Mstislav Rostropovich; *Persian Surgery Dervishes* by Terry Riley; and *Raag Bhairav (Excerpt)* by La Monte Young and The Theater of Eternal Music.

NOTES

CHAPTER 1: THE CHANCE TO BEGIN AGAIN

7 **"The old Koreans say** Later, in June 2016, this changed slightly, at least in relation to the building of new *hanok*s. "The Seoul city government announced a set of guidelines on providing subsidies for the construction of Korean traditional houses . . . amid efforts to preserve such buildings in the city. According to the new guidelines set up by the Seoul Metropolitan Government, those who erect (a) new *hanok*, or Korean traditional accommodations, can receive up to 100 million won (U.S. $86,700), including 20 million won in special loans." "Seoul City Announces *Hanok* Construction Subsidy Standards,"*Yonhap*, June 9, 2016.

CHAPTER 3: DO KOREANS DREAM OF ELECTRIC KIMCHI?

23 **As one Korean American writer** "Why Do Expats in Korea Complain So Much?" *Ask a Korean!*, July 13, 2008, http://askakorean.blogspot .com/2008/07/why-do-expats-in-korea-complain-so-much.html.

27 **"The core of the identity"** "What Is Korean Food?" *Ask a Korean!*, June 3, 2011, http://askakorean.blogspot.com/2011/06/what-is-korean-food .html.

28 **"The ingredients are really** Lucy Williamson, "Kimchi: South Korea's Efforts to Boost Its National Dish," BBC News, February 4, 2014.

CHAPTER 6: 1.5 DAK GALBI

50 **"Nearly half of elderly"** John Power, "Having Built Nation from Scratch, Elderly South Koreans Feel Abandoned," *Christian Science Monitor*, April 7, 2015.

55 **"The average Korean drinks"** Rachel Lee, "Coffee Beats Kimchi as Korean's Favorite," *Korea Times*, January 16, 2015.

CHAPTER 7: BUCKWHEAT PILGRIMAGE

68 **According to one survey** "Korean Men Use 13 Cosmetic Products on Average," *Korea Times,* May 31, 2015.

73 **In a 2015 survey** "South Koreans Spend the Least Time in the Kitchen: Survey," *New York Daily News,* March 31, 2015.

77 **The room took me back** "Hole in the Wall Restaurant in Gangneung," *Eating Korean,* December 4, 2011, http://www.eatingkorean.com/?p=602.

CHAPTER 9: IT'S OUR TIME NOW

92 **"Red pepper, the base** Daniel Tudor, *Korea: The Impossible Country* (North Clarendon, VT: Tuttle, 2012).

92 **And now, a little over** Rebecca Jang, "Women in Heavy-Drinking S. Korea Fuel Demand for Lighter Booze," Reuters, September 10, 2015.

92 **In addition, very few** "Four in ten South Korean adults are unmarried, the highest share among the 34 OECD countries. In Seoul over a third of women with degrees are single." "I Don't," *Economist,* July 25, 2015.

107 **The Korean coast guard** "Amid Ban, a Quasi-Legal Boom in Whale Meat and Culture," *Hankyoreh,* July 3, 2015, http://english.hani.co.kr/arti/english_edition/e_national/698766.html.

CHAPTER 10: LOW-RISE LEFTOVER

124 **"More and more university students"** "More Young Koreans Wolf Down Meals Alone," *Chosun Ilbo,* March 9, 2015, http://english.chosun.com/site/data/html_dir/2015/03/09/2015030900784.html.

124 **"Such options allow"** "Young Jobseekers, Singles Want to Spend Chuseok Alone," *Chosun Ilbo,* September 26, 2015, http://english.chosun.com/site/data/html_dir/2015/09/26/2015092600397.html.

CHAPTER 11: SLOW KOREA

128–9 **Most were baby boomers** "50,000 Koreans Moved to Countryside Last Year," *Chosun Ilbo,* March 21, 2014, http://english.chosun.com/site/data/html_dir/2014/03/21/2014032101633.html.

130 **There are more phones** "South Korea Has 4th Highest Smartphone Penetration," Yonhap News Agency, July 8, 2015, http://english.yonhapnews.co.kr/business/2015/07/08/91/0503000000AEN20150708000700320F.html.

CHAPTER 13: IN THE HAMLET OF YUCHEON-RI

144 **The event was** Marshall W. Stearns, *The Story of Jazz* (New York: Oxford University Press, 1956).

CHAPTER 14: SET THE CONTROLS FOR THE HEART OF THE SUN

149 **Genghis Khan's troops** "Going Back to Doenjang's Roots," *Korea Herald*, June 30, 2010, http://www.koreaherald.com/view.php?ud=20100630000615.

CHAPTER 15: ONLY K-POP SOUNDS HAPPY

158 **"Nowadays, many Korean people"** Beverly Bryan, "Korean Experimental Post-Rock Trio Jambinai Makes New Music with an Old Soul," *Noisey, Music by Vice*. May 18, 2016, http://noisey.vice.com/blog/jambinai-korean-instruments-post-rock.

CHAPTER 16: I DON'T KNOW

165 **South Korea's fertility rate** Jonathan Cheng, "South Korea 'To Go Extinct By 2750,'" *Wall Street Journal*, August 25, 2014, http://blogs.wsj.com/korearealtime/2014/08/25/south-korea-to-go-extinct-by-2750/.

166 **In 2008** Geoffrey Cain, "Korea Is Pulling Out All the Stops to Popularize Its Cuisine," March 22, 2015, *Global Post/PRI*, http://www.pri.org/stories/2015-03-22/korea-pulling-out-all-stops-popularize-its-cuisine.

CHAPTER 17: WITH YOU FOR LIFE

170 **When my parents** Luc Forsyth, "Under Pressure: Byun Ho San—Part 1,"*Luc Forsyth: Photo Journalist*, January 30, 2012, http://blog.lucforsyth.com/2012/01/under-pressure-byun-ho-san-part-1/.

171 **During the mid-fourteenth century** Marius Stankiewicz, "Hold Your Nose and Take a Bite: The Odd Appeal of a South Korean Fish Dish," NPR, *The Salt*, February 8, 2016.

CHAPTER 18: WE'RE THE LAST GENERATION

201 **Having known destitution** Kim Ji-soo, "Korean Food, Confident Enough to Go Back to Basics," *Korea Times*, January 6, 2014, http://www.koreatimes.co.kr/www/news/culture/2014/01/320_149298.html.

CHAPTER 19: THE AFTERLIFE

216 **And there were bigger plans** "Food Hub of the Northeast," *Asia Pacific Food Industry*, September 18, 2014, http://www.apfoodonline.com/index.php/features/item/400-food-hub-of-the-northeast.

216 **"It's much easier"** From an interview with Matt Van Volkenburg on *The Korea File* podcast. Van Volkenburg writes the *Gusts of Popular Feeling* blog, http://populargusts.blogspot.com.

217 **Even more alarmingly** Na Jeong-ju, "Koreans Drive Demand for Child

Prostitution in Southeast Asia," *Korea Times,* January 30, 2013, http://www.koreatimes.co.kr/www/news/nation/2013/01/116_129743.html.

CHAPTER 20: IT'S ALL IN THE WATER

224 **Wanna be healthy?** Joshua Hall, "How Not to Promote Korean Food," *Wall Street Journal,* May 21, 2013, http://blogs.wsj.com/korearealtime/2013/05/21/how-not-to-promote-korean-food/.

238 **"Drunkenness is an outstanding"** Isabella Bird Bishop, *Korea and Her Neighbours,* reprint edition (New York: Adamant Media Corporation, 2004).

247 **"Australian scientists"** Rob Waugh, "Science Has Just Found a Hangover Cure That Actually Works," *Metro,* August 3, 2015, http://metro.co.uk/2015/08/03/science-has-just-found-a-hangover-cure-which-actually-works-5324914/.

249 **"Some people call this** Elise Hu, "Korea's Most Famous Entertainer Is Now Its Most Infamous Landlord," NPR, October 21, 2015, http://www.npr.org/sections/parallels/2015/10/21/449918818/koreas-most-famous-entertainer-is-now-its-most-infamous-landlord.

CHAPTER 21: A WORMHOLE IN MYEONGDONG

259 **She dug out** Jung Mi-Kyung, "I Love You," in *My Son's Girlfriend: Stories,* Yu Young-Nan, trans. (Champaign, IL: Dalkey Archive Press, 2013).

CHAPTER 22: WE'RE NOT ALIENS

268 **When Marvel Studios** Steven Borowiec, "Some South Koreans Say 'Avengers: Age of Ultron' Shows Seoul's Ugly Side," *Los Angeles Times*, May 8, 2015, http://www.latimes.com/entertainment/movies/moviesnow/la-et-mn-south-korean-avengers-age-of-ultron-20150508-story.html.

CHAPTER 23: LIKE MOM'S FOOD

277 **Thomas Carlyle** *The Opera* by Thomas Carlyle. Published in 1852.

CHAPTER 24: THE PYONGYANG CONNECTION

285 **The statistics suggested** "Survey: Many S. Koreans Stressed, Unhappy with Their Lives," KBS World Radio, May 10, 2016, http://world.kbs.co.kr/english/news/news_Dm_detail.htm?No=118888.

285 **At the same time** "South Korean Children Feel Least Happy," *Korea Herald,* May 4, 2016, http://www.koreaherald.com/view.php?ud=20160504000574.

290 **Analysts reckoned** "Miscalculating the Cost of Unification," *Econo-*

mist, December 7, 2014, http://country.eiu.com/article.aspx?articleid
=812555265&Country=North%20Korea&topic=Economy.

CHAPTER 26: LONG DESERTED, THE DREAMS

297   Chapter title from "An Old Snake" by Philip K. Dick. First published in
W. J. Gulyás, *Child's Hat* (San Francisco: Bindweed Press, 1966).

297   **I lifted my bowl** Kim Sung-Ok, "Seoul: 1964, Winter," Marshall R. Pihl
Jr. trans., in *Land of Exile: Contemporary Korean Fiction,* Marshall R.
Pihl, Bruce Fulton, and Ju-Chan Fulton, eds. (Armonk, NY: M.E. Sharpe,
1993).